Barges

Frontispiece Two unladen spritsail barges in a squall. The nearest has rucked the topsail and both have the mainsail slightly brailed to reduce area. The mizzen of each is brailed to ease steering. The contrast in sterns suggests that the nearer barge is the older. A photograph taken on the lower Thames about 1900

John Leather

Barges

ADLARD COLES LIMITED
GRANADA PUBLISHING
London Toronto Sydney New York

Adlard Coles Ltd
Granada Publishing Ltd
8 Grafton Street, London W1X 3LA

First published in Great Britain by
Adlard Coles Ltd 1984

Copyright © John Leather 1984

British Library Cataloguing in Publication Data

Leather, John
  Barges.
  1. Sailing barges – England – History
  I. Title.
  387.2′24   VM466.B3
ISBN 0-229-11594-2

Printed and bound in Great Britain by
William Clowes Ltd, Beccles and London

Contents

Acknowledgements

The author wishes to thank friends Hervey Benham, Arthur Bennett, Keith Figg and Alf Pyner for the loan of photographs and Henry Higgs and Roger Finch for use of copies of paintings and drawings. Several photographs were also provided by Les Moore and by the late Commander H. Oliver Hill R.N.

The Director of the Science Museum and Mr. Tom Wright, Head of the Water Transport Department, have kindly allowed the reproduction of plans and photographs from the Museum collection.

The work of other researchers on this subject is noted in the Introduction but Frank Carr's study *Sailing Barges*, first published half a century ago, deserves special mention as it has long been an inspiration to many, including myself since I first read it at school in 1941.

The foundations of this book owe much to barge skippers Charles Sheldrick of the *Leofleda*, Bill Haisman of the *M. Piper*, George Cooper of the motor vessel *The Miller*, Mr. Bugg of the *Glenmore* and Bob Roberts of the *Greenhithe*. They are gratefully remembered for time spent on board their vessels and for patient answers to many questions in those last days of the cargo carrying spritsail barge, between 1945 and 1955.

John Leather
Fingringhoe and West Mersea
Essex

Illustration Acknowledgements

The photographs in this book appear by courtesy of the following; Hervey Benham, Nos: Frontispiece, 3, 4, 5, 8, 18, 19, 30, 35, 40, 42, 44, 46, 47, 50, 51, 72, 117. Science Museum, Nos: 15, 21, 22, 23, 53, 67, 80, 83, 85, 86, 88, 89, 92, 93, 94, 98, 99, 100, 104, 105, 106, 107, 111, 112, 113, 114, 118, 123. L. W. Moore, Nos: 2, 20, 119, 121, 122. Late H. Oliver Hill, Nos. 101, 102, 103. A. W. Pyner, Nos: 109, 114, 115. Arthur Bennett Nos: 12, 36. Keith Figg, Nos: 9, 10. Henry Higgs, No: 38. Roger Finch, No: 119. R. Hadlee, No: 13. A. Keeble, No: 11. A. Balmfour, No: 49. A. Bromley-Martin, No: 95 and San Francisco Bay Maritime Museum, No: 127.

Introduction

To write yet another book on sailing barges will seem to many unnecessary and to find something fresh on the subject impossible. When the publishers suggested this book I shared those views but realised that to many British sailing people a *sailing barge* now means only the spritsail rigged barges of the coasts of Essex, Kent and Suffolk and of the rivers Thames and Medway, whose story has been told in many earlier books. However, there remain some barge types and aspects of the once extensive sailing barge trade which have been neglected and these have been addressed in terms of the vessels and the way of life afloat. Also, a look at some less well known types of sailing barge will broaden the perspective of the subject.

For example, there were large English barges which were rigged variously as barques, barquentines, brigantines, schooners and ketches and are now little known. The stack barge trade has not been examined in detail elsewhere and the experiences afloat of a typical sailing barge skipper and a typical mate contribute to the human aspects. Yacht barges and barge yachts (two differing species) are a neglected subject, though no less interesting than the working barges of the east coast.

There were several other types of English sailing barge whose background is full of interest and which

contributed considerably to serving industry and agriculture in various areas. The keels, sloops and Billy Boys of Lincolnshire and Yorkshire are long gone and in Lancashire and Cheshire the bulky, workaday Flats were once part of the industrial growth and surging commerce of that now sadly declined area. Similar sized Trows once carried much of the trade of the river Severn and the Bristol Channel. Down channel, in south Devon and Cornwall, small sailing barges were part of the local transport system into the mid-twentieth century and barges of many types were built, owned and worked in the Solent.

In contrast, the sailing barge never developed widely in north America but large numbers of special types were built and used in some areas where shallow water, relatively sheltered conditions, prospects of continuous cargoes and usually a lack of railroad transport, made their construction and operation worthwhile.

There were of course also other types of sailing barge in many countries and some of these made interesting comparison with the English and American barges. Dutch cargo carrying, shallow draught sailing vessels which worked coastwise and inland were of bewildering variety of type and size. Further north, on the North Sea coast of Germany, the great ports of Hamburg and

Figure 1 An early nineteenth century, swim-bowed and stumpy rigged
spritsail barge aground. An etching by Cornelius Varley

Bremen were growing lustily in the late nineteenth and
early twentieth centuries and the ever increasing traffic
of goods as German industry became more organised
and productive, brought need for many small cargo carriers to collect and distribute bulk and piece goods over
a wide area, from the Ems in the south to the Danish
and north German coasts, accelerated by construction of
the ship canal from the Elbe to Kiel. They also sailed
the many rivers and waterways and occasionally made
voyages to Britain. Small sailing barges were used in
parts of Denmark and spritsail rigged kahns sailed the
coast and waterways of Pomerania, in north Germany
and Poland. Large, lateen rigged sailing barges carried
cargoes, often of stone, on Lake Leman and lugsail
rigged barges worked on many French rivers. Other,
very different lug-rigged barges worked from Venice and
along the coast of the eastern Adriatic. There were other
types of barge-like craft evolved for use in many
countries including New Zealand, Russia, Egypt, India,
China and the East Indian islands. At Singapore, craft
remarkably like the ketch barges of the east coast of
England, but of asiatic origin, traded for many years with
timber. These and other types of sailing barges have had
to be omitted for limitations of space but will form a
fascinating comparative study in the future.

This is not intended to be an exhaustive treatise on
every aspect of British and American sailing barges,
which would need many volumes, but a selective look at
a range of types and the trades they served in England
and north America. It examines many types of barge,
their conditions of operation and handling and evolution
and traditions. There has been no attempt at a detailed
account of the origins, evolution and decline of the complex range of types comprising the English spritsail
barges of the east coast, which have been extensively

Figure 2 A swim-bowed spritsail barge in the Thames, showing a stage of evolution beyond the early stumpy rigged barges to a topsail rig but without a bowsprit, for work in the Thames and Medway

dealt with by many other writers. However, an overview of the craft is given, to introduce chapters on hitherto neglected aspects of the subject and other types of sailing barge from that area.

It is appropriate to recall earlier works on the east coast barges. Frank Carr's *Sailing Barges* has been a standard book on the English sailing barge for over half a century and at school, it first explained to me the background of the brown sailed barges which passed our village on almost every tide, bound up and down the river Colne.

W. L. Wyllie's *London to the Nore* described that artist's affinity for the sailing barges of the Thames and Medway, a theme developed further in *A Floating Home* by Cyril Ionides, J. B. Atkins and Arnold Bennett, with its ingenious capturing of the south Essex dialect and the amphibious nature of the area.

That consummate sailing personality E. G. Martin, caught the essence of east coast barging in his splendid *Sailorman*, a study of several months spent in the Mistley barge *Vigilant* during the 1930s and too long out of print.

In contrast, Edgar Marsh produced *Spritsail Barges of the Thames and Medway* as a research work which fuelled the interest of many in post-war times, when there was still a fleet of about 80 spritsail barges in trade.

My old friends Hervey Benham and Roger Finch have contributed over the years to my understanding of the east coast sailing barge. Hervey has written of them comprehensively in his books *Last Stronghold of Sail, Down Topsail* and *Once Upon a Tide,* and more recently in *The Big Barges,* a work written jointly with Roger Finch, who has also published a study of R. and W. Paull's Ipswich barges entitled *A Cross in the Topsail.*

Genial Arthur Bennett put his long practical

Figure 3 The spritsail barge *Hyacinth* of Maldon was built there in 1889 for E. H. Bentall. She was owned by George Littlebury of Colchester when this photograph was taken, about 1907

experience of converting and sailing the yacht barges *June* and later the *Henry*, into the books *June of Rochester* and *Tide Time*. These are evocative studies of the swan-song of the commercial sailing barge in the 1930s and 40s. Fortunately he has recently continued with *Us Bargemen* and one hopes for more.

Bob Roberts, that irrepressible bargeman, caught the full flavour of skippering sailing barges over a thirty year period in his *Coasting Bargemaster* and *Last of the Sailormen*. His breezy personality is sadly missed on the coast and its watersides. James Uglow, another skipper, set down his experiences in *Sailorman* and John Allendale has well put the crews' viewpoint in *Sailorman between the Wars*. Another barge mate who has ventured into print is Marion Carr, who sailed as mate in the sailing barge *Clara* in the 1950s. I recall the astonishment with which we watched the strange spectacle of a tousle haired girl hauling at the topsail halyard as the *Clara* towed downriver past the shipyard. Her *Call of the Running Tide* is an account of everyday life on board a barge in their last days of working under sail and the transition to motor vessels.

Richard-Hugh Perks has crystallised some of his extensive research in the books *Sprits'l* and *George Bargebrick Esquire*, while Tony Ellis has produced an excellent précis of types in *Sailing Barges of Maritime England*. S. D. Sattin has written of north Kent barges in *Just off the Swale*, and *Bricks and Brickies* and *Cement and Muddies* by F. G. Willmott provide more background to the barge trade of that district.

No doubt the list of books will continue to lengthen and it would be repetitive to cover ground so well researched by these authors. Indeed, the volume and accuracy of their writings on east coast barges, enjoyable though these are, has tended to obscure the many other

Figure 4 Sailing barges awaiting work off Woolwich, in the river Thames,
during the trade depression of the early 1930s

types of barge, equally worthy and often operating under harsh conditions in other places: the Flats of the rivers Mersey, Weaver and Dee and the adjacent Lancashire, Cheshire and Welsh coasts; the keels, sloops and Billy Boys of Lincolnshire and Yorkshire waterways and rivers, which also sailed the east coast at times; the sloop, cutter and ketch rigged small barges of Devon and Cornwall, working the large rivers and the nearby coasts; the several types of sailing barge found in Solent waters and the variety of types known as Trows, once numerous on the river Severn and associated rivers and waterways, and in the upper Bristol Channel.

Again, others have written on many of these types but compared to the east coast sailing barges, these are relatively little explored. E. Paget Tomlinson wrote of them in *Mersey and Weaver Flats* and has included the flat in *Britain's Canal and River Craft*. Michael Stammers has referred to them in *West Coast Shipping*, as has Alan Lockett in *Ports and People of Morecambe Bay*, one of several excellent studies he has published on craft of the north west.

Lincolnshire and Yorkshire keels were described in a practical article in *The Mariner's Mirror*, 1955, by John Frank who had been master and owner of a keel. Keels and sloops are the subject of Harry Fletcher's *A Life on The Humber* and Michael Ulyatt's *Flying Sail* and *Inland Sailers*. The late George Holmes also included these and Billy Boys in his illustrated writings early in the century.

David Macgregor has researched and published much on sailing vessels from many periods including the sailing barges of the Fal which, with the Devonshire barges, were also studied by the late Commander H. Oliver Hill, to whom all interested in the history of British small craft owe much. Lawrence O'Toole has caught the

atmosphere of the hinterland served by these craft in *The Roseland*.

Those staunch westcountrymen Dr. Basil Greenhill and Grahame Farr have long studied and written on the craft of their favourite countryside and seaboard and both have written of the Trow; Farr in *Chepstow Ships and Somerset Harbours* and Dr Greenhill in *Sailing for a Living, a Quayside Camera 1845–1917* and *The Merchant Sailing Ship*; with Ann Giffard in *Sailing Ships* and with W. Slade in *West Country Coasting Ketches*.

I have deliberately avoided the sailing wherries and keels of Norfolk and Suffolk as these have been well covered by G. Colman Green in his attractively illustrated book *The Norfolk Wherry* and also by Arthur Patterson and G. Christopher Davies in books on their home waters. More recently, Robert Malster has extended our knowledge with *Wherries and Waterways* and Roy Clark's *Black Sailed Traders* gathered together much on the subject.

Few sailing barges were used in Scotland and lack of space has prevented some appreciation of the Scottish gabert or gabberd, the sailing barge of the Clyde and adjacent coast; forerunners of the hard worked Puffer. The many sailing barges of the Solent area, which carried considerable trade, have been almost overlooked by others and it has given me particular pleasure to record something of their story during several happy years living on the Isle of Wight.

Little has been recorded of American sailing barges apart from some research by Howard I. Chappelle, published in *American Small Sailing Craft* and by M. V. Brewington in *Chesapeake Bay* and by John Haskell Kemble in *San Francisco Bay*. George B. Douglas recorded several types and William E. Verplanck and Moses W. Collyer wrote from experience of the packet

Figure 5 A typical staysail barge with a load of softwood planks from ships at the Surrey Dock, in London, bound coastwise in the Thames estuary in the 1940s

Figure 6 The spritsail barge *Veronica* in racing trim before a barge match in the Thames about 1960. Originally owned by Clement Parker of Bradwell, Essex, she was latterly amongst the fleet of F. T. Everard and Sons of Greenhithe, Kent

and market sloops of the Hudson River in *The Sloops of the Hudson.*

It is hoped that this book will fill some gaps.

The maritime historian, the yachtsman and those who have been and are busy restoring and sailing barges of various types for pleasure inevitably regard the working sailing vessels of the past with varying degrees of romantic affection. However, it must always be remembered that the purpose of these vessels was to carry cargo and there was little or no pleasure in going afloat to earn a living in them. Hard work, often poor food, usually meagre pay and sometimes hardship, exposure and danger were the lot of their crews, many of whom were glad to see diesel engines supplement and then replace sails, and radar and radio aid their navigation.

Perhaps amateur bargemen and yachtsmen appreciated the sailing craft most. Cyril Ionides well expressed the atmosphere of the sailing barge at its most appealing in this passage from *A Floating Home*, which will do well to set the scene for this book:

'Perhaps the best time to see a barge is while deep laden she beats to windward up Sea Reach, on a day when large clouds career across the sky, sweeping the water with shadows, as the squalls boom down the reach, and the wind, fighting the tide, kicks up a fierce short sea. Then, as the fishermen say, the tide-way is "all of a paffle". As the barge comes towards you, heeling slightly (for barges never heel far), you can see her bluff bows crashing through the seas and flinging the spray far up the streaming foresail. It bursts with the rattle of shot on the canvas. You can see the anchor on the dripping bows dip and appear as sea after sea thuds over it, and the lee rigging dragging through the smother of foam that races along the decks and cascades off aft to join the frothy tumult astern. You can see the weather rigging as taut as fiddlestrings against the sky. Now she is coming about. The wheel spins round as the skipper puts the helm down and the vessel shoots up into the wind. She straightens up as a sprinter relaxes after an effort. The sails slat furiously; the air is filled with a sound as of the cracking of great whips; the sprit, swayed by the flacking sails, swings giddily from side to side; the mainsheet blocks rage on the horse. Then the foresail fills, the head of the barge pays off, and as the mate lets go the bowline the staysail slams to leeward with the report of a gun. The mainsail and topsail give a last shake, then fill with wind and fall asleep as the vessel steadies on her course and points for the Kentish shore. As she heels to port she lifts her gleaming side and trails her free leeboard as a bird might stretch a tired wing. She means to fetch the Chapman Light next tack.'

PART ONE

The sailing barges of
South-east England

An overview

For a better appreciation of the first section of this book it is necessary to review briefly the basic types of sailing barge built, owned and sailed with its variety of cargoes in south-eastern England until the 1950s.

Most of these barges were built of wood, a few of iron and after the 1880s a considerable number of steel. All had flat bottomed and relatively shallow hulls with a flush deck. A chine ran for much of the length amidships, merging into a shaped bow and a transom stern, or in some of the larger barges, a counter stern.

The early sailing barges of the Thames and Medway, common until the 1840s, had swim bows and budget sterns, that is, the bottom at the forward and after ends was raked upwards, producing the almost rectangular midship section in a decreasing depth to the almost square ended bow and stern. The rudder was hung on a budget or deadwood aft. The stumpy barge shown in fig. 1 has a hull of this type. Many of these barges were rigged as cutters and carried a topsail. Others had a sprit mainsail. By the 1840s barges having shaped bows were replacing this hull form.

The barges had one hold, usually with two hatches; the smaller one forward and the larger abaft the mast, except in the largest seagoing barges where there might be up to three hatches, to suit the mast positions.

Hatches were closed with wooden covers and battened tarpaulins.

To aid sailing these shallow draught hulls, particularly to windward, all except some of the largest barges were equipped with large wooden leeboards which were pivoted at deck level abreast the mainmast, or the foremast in those with a rig other than a spritsail or a gaff ketch. The leeboards were hauled up or lowered by pendants operated by hand winches on deck and almost all the halyards and the brails, in the spritsail barges, were led to geared hand winches. The anchor, on which the safety of the barge often depended, was handled by a wooden barrelled windlass worked by hand, with gearing to aid recovery of the chain cable.

The skippers and crews of the barges came from many places on the Thames and Medway rivers and from towns and villages in the nearby counties of Essex, Suffolk and Kent, with a few from elsewhere. Most skippers had no paper qualifications but were excellent practical seamen in their own type of vessel and in known waters. Their skill in handling the barges in all conditions was often remarked on by sailors from many other branches of seafaring. The crews varied in age and ability, but men commonly sailed with the same skipper for many years and the atmosphere on board these craft

Figure 7 Lines, sail plan and general arrangement of a typical, wooden hulled spritsail barge of the period 1870–1895. Such craft were built and owned in the counties of Essex, Kent and Suffolk and at places on the river Thames. A few were also built and owned in the Solent area

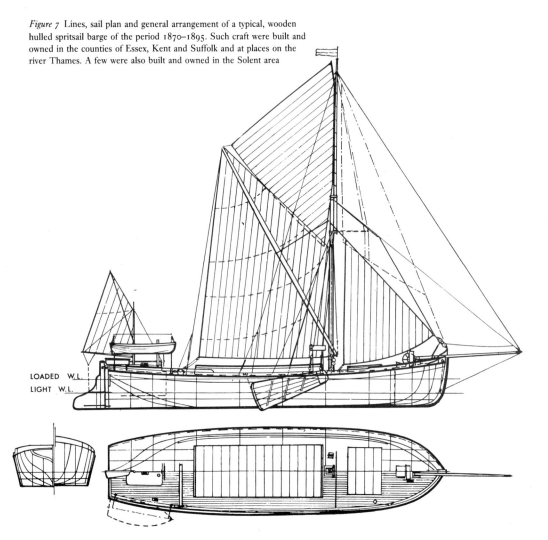

LOADED W.L.
LIGHT W.L.

Figure 8 A sailing barge port. Mistley, on the river Stour in north-east Essex on a summer afternoon in the 1930s. Four sailing barges on the hard, the fast *Sara* at left

Figure 9 The unladen mule rigged barge *Cetus*, built at Grays in 1902, shows most of her side in light airs

Figure 10 Sails were used by some barge owners to advertise their interests. Eastwood's *Delta*, built at Maidstone, Kent in 1898 drifts in light airs, 1935

port. It is believed that some 5,000 sailing barges were in use in 1860 but with the gradual increase in the size of the barges, the numbers fell to about 2,000 in 1900. Probably the heyday of these craft was approximately from 1870 to 1920. About 700 were still sailing in the 1920s and perhaps 500 in 1939.

Cargoes varied and included grain, cement, coal, stone, timber, manure, hay, straw, gravel, sand, linseed, bricks, sugar, rubbish, and many others from machinery to gunpowder.

Ownership might be by an individual, often a miller or a farmer in earlier times, or by a company of shareholders, often from a small community, particularly on the coast. More frequently it was by a company owning several barges in general trade or one which also owned works, whose raw materials and manufactures the barge would usually carry. Few barges were owned by their skippers, though many held shares in the barge they sailed and sometimes in others. Most of the sailing barge owners possessed little capital and usually obtained a new craft by paying a deposit at the placing of the order with a builder and obtaining the balance of the contract price by shareholding or by mortgaging her on completion, either to a bank or through brokers.

Most skippers and crew were paid from a portion of the freight money. If the barge was owned by a company whose goods she carried regularly they were usually paid by the week. When paid by the freight returns the crew of a weatherbound barge or one awaiting a cargo did not receive pay, which could result in hardship as they brought their own food and had families and homes to keep.

The sailing barges from the south-east could be broadly classified into types by their cargo capacity, dimensions and rig, all reflecting the requirements of the

was informal. The skipper and sometimes also the mate lived aft in a cabin abaft the hold. The fo'c'sle served as a store, and as necessary, for accommodation for others of the crew. This might vary from a boy or a man to perhaps two, three or four men in a large seagoing barge.

The period which saw greatest use of these sailing barges was between about 1820 and 1950, which spanned the rise of British trade after the Napoleonic wars to the post World War II advance of road trans-

Figure 11 The bargemen (1) Skipper and mate of a well found Essex or Suffolk spritsail barge in fine summer weather

trades for which they were built.

The stumpies were the smallest of these basic types and retained the original low and simple rig of the Thames spritsail barge into the 1930s. Most were built for work in the Thames and Medway, serving industry and the docks, and working into tributaries and canals where small size and little draught were useful and greater cargo capacity had yet to become important. Many early stumpies, like the contemporary cutter and sprit rigged topsail barges, were built with a swim bow and a buget stern, similar to the towed lighters of the Thames which are still in use. However, by the mid nineteenth century the stumpy usually had a shaped bow and stern like other sailing barges. They were often built to dimensions restricted to suit certain locks and waterways and rarely carried more than 75 or 80 tons of cargo but some managed up to 100 tons. Average dimensions were 70 ft × 14 ft × 5 ft load draught. The rig was a foresail, a sprit mainsail fitted with brails to reduce the area or furl the sail and a small sprit mizzen sheeted to the top of the rudder to haul it to weather and aid steering when coming about. Some stumpies did not have a mizzen. Many of these small barges were steered with a tiller and frequently the sprit was long and well peaked for efficient windward sailing. This two-sail arrangement was convenient for working in confined waters and making short passages in the rivers. The usual crew was two men, or a man and a youth. Of all the types of sailing barge, the small stumpy would be the most sensible and most economical to reproduce as a replica for pleasure sailing.

The next larger size of sailing barge worked generally between the Thames and Medway rivers and to the many small ports on the adjacent coasts of the counties of Essex, Suffolk and north Kent, usually between the

river Deben in Suffolk, to the north and Sandwich in Kent to the south, though many ventured further at times. These barges carried from 70 to 150 tons of cargo and typical dimensions were 80 ft × 17 ft 6 in × 5 ft 6in to 7 ft draught loaded. This was the most numerous type of English sailing barge. Five basic sails were carried; foresail, sprit mainsail, with brails, topsail, a spritsail mizzen and a jib topsail often set to the stemhead and known as a staysail to the bargemen. A bowsprit and a jib were not usually carried by barges of this type working in the Thames and Medway as it would be in the way in confined waters and was unnecessary for their short passages, but a bowsprit and jib was usual for others of the type making coastal passages as it could considerably increase speed. The sail area varied from about 2,500 sq ft in the smaller examples to about 5,000 sq ft in the larger. As in many barges, the centre of area of the sails was arranged to be forward of the centre of lateral resistance with the leeboard in use, which theoretical relationship usually resulted in good balance under sail and an easy helm in most conditions. Steering was originally by tiller but wheels were introduced in the 1880s and quickly became commonplace.

The masts were stepped in tabernacles and the entire rig could be lowered to horizontal in a short time for passing fixed bridges or maintenance. When shooting a bridge under sail, as at Rochester on the Medway, the time for lowering might not exceed two minutes, the forestay being surged away with the stay fall purchase, though it took much longer for the gear to be raised again with the fall of the purchase led to the windlass. The crew of these barges were usually two men, and in larger ones also a boy, until the 1920s, when it was reduced to two, one of whom was often a youth. This small crew handled the considerable sail area and heavy

9

Figure 13 Spritsail barges shooting Rochester Bridge, on the river Medway, Kent. Barges approached with a fair tide, sailing as long as possible and lowering the masts and sails while passing the bridge. W. L. Wyllie's painting shows three shaped and one swim-bowed barge heaving up the gear afterwards, with the stay fall led to the windlass barrel

Figure 14 Spritsail barges *John Bayly* and *Gratitude* racing in the 1920s.
Barges were entered for the Thames or the Medway race in various
classes. They were refitted beforehand but did not adopt extreme rigs
until the end of sailing barge racing in the 1950s and 60s. The *John
Bayly* was built at Sandwich, Kent in 1895 for the Margate Hoy Co. and
the *Gratitude* at Battersea in 1884

Figure 15 Structural midship section of the steel spritsail barge *Niagara*, designed and built by Forrestt and Co., Wivenhoe, Essex in 1898. Showing the modest hold space occupied by structure compared with wooden construction

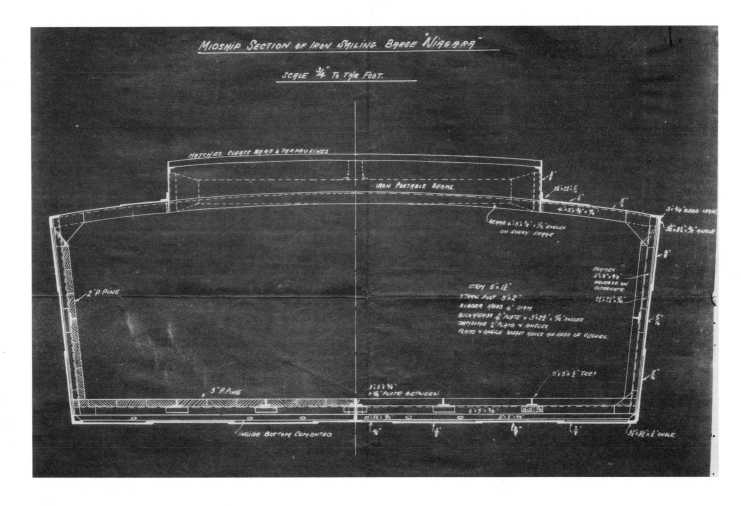

leeboards of the barge only by aid of many winches and carefully arranged gear. A barge under sail was, when unladen, a light displacement sailing vessel and needed careful handling in strong winds and a seaway.

This size and type of barge were the last of British sailing cargo carriers to survive the increasing competition of motor barges, motor coasters and road transport. A few remained under sail alone into the 1950s, when of the 80 or so still in use, almost all were fitted with motor auxiliary engines or were converted to motor barges. The decline was hastened by post-war commercial recovery, by major changes in the milling, cement, brick-making and other industries and by expansion of the tug and lighterage trade on the Thames and Medway, serving local industries and the docks and wharves.

A large type of sailing barge of similar but deeper hull form was built in considerable numbers to trade principally on the British coast to ports such as Ipswich, Yarmouth, Kings Lynn, the Humber, Portsmouth, Poole, Hull and many others on the east and south coasts, where they competed in many of the trades of the smaller coasting barges described above. More distant voyages were also made to places such as the river Tyne and south-west Cornwall and to ports in Germany, Holland, Belgium and France.

These coasters ranged up to 250 or 300 tons cargo capacity and had dimensions averaging 95 ft × 23 ft × 8 to 9 ft depth. Many were rigged with a foresail, sprit mainsail, topsail, a jib set on a bowsprit which could be topped up and a large mizzen which was stepped well forward, reducing the mainsail and topsail to a size suitable for the crew. The mizzen was often set from a standing gaff and was fitted with brails. This rig was known as a 'mule', a term the coasting sailors and fishermen applied to any hybrid rig or hull form. The total sail area might be 5,000 sq ft or slightly more and these were much more powerful, though not usually faster than the slightly smaller Thames estuary topsail barges.

Some similar sized coasting ketch barges had a gaff and boom mainsail and mizzen, both of which were often fitted with roller reefing gear which was a help to the usual small crew of three men, sometimes three men and a boy in the larger ones. Typical dimensions of a 'boomie' were 100 ft × 23 ft 6 in × 8 ft 9 in draught. These gaff rigged coasting barges often had the masts stepped on the keelson and wedged at the deck. The bowsprit in some was a standing spar. Many of these barges were built and owned at small ports around the coast from Yarmouth in Norfolk to Poole in Dorset, many being built at Littlehampton in Sussex. Handling the gaff rig was harder work for the crew than in the mule rigged coasters and some of these ketches also set square topsails and other sails when running or reaching on passage. Their hulls retained the flat bottom of the smaller barges but some had a counter stern instead of a transom and many had a small gammon knee at the stem head. Leeboards were carried in almost all of this type of barge.

There was a further, larger and less homogenous class of sailing barge which besides regularly working in the British coasting trade also made short sea and occasionally deep sea voyages to European ports and to central America and the east coast of north America. These vessels had the flat bottom and amidships chine of the smaller barges, often combined with a raking or a clipper bow and a counter stern. Their dimensions were considerably greater and the depth was proportionately increased. Many did not have leeboards, which in such craft were very heavy and cumbersome to handle, yet

Figure 16 One of the large coasting barges owned by F. T. Everard and Co. of Greenhithe, sailing in a Thames or Medway barge race during the 1930s. These mule rigged barges were amongst the finest craft of their type

made passages under sail when light. A typical example of these big barges would be 140 ft length × 26 ft × 12 ft 9 in depth. She might load 500 tons of cargo on a draught of about 10 ft.

The rig varied from ketch in the smaller examples, with or without square topsails to a two- or three-masted schooner, with or without square topsails, brigantine, barquentine and probably three were barques.

Voyages were regularly made to European and Scandinavian ports, many carrying coal, and some ventured across the Atlantic on a few voyages to central America and eastern north America, though these vessels were hardly suited to western ocean passagemaking. The crew were usually four or five men and a boy in the larger, or four men and a boy in the smaller. These barges were mostly built between about 1865 and 1890 and were extreme examples of the sailing barge.

In all these types of sailing barge the owners sought economy of construction, operation and maintenance. The design sought maximum carrying capacity on a limited draught with a rig capable of being handled by a small crew for the greatest profit, and without the use of costly ballast when light. Until the introduction of reliable marine diesel engines for barges and small coasters these sailing barges were commercially successful.

A small petrol auxiliary engine is believed to have been first installed in a spritsail barge in 1901 but it was soon removed, possibly for insurance reasons. The London and Rochester Trading Co. converted their barge *Arctic* to a fully powered vessel in 1907, the first on the Thames and Medway. However, auxiliary engines did not become common in sailing barges until the 1940s when compact and less expensive marine diesel engines of modest horse power were installed in most to meet the need for more regular delivery of cargoes, with reduced passage times and increased profits. By about 1950, a barge without auxiliary power was of little commercial value, though a few lingered under sail alone into the 1960s.

Part 1 of this book examines some neglected types and aspects of these sailing barges from South-east England; their origins, design, construction, rigs and operation.

2

The boomsail barges

Until the 1850s British coastal and short sea cargoes were carried by brigs, schooners, ketches, chubby hulled Billy Boys rigged as cutters and ketches and by cutter-rigged cargo smacks. On the east and south coasts the flat bottomed sailing barge hull, originally a craft developed for the rivers and estuary of the Thames and Medway, had proved capable of limited coastal passages under spritsail rig, if of suitable size, was increased in dimensions and was given a gaff and boom rig. A new type of ketch and schooner rigged barge resulted, whose owners needed a craft which could float up shallow creeks to load or discharge, would sail without ballast, which cost money to obtain, load and discharge, and was usually worthless on arrival, and were capable of coasting voyages in the North Sea, down Channel, to continental ports between the Elbe and Brest and sometimes even up European rivers, far inland.

These early boomsail barges as they were called, often shortened to 'boomies', were rigged as ketches and some had counter sterns, emphasising the influence on their origins of the round bottomed coasting ketches and schooners whose work they quickly began to encroach upon. However, there appears to have been little or no influence from the cutter and sloop rigged barges with gaff sails which were common on the Thames and Med-

way during the late eighteenth and early nineteenth centuries. By the 1840s spritsail barges were voyaging the Thames estuary and its rivers between the Suffolk Stour and Ramsgate in Kent. These were gradually increasing in size for occasional coastal work. Round bowed barges were steadily outnumbering the swim headers and the shape of the after body, the hull depth and the spritsail rig and its gear were improved for passagemaking and seakeeping.

It is impossible to determine who designed and built the first boomie barge, or when, but a ketch-rigged barge named *Elizabeth*, built at Maidstone, on the upper reaches of the river Medway, in Kent, in 1840 may have been the first. Hartnoll and Surridge of Limehouse, London, launched the 'dandy' rigged barge *Flower of Essex* for John Watts of Harwich in 1857. This rig was then fashionable in cruising yachts and some fishing vessels and approximated to that of a yawl but had a small standing lug mizzen stepped abaft the rudder stock on an old fashioned 'lute' counter and sheeted to an outrigger. Her tonnage was recorded as 67, compared to the 40 to 50 tons then usual for a spritsail barge. The hull form was shapely; a straight stem with slight rake and a well shaped run to the lute stern. She had leeboards. The mainmast was stepped well into the hull

Figure 17 The wooden ketch barge *Garson* was built at Great Yarmouth, Norfolk 1864 by Mills and Blake for Garson, Blake and Sons to carry bricks and tiles from the river Humber to Yarmouth and elsewhere. She was later owned at Mistley, Essex, and is seen here at Burnham-on-Crouch. The *Garson* was built with cutter rig but was converted to a ketch in 1884 and traded until the 1920s

16

and carried a long topmast. The jib was set on a long, running bowsprit.

While the *Flower of Essex* was building, John Vaux, another Harwich owner, was building the *Stour* at his own yard to add to his fleet of barges and schooners which carried coal for his own business. The *Stour* carried 200 tons, had a clipper bow, counter stern, a standing bowsprit with a jib boom, a mizzen stepped well inboard and having a fidded topmast. She could set a square course and a square topsail and the flat bottomed hull was adorned with shroud channels, catheads for anchor handling and whiskers to spread the bowsprit shrouds. She was a hybrid between a barge and a coasting schooner and was aptly designated a 'schooner barge'. But the large mainsail of the schooner rig was too powerful for the shallow hull and lack of after buoyancy and depth of the barge type hull, and the dandy or ketch rig suited the new barges better. The hull and rig of the *Stour* cost less than a schooner or brig of similar capacity. Later, Vaux also owned the schooner barges *Lymington* and *Jubilee*. His other vessels were schooners, square riggers or cargo carrying smacks.

John Watts had great faith in the boomsail barges and eventually owned the *Harwich*, *Dovercourt*, *Brightlingsea*, *May Queen*, *Lothair*, *Alice Watts*, *Emerald* and *Enterprise*. Most of these were sold in 1881 due to changes in his business. Middleton was another Harwich owner with the boomies *Gloriana*, *Mary Lynn* and *Laura*, besides the smaller *Ena* and two spritsail barges. There were soon many other boomies owned in Suffolk, Essex, Kent and at a few south coast ports.

The 1860s brought a flurry of boomsail barge construction, particularly at the Essex ports of Harwich and Brightlingsea and at Ipswich, Suffolk and Great Yarmouth, Norfolk. At Brightlingsea, in 1863, Aldous

Figure 18 The ketch barge *Record Reign* of Maldon. A ship portrait with square topsails set but without the leeboards, which were often omitted from such paintings to please the captain or owner. Built by John Howard and Son at Maldon, 1897

Figure 19 The *Record Reign* as a motor ketch. The bowsprit had been removed and a deckhouse and wheelhouse added. The leeboards are retained

built the *Eva* and the *Jabez*, in 1865 the *Dovercourt* and the *James Bowles*, which carried a simply rigged standing bowsprit. The *Harwich* and the *Antelope* followed down the ways in 1867 and 1869, the delightfully named *Startled Faun* in 1868 and the *Brightlingsea* and the *Antelope* in 1869. These boomies were built during the period of greatest activity of ship and boatbuilding which Brightlingsea had known. Aldous' yard was crowded with the rearing frames and completing hulls of ketch and cutter smacks, yachts and barges.

This boomsail barge boom was largely caused by the growing trade in coal for burning in household grates and at gasworks retorts. 'Sea cole' had been shipped to London from the north-east coast for centuries in larger vessels, with smaller communities receiving the cargoes of brigs and brigantines at their watersides. Growth in population and demand coupled with need for more economical carriage and the Victorian love of experiment and change favoured the introduction of the new type of coasting barge, which was more seaworthy than the spritsail type and could stand bad weather when reefed or when lying-to under a close-reefed mainsail. However, the early boomies were largely experimental, often reflecting the owner's experience with round bottomed craft. Some had clipper or fiddle bows, countersterns and a sweeping sheer. Others had plain, barge style hulls. Many could set a square course, perhaps with a square topsail above. A few which had standing bowsprits had a small figurehead, others had a knee decorated with scroll work and a standing bowsprit, sometimes a jib boom was also fitted. Square topsails, topgallants and gaff topsails set from hoops running on a metal jackstay were 'kites' carried by many.

A typical early boomsail barge had a mizzen which was large in proportion to the mainsail and was stepped well inboard. The mainsail head and topsail luff were short and the gaff was set at lower angle than in later craft and the jibs were cut low in the clew. There were three or four rows of reef points in the mainsail, two in the mizzen and one in the foresail. A few had reef eyelets in the inner jib, which was usually set hanked to a stay. The squaresail yard was slung in a truss and sling, and had lifts to the masthead and braces to trim it. The yard could be cock-billed out of the way when alongside or for discharge. The squaresail was set flying from it and in later years many skippers preferred the yard to be stowed on deck when not in use, the squaresail being bent to it before hoisting, and was unbent and stowed in the sail locker when it was sent down. With this arrangement the yard was hoisted on a strop by the foresail halyards. The weather clew was often boomed out.

Many early boomsail barges set a square topsail off the wind, hanked to an iron jackstay extending about half way up the fore side of the topmast to clear the topsail yard from the hoops for the gaff topsail luff. A few also carried a topgallant which was often hanked to an extended jackstay. Some boomies, like the Ipswich *Stour*, carried these square topsails on almost every point of sailing in suitable weather and dispensed with a gaff topsail. Smaller boomies were usually rigged like the contemporary ketch or dandy rigged smacks, having a plumb stem and a running bowsprit. Some had counter sterns, others a transom. The jib was sent out on a bowsprit traveller and was shifted for a smaller in bad weather. The bowsprit was often run in when alongside.

As the handy and economical boomsail barges grew in numbers on the east and south coasts, the schooners they supplanted were increasingly sold to owners on the south and west coasts of England and some also abroad. Few of the type were built to replace them. The boom-sail or 'ketch barges', as the type gradually became known, carried cargoes to English and European ports, generally between Hamburg in the north and Brest in the south. Sometimes they ventured further. The skippers' greatest worry after passagemaking was in finding a suitable berth for a flat bottomed craft. The boomies served patterns of trade which grew or declined with economic changes. Some craft were built for a particular trade but eventually worked in several and in later years all sought whatever cargo was available.

The carriage of coal from north-east England to small ports in the south-east provided work for many, as the steam colliers which had succeeded the old collier brigs in the coal trade to London were uneconomic for the smaller cargoes shipped to the towns and villages of the coast, often sited up shallow rivers. Ketch barges frequently loaded grain in Essex or Suffolk for Middlesbrough, to return with coal from the tips at Seaham. Prominent in this coal trade were the boomies *Thistle* and *Vanguard* owned by Smith Brothers of Burnham-on-Crouch, Essex. They often shipped coal to Dover and had a crew of five men who had also to 'jump' the cargo out by standing on a trestle or the edge of the hold hatch, each holding the end of a whip which led over a gin block and down to a coal basket. They jumped in unison and the combined weight raised the skip to the deck or quayside. Hard and thirsty work! The river Colne, in Essex, frequently saw the boomies *Alice Watts, Hesper, Antelope* and the *Startled Faun* bring freights of coal to the Colchester Gasworks or to Crosby's coal yard at Rowhedge, where earlier brigs and occasionally small coasting steamers discharged from the north. Some of the cargoes were also brought by Crosby's own ketch rigged smack *New Blossom*.

The *Gloriana, Startled Faun* and the similar *Reindeer* at

one time also traded frequently to Battlesbridge at the navigable head of the river Crouch. Ipswich, Suffolk was the home port and destination of many ketch barges too numerous to mention.

Sometimes the boomies sailed to the Channel Islands to load flints for roadmaking consigned to south or east coast ports. If a grain cargo was unavailable, a load of shingle from Shoreham or Orford would cover the expenses of a return voyage to the north-east for coal. Some boomies carried coal from Cardiff in south Wales. 'Big logs' was another staple cargo, loading and discharging with the barges' own gear and heavy work. Many loaded building stone at Portland, Dorset, a trade for which their broad, flat hold ceilings were well suited. The large blocks of stone were for the construction of public buildings, usually in London, and had to be carefully stowed against movement in a seaway. The constructon of breakwaters also needed large quantities of stone. That at Dover provided work for many ketch rigged and other barges for several years.

The ketch barges did not often discharge on beaches, as did many spritsail barges, but occasional cargoes were consigned to places without a harbour and the craft had to dry out and unload overside into carts. Herne Bay and Whitstable, in Kent, Southend in Essex and Skegness in Lincolnshire were some of the places where this occurred.

The *Mary Kate, Eustace* and *Northern Belle*, with others, carried china clay from the tiny port of Charlestown, near Mevagissey in east Cornwall to Poole in Dorset, to Dordrecht in Holland and to Goole in Yorkshire, amongst other destinations. Many cargoes of scrap steel were taken to Germany and Holland in the years before and after the 1914–18 war, and tiles, chemicals, bottles and bricks were loaded as return freights.

Some boomsail barges traded up the river Rhine, towing above Dort in Holland astern of powerful paddle tugs having perhaps six barges in tow; though in parts of the swift river current the tug had to tow them in pairs through the rushing narrows. It took eight to ten days to reach some of these inland ports, with anchor work all the way and a constant vigilance needed. Returning, the swift current bore them down in about thirty-six hours.

Several voyages were made by Ipswich and possibly by other ketch barges including the *Eastern Belle*, carrying pieces of assembled machinery out to Portugal, usually to Lisbon, and perhaps to other ports. The size and shape of these cargoes often precluded hatch covers being secured above it and ketch barges made several voyages out to that often stormy lee shore with only hatch cloths secured over an open hold, though the freeboard would be greater than with a usual cargo. How this was reconciled with their insurance was a mystery.

The boomie barge *Arundel Castle* sailed out to Christiana (now Oslo) in Norway to load with timber, returning with a 6 ft high deck stack. It is probable that ketch barges joined several of the larger schooner and brigantine rigged barges in the timber trade from Riga in the Baltic, but this cannot be established with certainty.

Many ketch barges were owned by firms having a mixed fleet of barges or other craft and were originally intended for a particular trade. Walker and Howard of London owned several. Many of them were built at Littlehampton in Sussex, and at least one at Topsham on the river Exe, in Devon, named *Western Belle*. She had a distinctive hull form with a flared bow and a suggestion of a clipper stem, unlike most of the south-eastern built craft. The company owned several fine ketch barges named with the prefix *Lord*. Their cargoes were often china clay to the river Rhine, where they were towed upstream to unload at Dusseldorf, in the industrial heart of Germany. A usual return freight was bottled mineral waters for London. On discharge, a cargo of clay or cement might be offered but this was a speciality of the Kentish ketch barges and was usually consigned to Holland.

Boomie barge earnings were divided differently from those of the crews of spritsail barges in more local trades. The returns on a freight were subject to the usual deductions for agents' fees, pilotage dues and tonnage charges. What remained was divided equally between owner and skipper. From his share the skipper paid the mate, the seamen and the boy a weekly wage. Maintenance and damages had to be paid for by the owner.

The men who manned the ketch barges were of mixed background. Most were spritsail barge men accustomed to handling flat bottomed, leeboard craft with their idiosyncrasies. A few were ex-schooner skippers and hands, but many of those seem to have preferred to remain with round bottomed craft. The usual crew of a boomsail barge until 1914 was four men, with five in the larger barges setting square topsails and carrying perhaps 300 tons of cargo on a draught of up to 12 ft or so.

The mate and skipper berthed aft in the cabin, or in two cabins in some craft. The rest of the crew berthed in the fo'c'sle, cooking on a small range for all hands. Some boomies carried a deck galley in the form of a large portable box lashed to deck ringbolts abaft the mainmast and having a door on each side which allowed the lee one to be opened when at sea. This could be lifted ashore out of the way when discharging or loading cargo, hoisted by ringbolts in its sides.

Like all seamen under sail the ketch barge crews frequently faced hardships and sometimes death, though their lot was usually better than the wretched conditions existing on board the deep sea sailing vessels. Sometimes a boomie was overwhelmed at sea or was sunk in collision or by stranding, but many of the hazards faced by their crews were of men being lost overboard. This was a danger compounded by the low bulwarks of the type and their liveliness in a seaway. Entering some harbours, particularly those with a bar or with an entrance confined by breakwaters, was a peril which often claimed lives. The *Daily Graphic* of December 11 1906 reported:

'The *Star* (barge) of Colchester put in as the church bells were ringing for morning service, and one hand was swept from the tiller and drowned in full view of the hundreds of persons on the piers, the coastguard, and the rocket battery. There was no time to man the lifeboat. In the present state of the bar, with a gale of wind from the north, Whitby is nothing but a death trap, and it is hoped that the Board of Trade will enable the town to mend matters very soon.'

So a seaman's life passed without even his name being mentioned. Others were drowned in less dramatic circumstances. Robert Taylor of Brightlingsea, Essex, master of the ketch barge *Antelope* drowned in the Berth Dock on January 24 1886, and another Brightlingsea seaman, Edgar Herbert, was fatally injured on board the ketch barge *Kindly Light* on October 27 1920 when lying in Lynn Deeps in the Wash. Five years later John Sawyer was lost overboard from the *Kindly Light* off Southend at the mouth of the river Thames. These are a small fraction of the toll of lives taken in the sailing barge trade.

As ketch barges were built in much smaller numbers than those of other types they tended to be more individual in design. There was considerable variation in hull form and dimensions. The average length, if transom sterned, was 95 to 100 ft with perhaps 21 to 23 ft beam and from 8 ft 6 in to 11 ft depth of side. Hull form varied from rather box-shaped amidship sections with a short run and a full bow to flared sided and fine ended craft with a narrow transom and a long run (fig. 21). On a typical load draught of 8 ft one of these barges might carry 220 to 240 tons.

During the later nineteenth century boomsail barges were built at many ports from Great Yarmouth, in Norfolk, on the east coast, to Topsham in south Devon on the south coast, though the furthest west these were usually built was at Poole in Dorset. Many were owned further afield. Many of these builders turned out a new ketch barge at about 12 or 18 month intervals, mostly of between 200 and 300 tons capacity. Ketch barges were built at Great Yarmouth by J. H. Fellows. At Ipswich, Suffolk, E. J. Robertson continued to build the type following what locals claimed was the 'first' ketch barge, the *Lothair* of 1872. William Bayley, the Ipswich shipbuilder, is credited with a few early examples and Orvis and Fuller launched many including the little *Blanche* (1884), *Zenobia* (1886), *Matilda Upton* (1887), *Lord Tennyson* (1891) and others. Vaux launched the *Gloriana* at Harwich in 1871 with a pineapple figurehead above a finely shaped clipper bow and she had considerable sheer. Two years later he built the *Laura* with a female figurehead. The *Alice Watts*, amongst the best remembered boomies, carried a figurehead representing her namesake.

The construction of boomies tended to be too light for their size, form and cargo capacity, and some were

Figure 21 Lines of the boomie barge *Pearl* of Ipswich. Built by Orvis and Fuller at Ipswich 1889. 85 ft 6 in length BP × 21 ft beam × 7 ft 9 in depth. Note counter stern and fiddle head under bowsprit. Loaded displacement 269 tons. Light displacement 101 tons 14 cwts. Deadweight capacity 167 tons 6 cwts

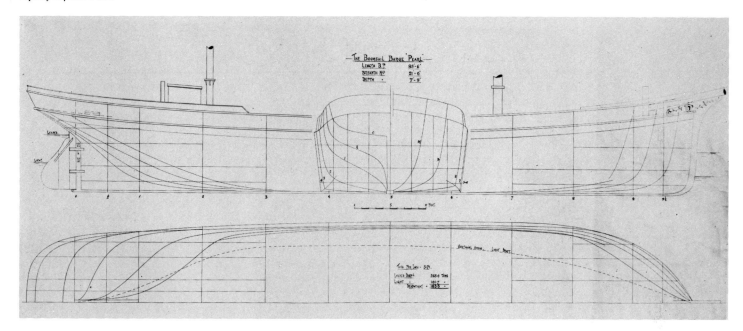

distorted and strained when loaded with a heavy cargo. Many were afterwards sheathed, often in mistaken attempts to stiffen the hulls.

Many well-built ketch barges were launched at Rye by G. and T. Smith, and further west on the Sussex coast, J. and W. B. Harvey of Littlehampton were respected builders of barges, barques and brigs when, in about 1878, they commenced building ketch barges and continued to do so until the building of the last of the type, which was abandoned incomplete on the slipway in 1921. Altogether twenty-nine ketch barges were launched by them into the Arun.

After the early years of exhilaration and experiment

the boomsail barge builders settled down to an arrangement of hull, and to some extent rig, which became common from Suffolk to Sussex. In most the square topsails had been laid ashore, though a squaresail was usually set when running. The boomsail barge *Pearl* of Ipswich, was a good example of these later vessels. She was built by Orvis and Fuller at Ipswich in 1889 and could carry 163 tons on a draught of 6 ft forward and 7 ft 6 in aft. Her chine hull was shapely within the limitations of a barge, having a counter stern and a 'fiddle' bow. The forward hull sections were well shaped from the chine endings and she carried the greatest beam abreast the mainmast. Her plans are shown in figs. 21–

Figure 22 Boomie barge *Pearl*. General arrangement profile and deck.
Typical of the ketch barges. The aft cabin plan is at left

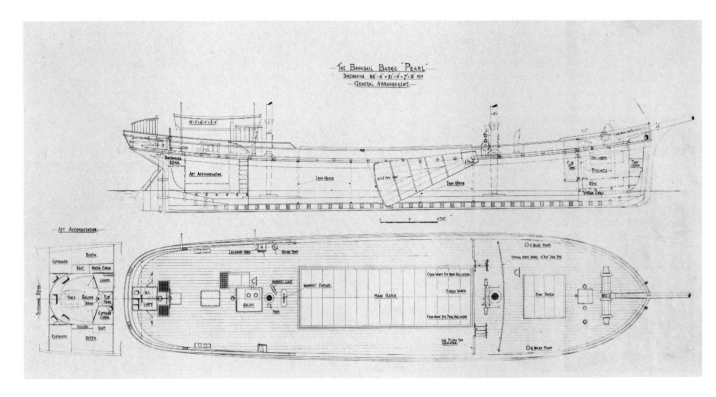

23. Construction of the *Pearl* was typical, with pitch pine hull and deck planking and ceiling on oak frames, floors and beams; durable construction which needed to be regularly wetted if it was to stay tight in summer weather and prolonged easterly winds in dry berths. The hold was continuous from the fo'c'sle bulkhead to the cabin forward bulkhead. Her crew was a captain, a mate, an able seaman and an ordinary seaman, who also acted as cook. The galley was in a small deckhouse immediately abaft the mizzen. The small 'whaleback' deckhouse on the counter abaft the steering wheel, housed a W.C. and a store. The crew berthed forward and the fore end of the fo'c'sle was often used as a sail locker. Gear for working cargo also often adorned their quarters. The skipper and mate berthed in the cabin aft, which was reasonably spacious and well kept, with polished panelling and brass fittings. In some boomies there was a tiny stateroom to starboard and port respectively, in ship fashion.

Figure 23 Boomie barge *Pearl*. Sail plan with roller reefing mainsail and point reefing on mizzen. Showing a squaresail for light weather, yard topsail on mizzen and alternative position of the boat on the hatches. The scantling midship section is shown at left

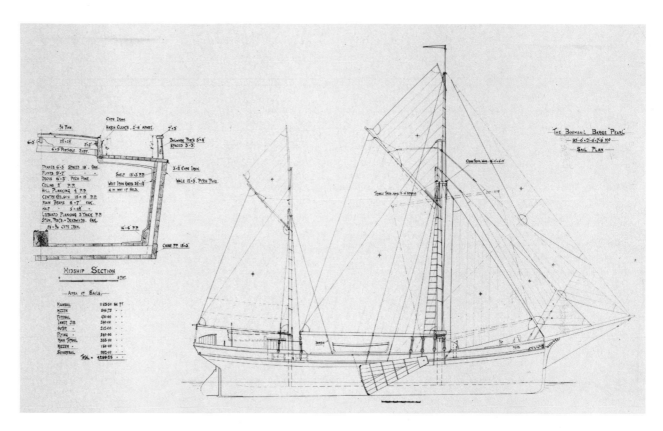

A ketch barge's fundamental difference from a spritsail barge was in usually stepping her masts through the deck to the keelson, instead of in a deck tabernacle; a more seamanlike arrangement. The rig of the *Pearl* was slightly unusual in having a longer lower mast and a shorter topmast than many boomies. There were four main shrouds on each side, set up with lanyards and deadeyes. Some early boomies, particularly those built at Brightlingsea, Harwich and Ipswich, where the influence of smacks and yachts was strong, had channels to spread the load on the frames and restrict hull distortion. The topmast shrouds were spread by wooden crosstrees. A runner pendant and tackle could be set up to support the lower mast when running in strong winds or in a seaway, and a shifting backstay pendant led from the topmast head to a purchase set up to the weather rail, port and starboard. The mizzen had two shrouds on each side.

The mainsail was reefed by the Goole Patent Reefing Gear which was commonly fitted in these barges for many years and enabled the small crew to roller reef the mainsail with certainty in any conditions.

The headsails were set hanked to stays; a flying jib, the 'boom' jib, the standing jib and the foresail. The bobstay was fitted with a bridle which was set up inboard. Some ketch barges had a chain bobstay led from the standing jib stay eyeband to the stem at the waterline. There were the usual sheets and downhauls and these sails were often stowed on the bowsprit. Many ketch barges set the flying jib (jib topsail) with a multiple part halyard in which the lower block, at the head of the sail, had a rope tail led through a block at the head of the lower mast and then to the deck. In strong winds this was set up to ease the strain on the topmast head. Many skippers preferred the halyards to be led to the topmast head in the conventional way and had the jib topsail stowed on the bowsprit when the breeze piped up.

Unlike the smaller spritsail barges there was little set pattern of ownership of boomsail barges. Some owners of small ships or of spritsail barges might own only one in their fleet. An example of this was the 97 ton *Olympia* ordered by Colonel Honeyball, who farmed at New-gardens, Teynham, on that incredibly active piece of the north Kent coast which owned and produced such large numbers of sailing barges. Alfred M. White of Conyer, Kent, designed and built this 100 ft transom sterned ketch which was intended primarily to carry coal for the owner's coal yard at Tyneham and appears to have been his sole vessel. After carrying cargoes for several years

the loftily rigged *Olympia* was lost by fire on passage in the English Channel.

Sometimes a village community found these larger barges attractive. At Tollesbury in Essex, a village bustling with fishing in winter and providing yacht crews in summer, there were several owners. Joseph Culf owned the *Mary Kate* and James Bowles ordered a fine ketch carrying his name from Aldous of Brightlingsea in 1865. Later she was bought by William Frost, another barge owner of the village, who manned her principally with his sons. They later took charge of his other boomies *Empress of India, Darnet* and *Lord Hamilton*. These craft were often in the coal trade and also voyaged to many North Sea and English Channel ports with cargoes of various kinds, the strangest being a complete wooden chapel shipped from Colchester Hythe to Bursledon, on the Hamble River in Hampshire.

There were few companies specialising in ownership of ketch barges but some fine boomies were owned by The English and Continental Shipping Co., including the *Eastern Belle* and *Northern Belle*, besides fifteen other barges with names prefixed with *Lord*. Four of these were built at Ipswich, Suffolk and the remainder at Littlehampton in Sussex. The smaller ones loaded about 150 tons and the larger around 250 tons. The *Lord Alcester*, launched by J. and W. B. Harvey of Little-hampton in 1891 was the largest at 101 ft registered length × 24 ft beam and 8 ft 10 in draught loaded. The smaller type was represented by the *Lord Tennyson*, built at Ipswich by Orvis and Fuller in the same year of 82 ft registered length × 19 ft 10 in beam × 6 ft 11 in draught loaded. The English and Continental Shipping Co. saw the heyday of the boomie barge between 1880 and 1900.

As the boomies had ousted the schooners and brigs

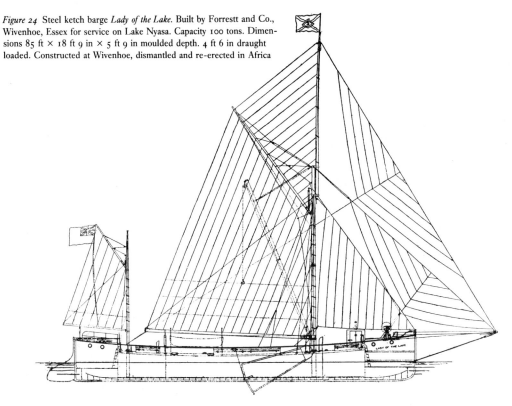

Figure 24 Steel ketch barge *Lady of the Lake*. Built by Forrestt and Co., Wivenhoe, Essex for service on Lake Nyasa. Capacity 100 tons. Dimensions 85 ft × 18 ft 9 in × 5 ft 9 in moulded depth. 4 ft 6 in draught loaded. Constructed at Wivenhoe, dismantled and re-erected in Africa

so, in the early twentieth century, the boomies began to lose trade to larger spritsail rigged barges, usually having a standing gaff mizzen and with this hybrid rig they were called 'mules'. Most equalled the boomies in average size but only needed a crew of three, perhaps two men and a boy, instead of the four hands then usual in a ketch barge. Railway competition, particularly in the carriage of coal, contributed directly to the decline of the

boomies, though the *Martinet*, the last of her type sailing, was still carrying cargoes to gasworks in the Thames estuary in the early 1940s; a trade perpetuated for another ten years by a few large mules.

Some ketch barges were sold abroad. Two sailed across the Atlantic before 1914 for service on the River Plate.

Numbers of steel, ketch rigged leeboard barges for service abroad were built at Wivenhoe, Essex, by Forrestt and Son, shipbuilders and engineers, who moved there from Limehouse, on the Thames, in 1889. The *Lady of the Lake* built in 1905 was typical of these craft and was constructed and erected at Wivenhoe before being dismantled for shipment in plates and angles to Africa and transport overland to Lake Nyasa, where the barge was re-erected to numbered drawings, rivetted up, launched and rigged. The spars, sails and rigging were also sent out as part of the job. This re-erection work, often with most complicated craft, was a speciality of the shipyards on the river Colne into the 1950s.

The dimensions of the *Lady of the Lake* were typical of the foreign barges built by Forrestt's. Length was 85 ft, beam 18 ft 9 in and the moulded depth only 5 ft 9 in. She drew 4 ft 6 in when loaded with 100 tons of cargo. Accommodation was provided forward for a native crew and aft for the European skipper, with another cabin aft for the few passengers who were occasionally carried. Her rig and arrangements were usual except for the raised deck above the forward and aft accommodation, which was flush with the sheer to gain headroom. Rails were provided around the quarterdeck. The cargo hatches were small, which suggests frequent carriage of deck cargo. The cargo derrick was unusual in English barges but useful for loading and discharge of heavy items in primitive places. The capstan-style windlass, the deck lavatory forward and the boat carried in davits well forward were also unusual but practical features, free from tradition.

The *Lady of the Lake* would have been designed in detail in the yard's drawing office, like almost all the other many, very varied vessels built there, ranging from sternwheel steamers for Russia to fast launches for South America. It is probable that this sailing barge and others from the yard were designed by W. M. Blake, who was a draughtsman there at the time and who had a special interest in sailing craft. The career and subsequent fate of the *Lady of the Lake* are unknown.

The first large coasting barge to be given motor auxiliary power was the *Grit* built by Messrs Everard at Greenhithe, Kent in 1912. She was sunk by a German submarine during the 1914–18 war. The war brought a gradual increase of freights which became a steady demand for shipments of bulk commodities to French Channel ports to support the allied armies. Seagoing sailing barges were well suited to this work and trade boomed, reaching a peak in 1917 to 1919. American independence day in 1917 saw just over eighty British sailing barges, spritsails and boomies, crowding the basins at Dunkirk. Owners, shippers and crews eagerly seized this chance to redress years of poor freights and scratching for odd cargoes.

From 1916 to 1919 large sailing barges earned more than anyone had thought possible from the freights of coke, coal, cement and other goods carried to France but several were sunk by enemy action including the proud *Cock of the Walk* whose motto inscribed across her counter was 'While I live I crow'. A few were converted to 'decoy' ships against German submarines, including the *Sarah Colebrook*. Others were lost by natural hazards of the sea, sometimes aggravated by wartime regulations.

The war stimulated development of the internal combustion engine for marine purposes and the ability to make more and regular passages induced some owners to install auxiliary engines, if these could be obtained. During the war the Wynfield Shipping Co. of Grimsby, Lincolnshire, bought several sailing coasting barges and fitted them with auxiliary engines made by the Dutch firm Kromhout. These included the *Pioneer* of 140 tons deadweight in which a 70 bhp engine was installed, and the *Worrynot* of over 200 tons deadweight, built in 1910 by J. and W. B. Harvey of Littlehampton in which a 90 bhp engine was installed. The firm also purchased the old established shipyard of J. and W. B. Harvey at Clymping, near Littlehampton, Sussex who had long been respected builders of large sailing barges and other craft. Wynfield commenced building large auxiliary barges for their own account at a time when shipping was booming because submarine losses and ever rising war freights were raising cargo rates to unprecedented amounts.

The 275 ton deadweight auxiliary sailing barge *Wessex* was one of the first to be launched there under their ownership. She was 100 ft 7 in long × 22 ft 2 in beam × 8 ft 4 in registered depth. A 90 bhp Kromhout engine was installed and such was the owner's faith in its reliability that the *Wessex* was designed to have a ketch rig which only set a boom and gaff mainsail, a foresail, jib and a gaff mizzen. A topsail, topmast and jib topsail were not carried. In 1920 the yard launched the *Moultonian* of slightly smaller size but of similar power and a start was made on a giant 500 ton barge of this type. However, the slump of 1921 set in and she was never completed. Two 100 bhp engines were to have been fitted and she would have been the largest and most advanced British coasting barge then built.

Figure 25 General arrangement and sail plan of a 250 ton capacity auxiliary ketch barge of 1922. Dimensions 100 ft length BP × 23 ft 9 in beam × 10 ft depth. Load draught 8 ft. Two 76 hp diesel engines. Speed 7¼ knots

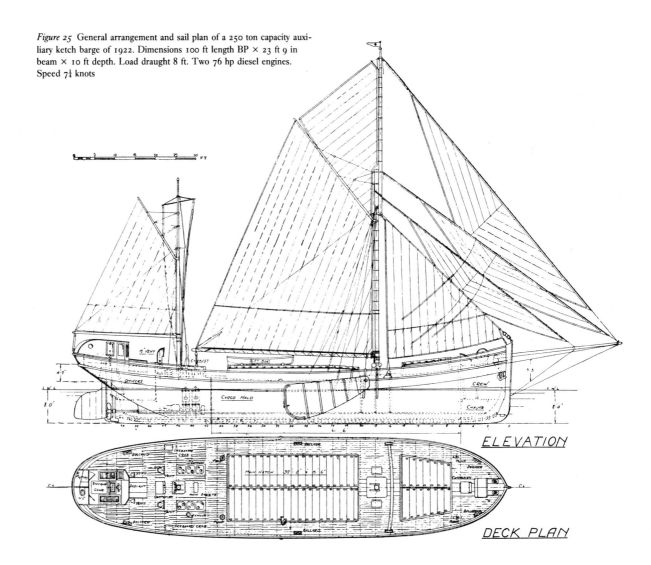

ELEVATION

DECK PLAN

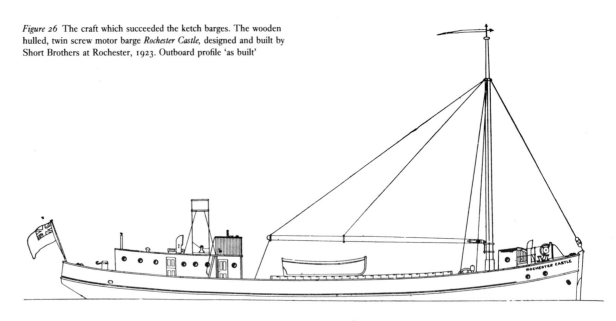

Figure 26 The craft which succeeded the ketch barges. The wooden hulled, twin screw motor barge *Rochester Castle*, designed and built by Short Brothers at Rochester, 1923. Outboard profile 'as built'

Auxiliary engines were installed in several ketch barges between 1918 and 1921 and some new craft were projected, with hulls of wood construction. Figure 25 illustrates an auxiliary sailing barge of 260 tons dead-weight capacity and having dimensions of 100 ft between perpendiculars × 23 ft 9 in beam × 10 ft depth. Load draught was 8 ft. Seventy bhp engines were installed, driving quarter screws. A seven and a half knot speed was attained. As in many similar barges a twin screw installation was preferred because of the excessive length of contemporary four cylinder engines producing about 140 bhp and also because of the light draught, when unladen, which would be insufficient to immerse a larger diameter single screw properly.

If an auxiliary sailing vessel could be worked by the same crew as a sailing vessel of similar capacity and if the sails were used on all occasions when the wind served, profits could be made. Even if an extra hand was shipped as engineer, the saving in time over a barge dependent only on the wind would outweigh the costs. However, as with all auxiliary sailing craft, the difficulty was to induce the crew to use the sails instead of the engine.

In 1921 a 250 ton wooden barge coaster was built at Chiswick, on the Thames, by Strand Shipbuilding Co. The hull form was similar to a Thames sailing barge but had a finer forward end and run. She was designed by G. J. Overy, the foreman of the yard and probably from

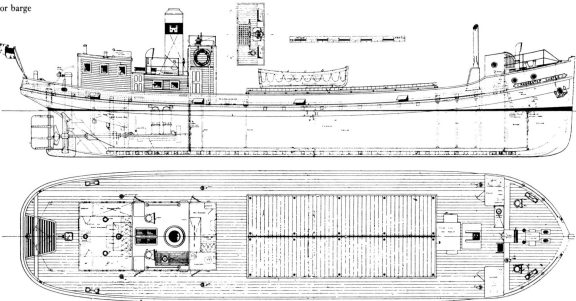

Figure 27 Profile and deck arrangement of the coasting motor barge *Rochester Castle* as designed

Lowestoft, Suffolk,. She was the largest vessel then built in the district. Several of these large wooden motor barges were built during the early 1920s, while the post war shipping boom persisted. The *Heather Pet* was typical. Constructed by Wills and Packham at Crown Quay, Sittingbourne, Kent and launched on April 1921 she was designed by the consultant R. C. W. Courtney, and was built by the firm 'to prove the suitability of a motor propelled barge for trading between ports which are generally served by the larger Thames sailing barges'. The *Heather Pet* was 100 ft 6 in long × 23 ft 8 in beam × 9 ft depth and could carry 250 tons on 8 ft draught when coasting. For river work she could load a further 30 tons. The propelling engine was a Vickers Petter, of 110 bhp with electric starting, direct injection and a reversing gear. She attained a speed of up to seven knots. The hull had the usual chine for much of her length, with shaped ends, a counter stern and a low fo'c'sle. Construction was on the builders' 'semi-composite' system where steel frames, beams and longitudinals and some stringer and tie plating was used in a principally wooden hull. This system was then common in yachtbuilding and in some small commercial craft, as it had been in some large sailing ships in the mid nineteenth century, but was infrequent in sailing barge construction. A somewhat similar motor barge was

Figure 28 Body plan of the motor barge *Rochester Castle* showing the evolution from the sailing barge hull form. Dimensions 100 ft length overall. 95 ft waterline length × 23 ft beam × 9 ft 6 in depth amidships. Draught loaded 8 ft 6 in. Capacity 250 tons. Two 90 hp diesel engines

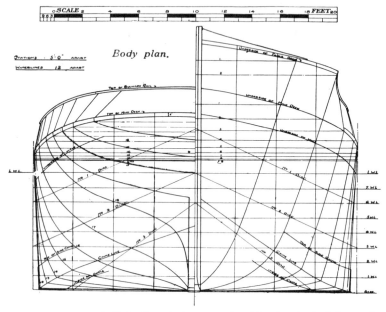

built in Canada in 1923, also following the hull form of the Thames barges.

Despite the growing interest in the full powered motor barge/coaster, many ketch barges continued to trade and several were given auxiliary engines. The large boomie *Sarah Colebrook*, built at Rye in 1913 was fitted with a Thornycroft 75 bhp auxiliary engine in 1922. Two years later R. C. W. Courtney, the naval architect and consultant who designed and supervised the construction of many Thames built craft for over fifty years designed a

large wooden auxiliary ketch barge having the hull form, construction and rig of the boomies, but which was intended for service in the New Hebrides Islands of the South Pacific. Her principal dimensions were 90 ft length × 21 ft breadth moulded × 8 ft 6 in depth of side amidships. She was to carry 180 tons on a draught of 7 ft 6 in. Details of her construction are shown in the midship section (fig. 32).

The keel was of three lengths of elm, sided 12 in and moulded $4\frac{1}{2}$ in. This was increased in depth at each end to take the stern and sternpost. The bottom was of $3\frac{1}{2}$ in Oregon pine laid in as long lengths as possible with a proper shift of butts. In some cases, notably amongst Thames and Medway builders, it was practice to lay the entire bottom of the barge first, starting with the garboard strakes, which were tie-bolted through the keel, and working out to the chine plank. The disadvantage of this system was that all the butts came in one line and this in a seagoing vessel eventually causes weakness and leaks. The best method is to erect the frames at the forward end and after ends and then work the bottom planking fore and aft up to the lower chine plank, which enables a proper and efficient system of disposing the butts over the whole bottom. The floors were of oak, in one piece, 8 in sided and $6\frac{1}{2}$ in moulded, fastened to the bottom planking by $1\frac{1}{8}$ in diameter treenails and 6 in galvanised steel spikes. At each end the floors were doubled so as to give additional strength, especially in way of the engine space. One of the chief features of a barge is the keelson which provides longitudinal strength for the flat floored and shallow hull. In this craft this was a single baulk of Oregon pine about 75 ft in length and 16 in square. A steel keelson was considered, as had been fitted in many wooden barges then recently built, because of the unavailability of long timber, but although this method offered greater rigidity, the steel keelson was likely to take a permanent set if the barge sat badly in a berth, whereas a wooden keelson would spring back unless it was so strained as to be broken.

The accommodation comprised the customary fo'c'sle, with two bunks and a cabin aft for the skipper and, in this craft, the engineer. Two cargo hatches were provided to the hold which was 60 ft long, enabling long lengths of timber to be carried if required. The engine was a semi-diesel of 65 bhp which was sufficient to maintain a speed, loaded, of 6 knots under power. A shelter was built at the after end to provide protection for the steersman. It also housed the screw steering gear, a W.C. to starboard and the entrance to the cabin to port. The engine room was entered by a companion hatch by the skylight, forward of the shelter.

The rig was a gaff and boom ketch with a roller reefing mainsail and mizzen, a single reef also being provided in each for emergency use. A topsail, a foresail (staysail), jibs of several sizes and a jib topsail could be set and the bowsprit was steeved in line with the sheer to keep the jibs as far above water as possible and adding a jaunty air to the bluff and boxy craft. Details of the keelson construction and of the floor and bottom construction and of the deck and hatch coamings are shown in fig. 33. By 1924 such a vessel was only of commercial interest in remote areas such as the South

Pacific, though it is not certain how suited she was to local conditions.

Ketch barges, auxiliary or otherwise, declined rapidly in the English coastal trade during the mid 1920s. Some were re-rigged as mules having a sprit mainsail and a standing gaff mizzen with brails to reduce the crew needed to two men and a boy, further reduced to two men in later years. Some which suffered this change were the *Dannebrog* and *Major*, owned by the Groom family of Harwich, the *Thalatta*, *Ena* and *Alice May* owned at Ipswich by R. and W. Paul Ltd, the *Matilda Upton* and the *Lord Churchill* and others. But the auxiliary engine, then the full powered motor coaster, were commercial forces against which no rig could argue and first the boomsail and then the spritsail barges were driven out of the trade, a process speeded by the competition of Dutch motor coasters in the British coasting trade during the 1930s. The *Genesta*, *Mazeppa*, *Davenport* and a few others struggled on into the inter-war years against falling freights, rising costs and increasing difficulties in finding crews. If possible they sought grain or coal cargoes, but most had to accept whatever was offered against the fierce competition of the small motor coasters and the deepening economic depression of the early 1930s. Everard's *Martinet* was the last fully rigged survivor, built by G. and T. Smith of Rye in 1913 and lost in 1941 when loaded with cement.

3

A ketch barge voyage

Harry Keeble of Maldon in Essex, son of a barge skipper, wrote an account of voyaging as mate of the ketch rigged barge *Zenobia* in 1912. It makes interesting reading as a typically straightforward account of a barge in the 'home trade', as the waters around the British Isles between Brest in France and the mouth of the river Elbe in Germany were called. It is reproduced by courtesy of his son Mr. Bert Keeble of Cowes.

The *Zenobia* was built by Bayley at the St Clement's Shipyard at Ipswich, Suffolk in 1886. Her registered dimensions were 85.6 ft × 20.6 ft × 6.9 ft depth of hold. The Registered Tonnage of 68 was typical of the smaller boomies, when compared with others built at the same yard such as the 103 ft *Park End* and the 94 ft *Moss Rose*. Such craft were then rivalling the last of the schooners sharing the trade and were yet to face the economy and competition of the early motor coasters, which would finally squeeze them out during the 1920s. So Harry Keeble wrote of them before their swift decline. At the time of this voyage the *Zenobia* was owned by Bushell of Dover. Her crew included skipper James Alliston, mate Harry Keeble, a man and a boy-cook.

'It was in the year 1912 that I was mate of the ketch rigged barge *Zenobia* of London. I was very proud to be second in command of a 150 ton coasting vessel, for I was only a lad and it was a big responsibility. Our crew consisted of Captain, Mate, Able Seaman and Cook. At the time my story commences I had been in the *Zenobia* for about three months. We had been away from home for about six weeks and were lying at the Town Quay, Poole, Dorset, unloading superphosphates from Ipswich for Dorchester. We had been lying at Poole Quay for about a fortnight and were having a very pleasant time there when one day the skipper came aboard and told us he had secured a freight for the continent. We were to load White Clay for the potteries at Bonn on the Rhine, I was very pleased and excited about this as it was to be my first trip abroad. It was about the second week in June when we finished unloading our phosphates and left Poole Quay for a place called Goatshead on the other side of the harbour. Anyone knowing Poole harbour will tell you what an interesting and picturesque place it is, and the harbour is quite a good one. The entrance is very tricky, on the port hand going in is a very high cliff known locally as "Old Harry", and in clear weather quite a good landmark for many miles, and on the starboard hand are long low lying sandbanks and at low tide there is a bar of sand which lies

the morrow. Wednesday morning we started loading, the foreman told us he could not finish loading until the thursday afternoon.

Close to the quay where we were loading was a long narrow fir tree grove, which we found full of squirrels, we had no gun on board but we thought we would try and catch one. We saw about half a dozen up one of the trees, so we climbed up, but the squirrels were too quick for us, and we did not catch any so we gave it up as a bad job. My two shipmates got down from the trees alright and left me up a tree about 20 ft from the ground. I trod on a branch and it broke and let me down in a hurry and it gave me a nasty shock for about ten minutes. After that I gave up chasing squirrels and went on board and turned in, ready to start loading the next day.

We finished loading on thursday afternoon and we had a cargo of 145 tons of pure white clay, and we battened down, with the boat lashed to her chocks ready for our trip to Germany. We cast off our mooring and sailed down to the harbour to get a berth for the night, ready to go to sea at our first opportunity.

The next day, Friday, was nice and fine, we made further preparations for sea and got some odd jobs done. At 4 o'clock we weighed anchor and sailed quickly out of Poole harbour with a fair tide to the east, and a fair wind from the west. As soon as we got outside the harbour we took our bearings from Christchurch Spit, that is a buoy about three miles out to sea abreast of Christchurch, and kept to the inner channel close to the shore as the tide was running fast and we wanted to make the Solent before dark. We were leaving Christchurch Ledge buoy on our starboard hand and were making for the inner Shingles buoy channel. Still making fair way we left the

right across the harbour entrance with only about eight feet of water at low tide over the bar. Facing the entrance of the harbour is Brownsea Island with its castle, which looks very nice during the summer months.

The short run from Poole to Goatshead is about two or three miles, so our captain ordered a tugboat to tow us round to our loading berth. We arrived at our berth without mishap, and got ready to load on

Figure 30 An unidentified ketch barge, unladen and sailing in the lower
Thames. She has a standing bowsprit and loose footed mainsail and
mizzen with reef points instead of roller reefing gears. Photo probably
taken before 1914

36

Needles lighthouse well on our starboard hand. It looked gaunt and fierce in the late afternoon of summer.

We were still holding a good breeze, and leaving the Shingle channel we were making Hurst Race with a fair tide leaving Hurst Castle on our port hand. I should like to point out, that going through Hurst Channel the tide at high springs runs about 5 knots or about 6 miles per hour, and with a fair wind and tide we were making good headway. At last we got through into the Solent before dark, passing Yarmouth, with the Isle of Wight on our starboard hand and Lymington on our port hand.

Half way between Yarmouth and Cowes it became dark but we were making good headway with a fair wind and tide through the Solent. At last we were passing Cowes, the harbour ablaze with lights from the big yachts moored there, on the other hand the wide stretch of Southampton Water looking lovely from the lights of shipping.

After passing Castle Point at East Cowes we shaped out for Ryde pier. By then the stars were out and the weather very clear, we could see for miles. Still making good headway we passed Ryde on the starboard hand, Gosport and Portsmouth on the port hand. Passing Ryde pier we took our bearings for to go through the Looe Channel, which would cut off about 8 or 10 miles. If we were to go around the Owers lightship we would lose valuable time and should fall in with the Channel shipping as most of the ships take their bearings at this point for up and down the Channel. We decided to go through the Looe Channel which was tricky especially as it was in the dark. I had great confidence in our skipper to get us through. We were now in the entrance to the channel and our

skipper said, "I can manage alright now Bob, you can turn in for a rest. It's now about 10 o'clock. If all goes well I will call you about 2 o'clock", so the cook and I turned in.

The skipper and third hand took the first watch; it appears all went well as we were not called until 2 o'clock. On saturday morning we were going past Brighton pier, the skipper gave me my course as I took the wheel. The skipper and third mate turned in, and cook and I took our four hour watch. We still had a fair wind from the west and we were sailing well, passing Newhaven in less than no time and at about 4 o'clock we were practically abreast of Beachy Head lighthouse. The wind had veered from the north and in less than a quarter of an hour we were faced with a head wind and an ebb tide. This beat up the Channel gave us only 2 miles headway in the next 2 hours and the monotony of watch on, and watch off, making no headway was wearing us out. The skipper got angry and growled. I was the same; we all growled about the weather, hoping the wind would shift. We hung on with dogged patience hoping for a fair wind, and about 4 o'clock on sunday morning the wind came again, this time from the southwest direction, and it was almost low tide. This pleased us as we had got a whole day with a fair wind and with any luck at all, a fair tide if the wind held for about 12 hours. This gave me an appetite for cold beef, hot coffee and hard biscuits before I turned in at quarter past six on sunday morning. I was called again at 10 o'clock and the sun was shining brightly, we still held our breeze from the southwest and were going along nicely. I took my turn at the wheel while the others turned in. Now we were well out in the Channel and left Dungeness on our port hand making good way until we got to Dover when we changed our watch. Arriving off Dover at high water or full flood, we took the ebb or north set with us. We were still holding our breeze from the southwest which had freshened as the day wore on. After leaving we were about six hours crossing to the Belgium coast and as darkness set in we were creeping up the coast at a good pace and we could just see the sand dunes in the twilight.

Darkness had fallen, and before long we could see the bright lights of Ostend in the distance. It was a lovely sight as we were about 4 miles out at sea and could just discern the harbour entrance. It was about 10 o'clock and a beautiful starlight night. Now for a night at sea on a strange coast, but our skipper knew the coast well and we had every confidence in him and we knew we could not hope to find the pilot cutter in the dark without his help. Of course we were still doing our watches. Our skipper was very pleased with the days run as I was. I was seeing and learning something every day, and quite enjoying myself. To think I was only just 20 years old and mate of a ship carrying four hands. I was trusted at the wheel day and night during my watch on deck. At last, the skipper called me and said he thought he could see the pilot cutter two or three miles away, so we sailed for it, and hoisted our pilot jack. When we got close enough we spoke to them and they told us they had got a Dutch pilot on board and that we should have to sail about 8 miles to the northwest where the cutter was cruising. We would find our pilot on board. Skipper said to me "Do you hear that Bob?", I said "Yes", "But don't you think it's a bit rough?". "Well", he said, "we will hail one of those fishing boats you can see in the distance". When we were near enough we hailed one and asked if they could spare a man to

pilot us up to Zurrick Zee, so we could get the customs on board, and a river pilot. They accepted and were pleased we had asked them.

The next thing was how to get him on board; we could not launch our boat soon enough, and they hadn't got one, so the fellow that was coming said, "I will jump if you can sail close enough". So we sailed as close as we dared and when we came about 5 feet apart I said, "Come on, jump or we shall lose you", and jump he did, like a greyhound, and landed on our quarter deck with me and the third mate ready to catch him but he landed quite safely. He asked where we were bound for and we told him we wanted to get to Dordrecht to take a tug for the Rhine, so our skipper said to me, "You take the wheel Bob, while I take a nap". So I had our Dutch friend to myself for a few hours.

By this time we were passing the West Cappelle lighthouse to get to the entrance of the Maas river and it was not long before we were into narrow waters again. The channel was well buoyed and we had a good pilot with us. I was quite enjoying myself to think I was practically in a strange country and everybody would be talking in a strange tongue, but it was surprising how many people spoke and understood English. Now I will try and tell you how our fisherman friend was dressed. His hat was made of fur and fitted close to his head with earflaps, he had a blue serge smock and short knickerbocker trousers buckled just below the knee, thick woollen stockings and wooden sabots or clogs. He could speak fairly good English so I could understand all he said. He explained the course of the channel to me and pointed out the places of interest most of which I have forgotten now. We were now passing Veere, a quaint old

**The sail and
arrangement
plans.**

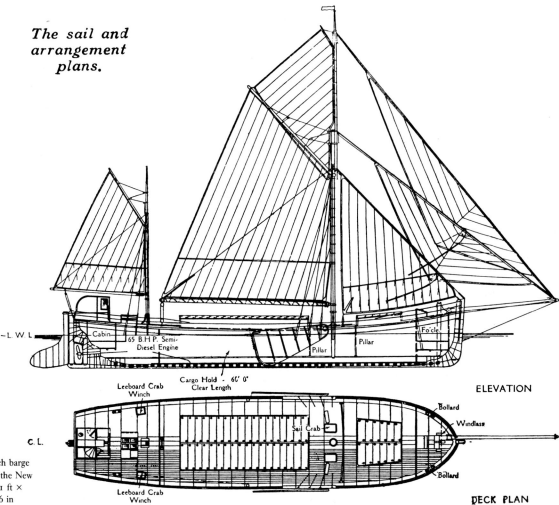

ELEVATION

DECK PLAN

Figure 31 General arrangement and sail plan of an auxiliary ketch barge
designed by R. C. W. Courtney and built in 1925 for service in the New
Hebrides, in the south Pacific. Dimensions 90 ft length BP × 21 ft ×
8 ft 6 in depth amidships. 180 tons capacity. Load draught 7 ft 6 in

Dutch town, but too far away to see the beauty of things on shore as I was still at the wheel which kept me busy, as we were now in very strange waters.

We were still keeping our breeze from the south-west and soon came in sight of Zurrick Zee. The skipper now came on deck, we hoisted our pilot jack and code signals for the pilot and customs to come on board. We were all questioned and asked if we had any goods to declare for duty. The ship was then searched and sealed down and no seals could be broken until we had crossed the frontier into Germany.

We received our orders for all clear, said goodbye to our fisherman friend and customs and shaped out for our long voyage up river to Dordrecht. Nothing special happened during our run to Dort as I was

turned in most of the time going up river.

I was called out about one o'clock on tuesday morning early and was told to get ready to stow sails and drop anchor as we were within an hour of our destination. By the time we were ready and stowed our sails we dropped our anchor in a good berth and I think we were all ready for bed. By the time we had finished it was about 3 o'clock and I think we had done well, leaving Poole on Friday afternoon, and arrived at Dordrecht at 2 o'clock on tuesday morning. Our A.B. was left on deck to keep anchor watch until 6 o'clock. At 6 o'clock we all turned out for hot coffee and breakfast which we shared with our pilot as he was leaving us at 8 o'clock for his home.

Now we were really in Holland amongst the Dutch people and some of them looked very quaint in national costume. Now for a busy time to prepare for our long tow up the Rhine to Bonn. The first thing to do, we had to put our pilot on shore to catch his train. As soon as we landed him our skipper was ready for the shore to order our tugboat. Then get all ready to lower our masts so we can get under the bridges, as there would be 8 or 9 to pass under. The afternoon of tuesday was well advanced and Captain shouts, "All ready Bob", and I was very pleased I can assure you to think we should have a rest and tea. After tea a good wash, change our clothes for the shore, we got on shore at last. I was a bit excited and things looked a bit different from our towns and the dress of the people in the town did not seem much different to our own until you got into the country, and things and houses looked very much nicer and cleaner. Instead of horses to draw the carts they had dogs which seemed very funny after seeing horses in our own land. We had a job at first to make people understand us, so

Figure 32 Structural midship section of the 90 ft ketch barge

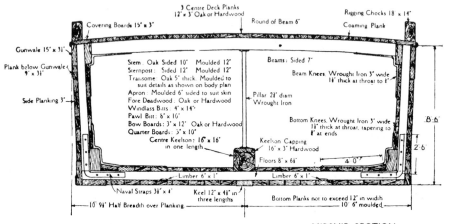

MIDSHIP SECTION

Figure 33 Structural details of the 90 ft ketch barge, keelson and deck edge and hatch arrangements

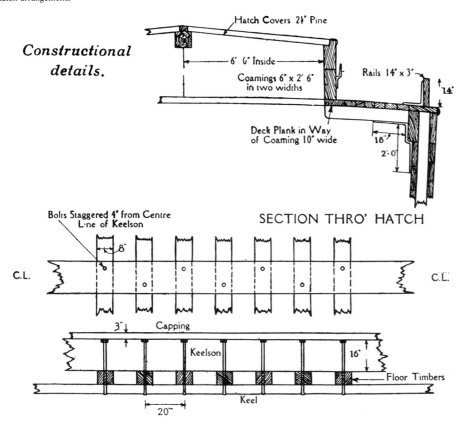

Constructional details.

Hatch Covers 2½" Pine

6' 0" Inside

Coamings 6" x 2' 6" in two widths

Rails 14" x 3"

14"

Deck Plank in Way of Coaming 10" wide

18"

2'-0"

Bolts Staggered 4" from Centre Line of Keelson

8"

SECTION THRO' HATCH

C.L.   C.L.

3"   Capping

Keelson   16"

Floor Timbers

Keel

20"

after going in one or two shops, we found someone who could speak English, so we bought our little store of cigars and tobacco, good cigars cost ½d and 1d each, tobacco from 8d to 1s 6d per pound. Cigarettes

were very cheap, so cigars were the only thing I smoked for a good many days to come. Nearly everything was fairly cheap, but sugar was 6d per pound and we had to bite a bit short on that. After a good look round the town and visiting one or two more shops we were ready to get on board again, so as we were ready to start our long tow in the morning.

I called our cook at 6 o'clock on wednesday morning to get breakfast ready, and as soon as breakfast is over we got our pilot for the Rhine on board and waited patiently for our tugboat. While waiting we watch the canal and river shipping, the like of which you will never use in English waters, big tugs, with two or 6 lighters which will carry anything up to 2 or 3000 tons of merchandise, little flat bottomed boats, with something of nearly anything to sell, sweets, tobacco, cigars, groceries, vegetables, provisions, boots, shoes and slippers and other things too numerous to mention. Dinner time and no tug; skipper orders dinner; dinner over and then our tug comes into view; he comes alongside, gives us the tow rope, we heave up anchor, and are ready at last and away we go. We leave Dordrecht about 2 o'clock. Now as we leave the town we can see lovely but very low country all round for miles. We all take about 2 hours each at the wheel except the cook. That means we have two hours on and six hours off as there is four of us to take our turn so we are not overworked. At 8 o'clock in the evening the bell rings aboard the tug, we all drop anchor for the night and until 4 o'clock in the morning. Thursday morning arrives, we up anchor at 4 and the day passes uneventful. Friday morning up anchor again at 4. The weather is lovely in the early morning and the country around us is all beautiful with flowers and growing corn, as the day gets well advanced we come to Emmerich the frontier town of Germany. The customs officers come on board and search us for contraband. They chat to the skipper and myself then give us the all clear. Then we have an hours wait, the tug rings the bell again and then away we go, the German people treating us all well as we come in contact with them. The days were much the same but the landscape is prettier and more hilly the further we get up the river. The pilot and I became good friends he tells me the names of the different towns and villages as we pass them. We passed the canal entrance that leads to Krupps ammunition works at Essen, the next town of note we passed is Dusseldorf, the scenery changing the while at last we came to Ruhrort. Here we wait half a day to change tugs as the Dutch boats are not allowed to proceed further without a special permit. The fresh tug comes alongside and gives us our towrope and we are off again. At 8 o'clock the bell rings and we drop anchor again until 4 o'clock next morning, and next day we proceed well up the river and mid afternoon we come in sight of Cologne, the bridge and cathedral which are very prominent from the river. We pass under the bridge which is about thirty or forty feet above river level and as soon as we have passed under the stone bridge, about a mile further on we have to pass through the bridge of boats. They haul some one way and some another and we pass through one of the queerest bridges I have ever seen. The city looks lovely in the afternoon sunshine and I wish I could get ashore and have a good look round. Just as we get clear of the city we see two aeroplanes and the pilot points out a big airship in the distance. It is coming towards us and we get excited a bit as it's the first airship we have seen so close. Later we find out it's a

Zeppelin; little did I dream we should ever see them over London causing death and destruction.

The days are still going on we are still towing sixteen hours a day and resting eight. On the eighth day after leaving Dordrecht we see Bonn in the distance and pass under the bridge, in a few minutes we are told to stand by for casting off, then a shout from the tug, "Let go". We cast off our tow rope and drop alongside the small jetty where we are to be unloaded. The small ship comes to life with the bustle of mooring, we get that done and the next order is to heave up the masts ready to start unloading on the morrow. After everything is done and all squared up we have tea and get ready for going on shore. Now for an evening in Bonn, we don't know a word of German and we are getting short of cigars and tobacco, so our first visit is to a tobacco shop, and asked the lady for what we wanted as well as we could, she said "Sprechen Sie Deutsch?". I said "We are not Dutchmen, we are English", so the lady then said "Englander he wait", then a man came to us and asked what we wanted in fairly good English, we bought what we wanted so got over difficulty number one. Now for a good look round, we hear a good band in the distance so we make our way to the river bank and listen to the singing and music but we cannot understand what is going on. Some people speak to us we don't know how to answer them, we walk away drifting into town again. We get tired of being on shore with no one to speak to so we make up our minds to go on board and turn in. On the way we pass a bakers shop and we see some cakes we should like, we go in the shop to buy some, then I told the girl what I wanted as plain as I could, she had a good look at us, and said, "You are English?", I said, yes. She called another young woman to serve us and she spoke good English, at that I felt we were among friends, after being served we had a long chat. The young ladies asked us about England and they told us they had learnt their English at school, and had never been out of Germany. Next day we started to unload our clay, it was put into iron buckets by two men and taken by a travelling crane into the potteries. The men using long handled shovels which you never see in this country. In the evening we had another walk around the town, sight seeing, there are two royal palaces and other places of great interest to visitors, we also had a look over Bonn bridge which is a very nice piece of architecture. After a good look round again we visit our bakers shop again and the young ladies told us our money which was a great help to us. We go on board again to get ready for the morning. We finished unloading on Saturday and the day passed uneventful. Next morning being sunday we get ready for our tow to Remagen; all being ready we have an hours wait for the tug, which comes alongside and gives us our towrope, we cast off from the jetty and away we go. The scenery above Bonn is more beautiful than ever, very high hills each side of the river. After about three hours tow we come in sight of Konigswinter and a very pretty town it is, and a mile or two above the town is a very high hill called the Gartenfels, and rounding the headland we pass Oberwinter on the starboard hand. We arrive at Remagen on sunday and find we have a long wait before we can start loading. There are three or four English vessels lying there awaiting their turn to load so we shall have plenty of company for a few days at least. Monday morning arrives I go ashore with our pilot and skipper to see when we can start loading and find we shall have

about a fortnight to wait, we are told to load Appollinaris waters for London. We had a very happy time with nothing much to do but enjoy ourselves. While we were there three English ladies came on board and took our photos and gave us an enjoyable afternoon and promised to send us our photos home if they turned out alright, which they did. The Appollinaris church and grounds were very beautiful with stones bearing carved figures from the birth to the crucifixion of our saviour. The church had four spires one at each corner. An abbott and six monks lived at the church, and to view the church inside they charged 6d per head. There were several people who could speak English and the police were more like soldiers carrying sabres and revolvers.

After we had been there about ten days we started to load. We took our berth alongside of the jetty and it took about three days to load us with wheelbarrows along planks ready for the men to stow the bottles away in the hold. The foreman speaks good English and we get on alright with him, during our stay in Remagen we have several good rambles around the countryside climbing the hills to watch the lovely scenery all around. Along the sides of the roads fruit trees are grown and the people who pass us all speak to us and bid us Guten Abend, which means "Good evening". At last we are loaded and get ready for our long journey home, we bid goodbye to what friends we have made. The tug comes alongside again, we cast off from the jetty and the shout is all ready and away we go. The run home is much quicker as the river is always running towards the sea. Nothing much happens until we have passed Bonn, then a small Dutch schooner is picked up in tow, and the first evening after leaving Remagen we arrive at Cologne, and were very pleased to get a run on shore so we could have a look round, we visited the cathedral and had a good look round. Then it was time to get on board and turn in to get ready for the morning. We are under weigh again at 4 o'clock and everything is going on well and that evening we arrive at Ruhrort. Next morning we change tugs again but do not get a start until midday. That evening we arrive at Emmerich. The customs come on board to clear us and seal us down. We start off again next morning still taking our turn at the wheel with nothing else in particular to do. Towards evening we sight Dordrecht again and arrive there in the early evening. We slip our bow rope and drop anchor abreast of the town, say goodbye to our pilot friend and put him on shore. We have tea and then all go on shore for ships stores and make our own purchases for our run to London. Next morning we all turn to at 6 o'clock and heave up our masts, get shipshape and when all is ready for sea we fetch our pilot for the river, get more stores and then on board again. After a hasty meal we all turn to weigh the anchors set our sails and away we go. The trip down the river is very interesting and pretty. Our pilot told me if the wind held we should get to Zurrick Zee some time in the early morning so we had to go to watch and watch again to get our rest. We arrive at Zurrick Zee just after daylight, so again we hoisted our pilot jack and code signals for the customs. They arrive after about half an hours wait, hove to. They clear us for London and say goodbye to our pilot and away we go. We arrive at Veere Gat in the late afternoon, get a good anchorage for the night, and we are in high hopes of a quick run to London next day. But unfortunately there was half a gale of wind blowing when we turned to the next morning, so

our skipper said "Bob, Bob I am afraid we shall have to give it up for today the wind is S.W. and right in our face, it would be foolhardy to go to sea a day like this," so we gave it up. After breakfast he said how about a run on shore and have look round and I said I would like to go. When we got on shore I was surprised to see the thickness and height of the sea wall, two carts could easily pass one another at the top and the sea at high water was much higher than the land. We next visited a windmill about a quarter of a mile away and they were grinding corn when we arrived and the miller showed us all over the mill. Everything in the mill was made of wood, cog wheels, driving wheels and spindles made of wood seemed very funny to me as I had never seen the like before. After leaving the mill the first thing that caught my eye was one of Bentall's chaff cutters and that seemed like home to me. (Bentall's were a noted firm of agricultural machinery manufacturers at Heybridge, near Maldon in Essex, the home of the writer.) We could not make the people understand us as they did not know a word of English. The day wore on and we went on board to get ready for the next morning, but the wind was still blowing and we had to keep our anchorage for a whole week windbound. Each day very much like the first, until friday afternoon when the wind changed into the S.E. so we turned in early so as to get an early start on saturday morning. This was the saturday before August bank holiday and we all wanted to be home by then if possible. Saturday morning we turned to at half past three and the wind was a light breeze from the east so we expected a quick run. We set the sails and weighed anchor and we were soon leaving Veere in the distance and it was not long before we were out in the North Sea. After breakfast the wind fell and we were becalmed three or four hours. In the afternoon a breeze came from the east and we were soon making good headway along the Belgian coast. Towards evening the wind fell to a calm again and our skipper predicted some rough weather next day. Now for a night at sea still becalmed and the tide taking us in a southerly direction which we wanted. About midnight there came a breeze in fitful gusts, and about 4 o'clock with the wind freshening still from the N.E. we were making good headway and presently our skipper said land ahead but a good many miles away. It was the North Foreland he had sighted and by his good seamanship we were getting close under the English shore. As the day wore on it came more squarely and a heavy sea running from the N.E. We passed the Foreland in quick time and as we neared Margate Pier we ran into a thunderstorm, the rough weather had come as our skipper had predicted. We were soon passing Herne Bay and Whitstable and as we got under the land of the Isle of Sheppey another storm caught us but we still hung on with a fair wind but plenty of it. After a time the wind lulled for about half an hour and then another storm broke catching us as we were passing Sheerness, and doing a good deal of damage to other shipping. By this time we had shortened sail and the wind began to blow harder than ever, but we were in a good harbour and fairly safe.

About half an hour later the wind dropped to nearly a calm and at high water, about 8 o'clock on sunday, we stowed sails in a good anchor berth and turned in for the night. The morning broke nice and fine and had a nice quiet run up the river as it was August bank holiday and not many craft about, the customs clearing us at Gravesend. We managed to get as far as Limehouse Reach that tide, and had another night in bed for which we were thankful. Our skipper called us at 6 o'clock next morning, breakfast at 7 o'clock and told us to get ready for the customs officers when they came on board to search. We then weighed anchor and drove up river stern first as far as St Katherines Dock. We docked that day without any mishap and we were glad to be back in London again I can assure you and that is the end of my trip to Germany.'

The *Zenobia*'s return cargo was Appollinaris water, a mineral water from the spring of that name in the Ahr valley. It was popular to blend drinks from its discovery in 1857 until 1939, and before 1914 was shipped to London in quantity, mainly by sailing barges. The empty bottles often formed a return cargo. The trade stopped in 1914 but was revived between the wars to finally end in 1939.

Harry Keeble remained a bargeman, eventually becoming a skipper, like his five brothers, before working ashore in an electrical factory. He retired in 1950 and died in 1975 aged 83.

The *Zenobia* was later owned at Gravesend and was broken up there in the 1940s.

4

The big barges

Besides the comparatively numerous ketch rigged boom-sail barges there were also larger flat bottomed barges designed and built for seagoing and rigged as two and three masted schooners, brigantines, barquentines and a very few as barques. All had the flat bottom of the sailing barge and were similar in basic hull form to the smaller sailing barges which were also usually constructed by their various builders. However, all were proportionately deeper and, though some carried leeboards, many did not. The largest was the 800 ton capacity *Emily Smeed*, built in 1868. At various times there were, besides the very few rigged as barques, at least three rigged as barquentines; three or more three masted schooners; fifteen two masted schooners, and probably more in all categories. In comparison there were at one time more than 144 ketch rigged barges of slightly smaller size, many of these carrying square topsails.

The true reason for the concept of the big barges is obscure, but as with any barge, shallow draught was the first consideration, either for working regularly in shallow waters, to cross river bars or to sail well up certain rivers to load or discharge cargo. Although many worked in the coal trade from English north-east coast ports to gasworks and coal wharves on the east and south coasts of England, where their large capacity on relatively shoal

draught were an ideal combination, several were built for overseas trade. The principal attraction seems to have been the ability of a flat bottomed, barge-shaped hull to make sea passages with little or no ballast, coupled with relatively inexpensive construction due to the considerable use of straight timber and the low labour rates in barge building yards.

As with the smaller ketch rigged barges, incentive to build probably also arose from increasing competition in coal carrying and other coastal and short sea trading from steam cargo vessels which offered more regular delivery and usually faster passages, besides which steam colliers received priority for loading at the north-east coast coal staithes. This coal carrying trade to gasworks around the coast by sailing barges survived until the 1960s and was a staple of the boomsail and big barge carrying during the late nineteenth and early twentieth century, along with bunker coal for some commercial and naval ports. Many gasworks were sited at harbours for the convenience of sea transport. Others were by foreshores of seaside towns where unloading on the beach was usually necessary.

Most of the big barges were built and owned, at least originally, on the north coast of Kent at the small barge ports on the Swale, the channel which divides the Isle of

Sheppey from the mainland. However, the earliest traceable example of these flat bottomed big barges was built at the rural village of Fingringhoe, in Essex, on the river Colne which is navigable to the town of Colchester and shares a common estuary with the river Blackwater. This then unusual vessel was designed and built by Philip Mosely Sainty, son of a noted shipbuilder of Wivenhoe, who was well known for designing and building fast ships and small craft and was implicated in smuggling. Philip M. Sainty seems to have inherited something of his father's flair for experiment and in 1856 the flat bottomed barque *Leading Star* was launched from his

Figure 34 Structural midship section of the barque rigged barge *Leading Star*, built at Fingringhoe, Essex, by Philip M. Sainty in 1856. Note side keels, arrangement of bulwark stanchions, deck edge construction and iron tie beams in the hold. She was one of the largest barges built. Dimensions 130 ft × 23 ft 9 in × 14 ft depth amidships, 13 ft 1 in depth moulded

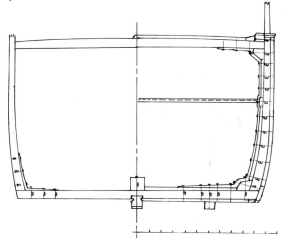

Fingringhoe yard for William Cross. Of 210 Registered Tons and 130 ft overall length she was classed with Lloyd's Register of Shipping and her dimensions suggest that she may have been intended for voyages to the Mediterranean, besides the usual coastal and short sea trades. Described as 'built upon a new principle', she had perfectly flat floors which were a novelty in those days of fine bottomed, heavily ballasted hulls. From this it appears that Sainty mastered the problem of designing a seagoing vessel to sail without ballast, though the feature may also have been encouraged as a result of change in the tonnage rules then current. Exactly where she was built remains a mystery though I believe the only suitable spot was at the foot of the lane which runs by my farm and which then ended in a small hard cum barge berth used for shipping farm produce and manure and bringing in road stone. This would offer a suitable declivity for launching and ample space for construction of what was then a large vessel for the locality.

Launches then, as now, seem to have been festive occasions for it was reported, 'About noon the company began to arrive and by 2 p.m. the shipyard was well nigh filled'. A cabinet minister, local squires and a military band from Colchester barracks attended. With this flourish the barque slid into the Colne and was moored alongside so that a reception could be held on board. They did themselves well as 'about three o'clock the attack commenced and fowls, tongues, pigeon pies, ale and stout, port and sherry, speedily vanished'. What a picture of activity existing over a century ago on the now rustic Fingringhoe shore. The yard was still launching craft in 1864. The *Leading Star*'s maiden voyage was to Sunderland where she loaded coal for Ipswich, Suffolk. Her subsequent career and fate are unknown.

Many of these big barges were intended for trading to

the ports of the north-east coast of England where the then shallow bars and berths made light draught almost as desirable as at the usual small ports of discharge. The chine hull form also enabled them to sail light without need for ballast or a return cargo.

Many of these large barges were owned by George Smeed of Sittingbourne, on the north Kent coast, a brick maker, merchant, farmer and barge owner whose rise from humble circumstances to an epitome of Victorian entrepreneurial success is well told by Richard Hugh Perks in his fascinating book *George Bargebrick Esquire.* Sittingbourne was one of the largest brick making centres in Britain. The trade was established there about 1740 but it was considerably developed after about 1830, principally by George Smeed and later by his partner G. H. Dean. The brickfields and other activities of the area needed quantities of coal to be brought in and bricks and other manufactures shipped out. Gradually George Smeed became owner of a fleet of sailing barges and a yard where these were maintained and occasionally built. In the 1860s he embarked on a programme of building big sailing barges. The design and construction of these appear to have been superintended by the manager of the yard, Fredrick Sollitt, a Yorkshireman who had been a foreman shipwright at Chatham Dockyard. His knowledge and Smeed's business sense combined to produce a series of large, flat bottomed seagoing barges; the 'bulk carriers' of the sailing barge fleet.

The first was the schooner-rigged *Seven Sisters*, launched in April 1862 and having an elliptical counter stern and registered dimensions of 125 ft × 23 ft 6 in × 9 ft 6 in depth of hold. She could load 300 tons of cargo. The three masted clipper schooner *Eliza Smeed* was next, launched in March 1865 having been twelve months building. The Sittingbourne Town Band played as she slid into Sittingbourne Creek. Her dimensions were 140 ft × 27 ft 10 in × 13 ft 2 in depth of hold, and she could load 750 tons. Her skipper for some years was Captain Waters of Whitstable, who recalled that she was stiff and able for her size and type, and sometimes made ten knots off the wind. After one rough passage trying to round the Longships, off Lands End, she put back to Cardiff, in south Wales, leaking and was later sold to American owners who placed her in the trade between New York and the West Indies, where her moderate draught would be advantageous. She went ashore on the New Jersey coast in the 1870s and broke up in the surf.

She was soon eclipsed by the barque-rigged *George Smeed*, designed to carry 750 tons with dimensions of 156 ft × 30 ft 6in × 15 ft depth of hold. She was launched in November 1866 and was sold to Norwegian owners in 1879. The barque-rigged *Esther Smeed* was next built in 1868 and could load 800 tons. She is believed to be the largest sailing barge built in Britain. Her nett tonnage was 494. She last appeared in the Mercantile Navy List in 1878. The *Esther Smeed* was reputedly fast off the wind, as would be expected from her hull form but 'beating to windward in a jumpy sea, (they) sagged badly to leeward', as Lord Runciman wrote of the type from experience. Some of these craft had leeboards but because of their draught and general size, most did not. Only one of these big barges, built on the south coast, was fitted with a centreboard, which was then common practice in American coasting vessels up to the largest sizes. The objections to use of the centreboard in British shallow draught coasters and barges were based principally on leakage of the trunk, weakening of the centreline structure and the bulk of supplementary stiffening necessary to preserve longitudinal and transverse strength, difficulty of repairing the centreboard if damaged and of painting and maintaining it and the inside of the case. There was also a certain prejudice against centreboards in most British sailing craft, commercial or pleasure, except for small boats and sailing dinghies. This lasted into the twentieth century. But probably the major influence in preference for lee-boards by sailing barge builders and owners was that until late in the nineteenth century their trades were in comparatively sheltered waters, where the craft had frequently to take the ground, light or loaded; conditions which would often rack and strain a central installation.

In 1871 Smeed's firm bought the Burham Lime and Brick Co. and their fleet of barges, including the gaff-rigged cutter barge *Henry Everist,* which was placed on the slip and under Sollitt's direction was cut in two, was lengthened and rebuilt to emerge a year later as the three masted schooner barge *Ellen Smeed* of 134 Gross Registered Tons.

It was difficult to obtain well seasoned timber in north Kent at economical cost and to assist in building the 272 ton G.R.T. barquentine-rigged barge *Emily Smeed* in 1872 Sollitt had broken up the hulls of several small and uneconomical barges and much of their oak timber went into the new barge's framing. She was 133 ft 4 in Registered length × 25 ft 10 in beam and 13 ft 4 in depth, presumably depth of hold as her moulded depth amidships was probably 15 ft; deep for a sailing barge. She carried 500 tons on a draught of about 13 ft; less than a contemporary coasting brig which would carry about 250 tons. She set roller reefing topsails, then common in short handed coastal ships and sailed under the Smeed and the later Smeed Dean flag until sold in 1881. In later years she was owned by J. Bull of Newhaven, Sussex, carrying gasworks coal, principally from the north-east ports to Eastbourne gasworks. She had frequently to be beached there for discharge on what could quickly become a lee shore and good anchors and cables were needed, laid seaward to be sure of haul-ing off in onshore winds. The *Emily Smeed* and Bull's other ships also took the firm's Bull house flag to the Baltic and many other European ports. In 1903 the *Emily Smeed* was sold to become a lighter at Aberdeen.

The *Ellen Smeed* was a three masted schooner built at Sittingbourne in 1872: 107 ft 10 in Registered length × 22 ft 8 in beam and about 10 ft 6 in depth moulded. She traded for 40 years.

The Smeed firm must have found these big barges profitable as the 241 ton, three masted schooner barge *Sarah Smeed* was completed for them in 1874 at Murston, near Sittingbourne. She was also partly built from timber recovered from warships broken up at Chatham Dockyard. Her dimensions were 125 ft 8 in Registered length × 25 ft 8 in beam and a moulded depth of about 12 ft 6in. She last appeared in a ship register in 1882.

In 1875 Smeed entered a partnership with his son-in-law G. H. Dean and the firm became styled, Smeed, Dean and Co. Ltd.

George Smeed's big barges were principally employed to carry coal but also often shipped cargoes of bricks, chalk to the north-east coast ports, cement and ragstone to south coast ports and sometimes returned with large blocks of building stone from the quarries at Portland, in Dorset. After Smeed, Dean and Co. was formed in 1875 the company policy concentrated on the manufacture of bricks and cement and the big barges gradually became redundant in their future plans. They were at first placed in partnership with other owners, many of whom were their skippers, usually on equal shares. By the time of Smeed's death in 1881 most of them were sold to owners on the south coast and a few abroad. By the early 1870s the *Esther Smeed* had her rig reduced to a three masted schooner and frequently traded to the west coast of Ireland. In September 1878 she went ashore on the island of Gotska Sandon in the Baltic, when on passage to Riga, presumably for timber. In 1879 the *George Smeed* was sold by her then skipper-owner Captain King, to owners in Norway. The same year the *Seven Sisters* was bought by Margate, Kent, owners to carry coal for the local gasworks. In 1901 the *Ellen Smeed* was loaded with scrap steel bound from Faversham in north Kent where she was then owned by Charles Marshall. Off the Lincolnshire coast she encountered a gale and with sails blown away and pumps which could not contain the bilge water she drove ashore at Sea Palling, Norfolk where her captain and two hands got safely ashore but the mate and a seaman drowned. The hull of the *Ellen Smeed* was got off and after rerigging she continued trading until 1913.

Neither George Smeed nor Charles Marshall insured these barges, preferring to stand the risk themselves and save the premiums demanded of others who prudently joined the 'Barge clubs' or mutual assurance societies which were established to insure against the loss or damage to sailing barges.

Elsewhere other builders were designing and building larger barges. Bayley of Ipswich launched the large three masted schooner barge *Parkend* in 1873; 101 ft 9 in Registered length × 24 ft beam × 9 ft 6 in moulded depth. She was later increased in depth by 2 ft 6 in and was re-rigged as a ketch. By 1896 she was owned at Bridgwater, Somerset and in 1919 at North Shields. The *Parkend* had disappeared from the Register by 1922. In 1874 Keep's yard at Greenhithe, Kent, launched the three masted schooner barge *Greenhithe* which could load about 400 tons. She was later sold to French owners in 1876.

The big barge type also had a limited appeal to owners on the south coast. James Duncan Foster of Emsworth, Hampshire, on a creek of the watery complex known as Chichester Harbour, was a man of business enterprise and one who liked experiment. He owned a fleet of fourteen fishing smacks and the yard which built them and other vessels. The fishing craft included three auxiliary steam ketches which were amongst the largest and most advanced sailing fishing vessels built in Britain, and smaller craft from the yard were equally innovative. In 1870 Foster's yard launched the barquentine rigged flat bottomed schooner *Thorney Island*; 102 ft length overall × 27 ft 9 in beam and about 13 ft moulded depth. Her raised quarter deck was unusual for the type in Britain. At first Foster managed her himself in the coasting trades. Later she was sold to S. Ash. Like so many of Foster's vessels the *Thorney Island* lay as a hulk at Emsworth from 1898 until after 1920.

In 1878 Foster's yard launched the brigantine-rigged barge *Annie Florence* for J. T. Crampton of Portsmouth. Her dimensions were 96 ft 6 in Registered length × 23 ft 1 in beam × about 10 ft moulded depth. In 1884 she was sold to Stapleton Payn of Faversham, Kent and was re-rigged as a schooner. She disappeared from the lists in 1894.

The most interesting of Foster's large barges was the *Fortuna*, launched in 1892 with dimensions of 100 ft Registered length × 24 ft 4 in beam × approximately 9 ft 3 in moulded depth. Described as a schooner but more properly regarded as a brigantine, with the mainmast shorter than the foremast and a gaff and boom foresail between the usual staysails. The square fore-course was set flying from the yard, a rig typical of Foster's scorn for the orthodox if an improved method was obvious. The *Fortuna* had a large wooden centre-board instead of leeboards but, unfortunately, the wooden trunk leaked and proved almost impossible to make tight. In desperation her crew poured chaff down it, which might cure it for a time. She seems to have been the only British sailing barge equipped with a centreboard, in contrast to its successful use in the sail-ing scows of America and New Zealand. One of the *Fortuna*'s skippers was Captain William Bate, an experienced seaman in coastal and deep sea ships. He liked the *Fortuna* and in 1929 wrote enthusiastically of her in the *Sea Breezes* magazine. J. T. Crampton of Portsmouth, Hampshire, had the flat bottomed barque *Enterprise* built for the coal trade which employed so many colliers maintaining stocks of bunker coal for the fleet at Portsmouth.

Ipswich, Suffolk, builders were amongst the first to construct big barges. Bayly launched the schooner rigged *Problem* in 1861; 92 ft 1 in × 22 ft 7 in × approximately 11 ft moulded depth. She was sheathed with zinc in 1867 for voyaging to the Mediterranean, which was her principal intended trade. The *Problem* was considerably repaired in 1874 and was again zinc sheathed in 1877, indicating she was some time in the trades to the Italian and Greek ports. She was of unusual interest in having the flat bottom of a barge but instead of leeboards had three longitudinal keels, the central one being com-paratively shallow and the two outer ones to act as bilge keels for windward sailing, an arrangement which still allowed her to ground upright. Similar bilge keel arrangements were tried in various experimental craft during the nineteenth century and since the 1950s the

arrangement has become common in many small sailing yachts. However, the *Problem* was a poor performer to windward due to the relative shallowness of her keels and probably because of their length. She was lost in 1886.

The old port of Whitstable with its drying harbour was another of the north Kent homes of builders and owners of big barges. In 1873 H. Gann and Son launched the three masted barquentine barge *Zebrina* from their Whitstable yard. The *Zebrina* never carried leeboards and was built to trade in the River Plate. Her oak hull was copper fastened for deep water passage-making and had dimensions of 109 ft 1 in Registered length × 23 ft 11 in beam × 9 ft 11 in draught. She loaded a freight of cement for the passage out to Argen-tina and sailed in the River Plate for eight years until she was brought back to Whitstable in 1881 with a crew who were mainly negroes, which was the talk of Whitstable long after.

Under the ownership of the Whitstable Shipping Co. the *Zebrina* was placed in the British and European coasting trade under Captain R. Skinner. She joined the company's barquentines which went seeking cargo as tramps and were often in the coal trade from the north-east coast of England, taking a freight of chalk from Gravesend or Northfleet on the passage north.

The *Zebrina* was launched as a barquentine having a forecourse but no fidded topgallant mast, as that was combined with the topmast into one spar. She had the reputation of being a lucky ship, usually getting a freight on both passages. But if she had no cargo for a long passage she needed some ballast, which of course cost money and was troublesome to discharge in some ports. Her 'knee head' or fiddle bow made her recognisable at a distance as the stem raked aft above the water, prob-

ably because it was sheathed to resist the floating debris of South American rivers. She had a counter stern and a raised cabin top above the after accommodation, like the 'den head' of a small spritsail barge.

Captain Skinner sailed the *Zebrina* until 1896 when he handed over to Captain Bedwell who sailed her until the 1914–18 war when she featured in a curious mystery. The *Zebrina* sailed from Falmouth during October 1917 loaded with coal and bound for St Brieue. Two days later she was found ashore at Rozel Point, south of Cherbourg, without damage except for some disarrange-

ment of rigging, but without her crew, who it was eventually assumed had been taken off by a German submarine which was about to sink the *Zebrina* with charges (their favourite method), when she was forced to dive to escape detection and was afterwards sunk with all hands, including the *Zebrina*'s crew. The *Zebrina* was salvaged and refitted, having a small paraffin auxiliary engine installed, and she was re-rigged as a three-masted schooner for her Cardiff owners. By 1928 she had become a coal hulk at Ramsgate, Kent. However, in 1930 she resumed trading as a three masted auxiliary schooner with a 55 hp motor, again mainly in the coal trade from the north-east ports to the south and west coasts. During one passage from Blyth for Truro in Cornwall she caught fire and put into Spithead. She was condemned as unseaworthy after this and her hull lay in Vedder Creek, off Langstone harbour for many years.

The barquentine *Nellie S* is amongst the best remembered of the big barges and was about the same size as the *Emily Smeed*, but was a little shallower. She was built at Whitstable by H. H. Gann and Co. in 1876 with dimensions of 131 ft 3 in Registered length × 26 ft beam and had a moulded depth of 13 ft 7 in. She was salted, copper fastened and the underwater hull was felted and then sheathed with yellow metal. Considerable amounts of oak released from Chatham Dockyard were used in her construction. She was classed A1 by Lloyds Register of Shipping. In 1896 she had passed to ownership of J. H. Bull and was registered at Newhaven, Sussex as part of their small fleet of similar vessels. Her rig had been altered to a three masted schooner, probably to reduce the number of crew needed. Her skipper was J. Bennett who joined her in 1882. In 1898 she was for a time sold to Brazilian owners but returned to British owners and in 1908 Captain A. Garner took

Figure 36 Alfred Revell of Whitstable in old age. He sailed in the brigantine rigged barge *Nellie S* from Cumberland to Mexico in the 1880s. The passage out took 63 days, loaded with steel rails. Return passage to Plymouth was with mahogany

command. In 1919 she was owned by Craske and was registered at Aberdeen, Scotland and was still rigged as a three masted schooner. By 1930 she was Registered at Peterhead and was owned by Frederick Mulliur, being in use at Lowestoft as a lighter. Her usual freights were from the north-east ports to Dover and Folkestone with coal. She was a slow ship and was once given up as lost after boxing about the North Sea on passage without being reported.

Most of the principal barge building ports launched big barges at various times. In 1880 J. H. Vaux of Harwich, Essex, built the three masted schooner rigged barge *Lymington* for their own trade and seven years later the *Silver Jubilee*. These left the register in 1888 and 1910 respectively. Vaux also built several large barge ketches and some schooners, besides round bilged cargo schooners and the barque *Princess of Wales*; a deep water 350 tonner.

Further north, in Norfolk, the leeboard schooner barge *Enterprise* was built at Southtown, Great Yarmouth in 1891 for local coal merchants Bessy and Palmer. She reflected the general dimensions of these craft in being 109 ft 6 in Registered length × 24 ft 10 in beam and 11 ft moulded depth. Rig was a three masted schooner with double topsails and a topgallant on the foremast. She was not a great success in the trade and was clumsy to handle. The *Enterprise* retained her three masted topsail schooner rig until the First World War, carrying coal from the north-east coast to Great Yarmouth for the steam drifters and trawlers bunkered by her owners. Later her squaresail yards and the leeboards were sent ashore and an engine was installed. She was lost at sea.

At Milton, near Sittingbourne, on the north coast of Kent, Taylor built several big barges of various rigs. The three masted schooner barge *Friendship* was built in

Figure 37 The scantling midship section and table of scantlings of the
130 ft schooner rigged barge *Nellie S*, built at Whitstable, Kent in 1876

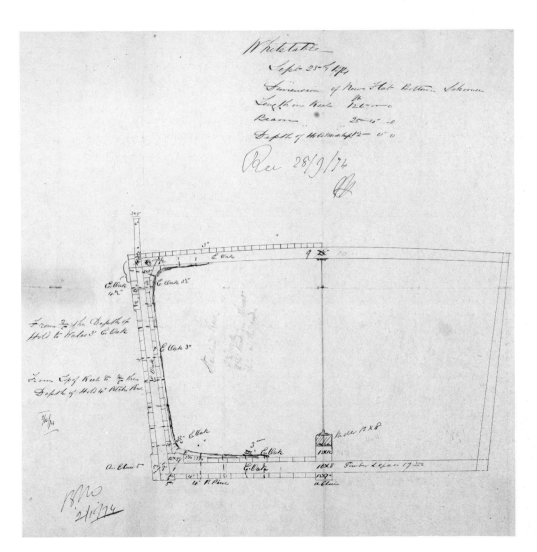

"NELLIE S" Port "FAVERSHAM" P.T.K.Q.
Built by H. & H. Gann, Whitstable, Kent.

Launched 22nd June 1876.

First master's name:– Thacker.

Rule Length = 130'	One deck
Length of Keel = 126' 6"	Under Deck Tonnage 282.69
Extreme Breadth = 20' 0"	Gross Tonnage 282.69
Depth of Hull = 12' 6"	Register Tonnage 262.16

Frame Space 17". Space between timbers = $4\frac{1}{2}$".
E. Oak and Italian Oak (Floors 15", 12", 10", some 9" sided. 8" moulded
(Side Timbers 14, 13, 12 and some 9" sided. $6\frac{3}{4}$" moulded in middle
Keel 12" sided 7" moulded E. Elm. $5\frac{1}{2}$" moulded at ends
Keel scarphed 4' 0"
Keelson 12" × 12". E. Oak and Teak
Rider 12" × 8"   E. Oak and Greenheart
Bottom planking 4". Elm and pitch pine
Chine 5".
Side planking 4" and 3" E. Oak
Sheerstrakes $4\frac{1}{2}$".
Planksheer 3"
Decks Danzig Pine
Ceiling 3". E. Oak
Inside Chine 12" × 9".
Deck beam clamp 4".
Deck beam shelf 8" × 8"
Deadwood – E. Oak.
Stern and Sternpost – E. Oak.
Deck beams – E. Oak.
Breasthooks – E. Oak.
Knees – Iron 7 pairs as midship section. Ordinary hanging knees to
        intermediate beams.
Rudder – E. Oak.
Windlass – E. Oak.
15 pairs of iron diagonal straps fitted on outside of frames from beams to
bilge.
Rudder Pintles $2\frac{1}{2}$" dia.
Fore Hatch 6' × 5' 6".
Aft. Hatch 8' 7".
Main Hatch 16' × 8' 6"

```
Anchors:- 3 bowers        12¼ cwt
                          11½ cwt
                          11¼ cwt
            1 stream anchor  5¼ cwt
            2 Kedges         2½ cwt
      30 fathoms 1¼" chain cable
      30 fathoms 1 3/16th" chain cable
      151 fathoms 1⅛" chain cable
      60 fathoms 9" hemp storm cable
      90 fathoms 7" hawser
      90 fathoms 6" warp
      4 pumps, one long boat, and one boat
Keelson and frame of vessel was salted, as rule, 12 tons of salt used.
            Classed A1 for 15 years
            "Copper fastened and salted"
```

1890 as one of several similar small ships built by Taylor and costing around £1,000 each, which was a low price for such a vessel, though the scantlings were reputedly slight. The *Friendship*'s hull lacked the form of some of her contemporaries. She carried, besides the usual double topsails on the foremast, staysails between the fore and main masts. Dimensions were 117 ft Registered length × 25 ft 6 in beam × about 12 ft moulded depth. By 1907 she was owned by E. J. Smith of Southminster, Essex and was Registered at Colchester. She could carry about 420 tons. The *Friendship* was run down by a steamer in the Yorkshire river Humber in 1912.

The Faversham, Kent builders J. M. Goldfinch launched the small schooner barge *Nancy* in 1890 for J. Greenstreet. She traded mainly on the east and south coasts under skipper G. Smith of Sandwich, Kent, who later bought her. In 1908 she was run down and sunk at anchor during a passage from Boston, Lincolnshire to Sandwich.

Many of these Kentish owners, and probably others, did not insure their vessels and the consequent saving on premiums was sometimes used to have a new vessel built. An instance of this was the 139 Registered Ton schooner barge *Belmont* built in 1895 at the yard of the Whitstable Shipping Company. She was 104 ft Registered length × 24 ft 1 in beam and 10 ft 8 in moulded depth. The loaded freeboard amidships was a meagre 1 ft 5½ in. She was not fitted with leeboards and had a counter stern. The rig was chosen by her skipper to be a two masted schooner having a square topsail and topgallant on the fore and a jib boom on the bowsprit. The *Belmont* was principally in the coal trade. She disappeared from the Register in 1920.

Probably if these big barges had been able to be built of steel their popularity would have increased, not least with their crews who must have spent many weary hours at the pumps as the wooden hulls aged. The Essex bargemen were not envious of the big Kentish barges. 'Look at them ole boys', they would say, 'a-pumping up chalk ballast bound down the north and coal dust south agin'!

The two masted schooner barge *Goldfinch* was launched at Faversham in 1894. She had a fiddle bow and a rounded counter stern and drew 9 ft 3 in aft when loaded with 250 tons. She once carried 265 tons of pitch. Like many similar barges she was built with a full topsail schooner rig; gaff foresail and mainsail, each having roller reefing; a main topsail, staysail, inner and outer jibs and a flying jib (or jib topsail). A patent reefing square topsail and a topgallant were carried on the foremast and a staysail could be set between the masts. Her normal crew with this rig was six but this was soon reduced and like all small sailing cargo ships, life on board these Kentish coasters was hard and the pay meagre. The romantic notions of many would quickly be dispelled after a week on board one of these workhorses.

Captain Waters was skipper of the *Goldfinch* from 1903 until 1930 and for part of that time was the owner, gradually buying shares in the barge until he achieved a controlling interest.

These barges were usually constructed in the same way as the smaller spritsail craft, without caulking in the side and bottom planking which was bedded with tar and hair 'setwork' or in pitch. Once when the *Goldfinch* was damaged aft in the river Humber through sitting on a pile, the local shipwrights replaced the plank and caulked the seams in way. The caulking worked out in a seaway and eventually caused a serious leak when the barge was loaded with a valuable cargo destined for France, emphasising the amount flat bottomed barges worked in a seaway and that the repair had not been well supervised to ensure compatibility with the rest of the construction. During the First World War the *Goldfinch* carried government stores to France in company with many other barges, usually discharging at Boulogne or Dunkirk, where the harbour was often attacked by German aeroplanes. Afterwards most of her peacetime trade was with coal from Keadby to Margate, Kent. The freight rates ranged from 8 to 11 shillings per ton. Although she could sail well the *Goldfinch* was difficult to steer. After a few years her square topsails were removed and the main topmast was sent down, convert-

ing her to a ketch rig and allowing the crew to be reduced. But she needed the square sails and a single topsail was replaced. In 1925 she was still finding freights and the foremast was lengthened by about 10 ft and the topgallant was also replaced. The mizzen and its rigging remained substantial to resist the pull of the braces for the square yards.

The *Goldfinch* was sold in 1930 for service in Demarara, South America. She was refitted and the bottom was sheathed with zinc sheet against worm. She made the passage from Plymouth to Demarara in forty-five days and entered the sugar trade out of Georgetown, where it is believed she was still carrying cargo in the late 1940s as a motor vessel.

By the start of the twentieth century competition from steam coasters and the changing economics of the coasting and short sea trades forced the big barges gradually to be laid up and sold; factors also affecting the boom-sail barges to some extent. Their prime had lasted about thirty years and, like many things maritime, had started in hope and ended in disillusion. While they lasted in useful trade the big barges had needed a unique mixture of square rig seafaring and the ability to ditchcrawl from their crews, and foresight and innovative courage from their owners and builders.

5

The stack barges

Until road transport of passengers and goods was revolutionised by the development of petrol engines and self-propelled vehicles, horse traction was supreme, and in the city of London hundreds of thousands of horses were in everyday use, all needing hay fodder and straw bedding in vast quantities. Some of this came in by wagon from the countryside beyond the ever-spreading capital. Much of it was carried up the Thames under sail in barges which loaded principally at the watersides of Essex and Suffolk farms.

Like contemporaries in Holland, India, western America and New Zealand, these English 'stack barges' carried much of their cargo on deck as well as in the hold. The deck stack rose perhaps 10 ft above the sheer and with the mate on top and the skipper at the helm, they set off every tide in the season, in an almost continuous procession of floating rickyards from the quiet rivers and creeks of the coast to the grime and hustle of London's wharves.

The hay and straw trade provided work for some barges before the end of the eighteenth century. After the French wars, in 1815, the capital grew constantly and demand increased until by the end of the nineteenth century the trade employed hundreds of sailing barges. It reached a peak around 1900 and soon afterwards declined with the introduction of motor transport.

The building of a haystack on the deck of a sailing craft and its carriage even on a coastal voyage of short duration, was a serious business. The stacks of hay or of straw were built from trusses made in the farm hand-lever presses. Straw was tied with straw, the hay with three string bindings. The trusses were carted to the barge and put on board but the barge crew built their own stack. First the hold had to be loaded. The first trusses were laid in with sufficient space left for a man to get his back against one and feet against another to press them to a tight stow. The remaining space was then filled tightly with trusses. When the cargo reached the coamings the outer trusses were laid with one end over the rail and the other on deck, so the sides of the stack canted inboard and so assisted in improving stability by reducing weight progressively to the top of the stack. Six 'stack irons' were placed in sockets in the rails; one pair forward, one amidships abaft the shrouds and a pair aft. These eight feet long irons shipped into square sockets in the rail. The trusses of the deck stack were pressed against these and the shrouds to pack the stack tight against shifting. Three main hatch covers were left off and all the covers of the fore hatch. Throat lashings were rove from the stack irons, through a scup-

Figure 38 Cutter and sloop rigged barges in the Thames loaded with hay. A painting by the noted marine artist E. W. Cooke, R.A., approximately 1826. Courtesy of Henry Higgs Esq.

per in the rail, one pair forward, two pairs aft.

A pair of wire breechings were made fast to the mast and were taken round the stack, leading aft to an eye in the rail on the opposite side. When a hay stack was built the top was given a covering of two layers of straw trusses to provide firmer foothold and the unshipped hatch covers were placed on top, two forward, one on each side of the mast and two abaft the mast. Three 24 ft square stack cloths were covered over all, lashed down by the bights of the throat lashings. The stack was held in place by the stability of its construction and its weight. The lashings were merely to hold the protective cloths down to prevent rain and spray penetrating the stack top. Another cloth was lashed over the after side of the stack to protect it against catching fire from sparks from the cabin stovepipe. Two men were expected to build the stack in a day, coping with the heavy work of lifting and placing the trusses and the intermittent arrival of more wagon loads, with country boys flinging trusses on to the barge. Much of the barge's sailing gear was buried under the stack, including the foresail horse. So a temporary rope or wire rope horse was rigged over the stack for the sheet of the small 'stack foresail' which was bent on for the work. Additional cleats were permanently seized to the shrouds of barges in the stack trade, ten feet or so above those used from the deck, near the mast. A spider band was clamped to the mast to provide belaying pins for the topsail halyard and sheet. Stack barges had a tall, high peaked mainsail and in some cases the long sprit resulted in the leach leading aft from the clew in rakish fashion. The main brail was taken from the winch on deck near the mast and was led to the dolly winch on the bitts. Lower brails were unnecessary as the bottom of the mainsail was reefed to clear the stack, using the second set of reef points fitted

to a stack barge mainsail, or a reefing line laced through eyelets, in the manner of a racing yacht's mainsail. As the stack projected through the shrouds, ratlines were not fitted and the mate, going aloft to stow the topsail in an unladen 'stackie', had to scramble up the shrouds.

A stack perhaps ten feet above deck and projecting outboard a foot from the rails on each side might weigh forty tons and the broad beam and flared sides of most stack barges were features intended to aid stability. Sometimes a freight of mangles or other root crop were loaded in the hold with a stack on deck above.

Although stack-laden sailing barges appeared to be the unhandiest of sailing craft, they would sail in any reasonable weather. The skipper at the wheel could not see directly ahead and relied on directions from the mate on top of the stack. In open water he might steer by observing the wake of the angle of a buoy the barge passed. Otherwise it was instinctive ability which kept her sails full and drawing. In some tiller steered barges the skipper rigged lines from the tiller in fine weather, through blocks leading to the top of the stack. He could then sit on top and see what he was doing. A loaded stack barge had so much windage at anchor that she usually kept sheering to it, checking on the scope of cable and then sailing off on the other 'tack'. So familiar was this constant movement that if it ceased the skipper usually guessed she was dragging.

On arrival, if bound above the Pool of London for discharge, the barge brought up and the centre trusses of the stack were cleared away to allow the mainmast, sprit, topmast and rigging and sails to be lowered so the barge would pass under the many fixed bridges. Trusses were removed aft of the mast case (tabernacle) but the after end of the stack on the centreline was not completely removed as once the sprit was down on it the

Figure 39 A swim bowed spritsail barge with a load of hay or straw bound into the Thames. A painting by R. H. Nibbs, 1878

Figure 40 A loaded stack barge ready to leave the quay at the head of Pyefleet Creek, where it meets the causeway to Mersea Island, Essex, about 1905. The carrier's cart crosses at right

Figure 41 Stack barges discharging hay and straw at Westminster. From a painting by Samuel Bough, 1858

Figure 42 The barge *Unity* with a stack of hay well up the mast
approaches the Pool of London in 1884. The skipper or the mate stands
on the stack to direct the other at the helm

stay-fall holding the mast was surged around the windlass and the momentum buried it a foot or so in the
cargo.

Many of the Maldon stack barges unloaded at Nine
Elms and a huffler was shipped to assist the crew
upriver. He often steered from the stack top with ropes
rove through blocks on outrigger irons shipped on the
barge's quarter rails, a late development in stack barges.
The skipper and mate rowed the barge with long sweeps
worked in rowlocks shipped in the forward rails. If there
was a favourable wind a 'bridge sail', usually an old lugsail, was set on the topped-up bowsprit which had to be
lowered at each bridge by a lead from the dolly winch.
Sometimes the crew towed the barge with a line from
the boat. Stack barges rarely, if ever, took a tug because
of the expense.

When the barge was alongside the wharf for discharge
the mast and rigging had to be hove up again before the
crew commenced helping to unload, which was
sometimes complicated. A dock just above Lambeth
Bridge accommodated only two sailing barges with bows
inwards, so each truss had to be carried ashore up a
plank off the fore stack. The bargemen placed one hay
truss weighing about 56 pounds on their heads. If
loaded with straw they took two trusses each weighing
about 36 pounds under each arm. The payment for all
this labour, often carried out by men who had had little
rest for many hours before, while sailing and mooring
the barge, was 5 shillings a ton for hay and 3 shillings
and 6 pence for a 'load' of straw composed of 36 trusses.
One half of this sum was shared between skipper and
mate. The freight of a stack to London was divided into
half for the barge owner and half for the crew, who had
to pay their share of the huffler's charges. Fire was the
greatest danger to the stack barges and several were

burned out by accident, sometimes when lying aground alongside each other for loading or discharge. A usual return cargo was stable manure for the farms and some barges carried sludge from London sewage works for the fields.

Essex barges predominated in the stack trade, joined by others from Suffolk and fewer from Kent. Maldon, at the navigable head of the Essex river Blackwater was noted for the number of stack barges built, owned and working from there. Many were built by John Howard at his yard at the foot of North Street.

The first sailing barge he designed and built was the *Surprise*, in 1879, and she was followed by many more. Sometimes he had three building at once, besides smacks, small yachts and an occasional larger sailing barge. Howard's stack barges were distinctively shapely; flat sheered, comparatively fine in the bow and stern form and unusually handy and fast, though stackies necessarily had moderate sail area to preserve stability with a stack of hay or straw half way up the lowermast. Howard was different from most other barge builders in being a competent naval architect, designing his craft on paper with accurate calculations before they were laid off and built. The result was predictable improvement in performance and speed and steady progress in the ability of his vessels. Nevertheless he draughted lines with the eye of an artist and his barge sterns have never been excelled. Howard's stackies generally had moderate draught, a healthy beam, little sheer or flare, yet the whole was a pleasing and shapely hull.

The 'farm barges', as some called them, were refitted from mid-July until mid-September for their season's work and Howard's yard often had a dozen, and once sixteen, in the yard at one time, bottom cleaning, re-rigging, replacing spars and having sails and rigging

fitted. The black hulls were 'breamed' by burning off old tar and black varnish with a basket of coals in the days before blowlamps.

Scale half models of barges, smacks and yachts lined the walls of Howard's office. He usually built his barges with single skin oak planking having rebated seams, but a few were planked in softwood with double skin.

To satisfy the busy stack trade Maldon had several hay and straw merchants. Some of the Keeble family were as well known on the floor of the London Exchange as others were at the helm of their sailing barges. James Keeble was a well known Maldon merchant and his nephews James (Jim) and Ebenezer carried much of his trade afloat with a fleet of barges which at various times included the *Sunbeam, Eva Annie, Ready, Burnham* and *Diligent*. Many other barges were owned by local hay and straw merchants and some by local farmers. Harry Stevens of Purleigh Hall owned the *Albion* and afterwards Keeble's old *Burnham* and *Eva Annie*. James Cardnell who farmed at St. Lawrence on the south shore of the Blackwater had the *Mayland* and *Mundon*, named after nearby creeks where they loaded many a stack.

Richard Seabrook farmed at the village of Tolleshunt D'Arcy, near Tollesbury, on the north shore of the Blackwater. He also owned barges including the *Pride of Essex* built at Limehouse, London in 1857 and the well-formed *D'Arcy* and *Defender*, both by John Howard of Maldon. Seabrook's red and white house flag with its blue S on a white circular ground flew above well-kept and well-sailed barges which were frequently in the stack trade to London. These were maintained at Seabrook's now forgotten wharf at Skinner's Wick, at the top of Thirslet Creek. The little fleet also loaded at waterside berths in creeks and by the seawalls of the various farms of the district, including nearby Gold-hanger Creek where openings known as 'hatches' were cut in the river walls to facilitate loading and discharge. These were closed with wooden baulks when not in use.

Across the river, Bradwell Creek, now dominated by a marina and a sailing school, was a home of bargemen and barges. Thomas Kirby and his five sons were all bargemen, owners and skippers. Their best barge was the *Water Lily*, built at Rochester in 1902. She left an unforgettable impression on the author when he sailed past her off Bradwell one day in 1948 when she was fresh off the yard after being rebuilt at Pin Mill. Bill Kirby was at her wheel, though she had long since passed, via the Parkers, to the Thames firm of Wakeley, whose barges continued the carriage of stone for the maintenance of the extensive Essex sea walls, which had been one of Parker's trades.

Until 1914 the Bradwell craft were principally in the hay and straw trade or carried root crops or grain to London, returning with manure for the vast fields of the Dengie Hundred farms. They loaded and unloaded at lonely berths on the foreshore of the Dengie Hundred or in outfalls leading from its hinterland. Barges also worked to the marshy island of Foulness, further south, divided from the low Essex shore by the entrance to the river Crouch and by the river Roach and its many creeks. William Hatch also owned barges at Bradwell and T. Goymer of Wick Farm was another owner whose craft worked to the village quay and included the *Bradwell*, *Dover Castle*, *Mary Ann* and the aged *Denton*. He was a better farmer than a shipowner and after a few years the barges were sold, leaving the waterside dominated by the hand and heart flag of the Parkers. James Parker's barges were sailing from the creek in the mid

nineteenth century and by its end Clement Parker was operating a fleet of well found and sometimes notably fast barges, besides farming on a large scale. The craft included the *Blackwater, Gillman, James, Sophia* and the *Triton*. He acquired the *Water Lily*, which had been Kirby's pride and which became the unofficial flagship but the fast *Veronica*, built on the Thames by Shrubsole in 1906 was crack of the fleet and amongst the fastest of the spritsail barges in the races on the Thames and Medway.

Clement Parker first entered his barges in the races on the Thames and Medway in 1905 when the *Violet Sybil* won the coaster class and his new *Verona* was second to the famous *Giralda* in the topsail class and went on to beat her in the Medway race. Bradwell men and their small community were exuberant. They felt like the 'giant killers' of modern football. Next year saw the Parker fleets triumph. The *Violet Sybil* won the Thames and the Medway races and the newly launched *Veronica* the topsail class in both races, with the *Verona* second and the *Giralda* third.

The *Veronica* was as fast when working. She was reputed to have once loaded a stack in the Crouch, sailed at noon and began discharging at Woolwich, on the Thames, twenty-six hours later. One of her skippers under Parker was H. Bell who recalled the keenness of the firm's skippers to get the craft going well:

'I have known skippers tie a piece of spunyarn around the standing part of the fore stay fall as a mark for the best position of the block and this would be moved half an inch at a time until the best rake of the mast was found – that was our usual practice in the *Veronica*. When one remembers that it was a three-fold purchase, the infinitesimal difference that one half inch could make shows to what lengths we would go to get the best out of these lovely craft.'

Parker's barges were allowed one week a year to refit, going on to the blocks at Bradwell waterside where the mast was lowered, sails were unbent and were taken up the hill to a small meadow where they were overhauled and sometimes recut by the firm's sailmaker 'Yankee' Bill Phillips. Clement Parker was fond of his barges and although he had the reputation of being a hard man of business, liked to sail a barge and sometimes took a party of family and friends away for a pleasure cruise in one of his better craft. His barges carried their 'bob' on flag halyards and these had to be lowered when alongside the quay, by the owner's order.

Barges occasionally worked up Salcot Creek, one of the four long fingers of water which probe deep into the marshes between Mersea Island and the agricultural hinterland of the north shore of the Blackwater. This quiet creek, filled in its lower part with oyster layings, leads at high water to the twin villages of Salcot and Virley, each with its church, pub, couple of dozen houses and extensive surrounding farms. Somehow the barges worked their way up its tortuous, narrow upper reaches to load a stack at improvised wharves by the sea walls. Barges sometimes berthed at Church Wharf at the head of the creek to load a stack and the *Lord Warden* was reputedly the last to do so, close by the village church of Salcot.

Tollesbury, a village of fishermen and later also yacht hands, was another loading port for the stack barges which could lie on the village hard allowing horse drawn wagons to stand alongside. Fisher was one local owner who proudly named his new barge for the village when she sailed up the creek in 1901. This bold sheered barge was a stout sailer and remained under canvas until 1950. In the darkest days of England's history, in 1940, the *Tollesbury* brought more than 200 soldiers off the beach at Dunkirk. The large ketch barges owned at Tollesbury by the Frost family were not in the stack work but the *Mary Kate*, owned by J. Culf, sometimes shipped a stack on the hard and returned with manure.

A now almost forgotten 'harbour' reached by the stackies was in Old Hall Creek, a community of 50 people to the north of Tollesbury village, where now only the wildfowl and distant farm tractors break the silence. Before the First World War there was a coal yard, a brickworks, a lime kiln, a pub and a barge quay there where spritsail barges discharged coals from the north-east coast, chalk and lime from Kent and manure from London. They carried away bricks, root crops, hay and straw. Banyard's barges were joined there by craft owned by Seabrook from nearby Tolleshunt D'Arcy and others from elsewhere. There were other owners with interests in the stack trade from the Essex rivers Crouch and Roach; from the Colne; from Walton backwaters and from the Suffolk rivers where, on the north shore of the Stour, the extensive farms of Wrinch of Ewarton sent large quantities of hay and straw to London. His craft included the *Bluebell, Butterfly, Farmers Boy, Primrose* and *Snowdrop*, with others, principally employed in supplying his contract for the army horses' fodder and bedding in London, unloading at a wharf which he owned in Vauxhall. These barges and many others loaded stacks in the rivers Orwell, Deben and Alde, though their principal cargoes came mainly from the Stourside farms.

Barges also loaded stacks on the foreshores of farms by the lower Thames, particularly from Benfleet and Grays in that area of Essex now dominated by a population from London. Most of these were owned at Grays,

Figure 43 A latter–day stack barge, the *Violet* of Maldon, owned by Francis and Guilders of Colchester, towing down the river Colne off Rowhedge in 1948. The hold and deck are filled with bales of straw bound for the paper mill at Ridham Dock, on the Swale in Kent during the short revival of the stack trade

Leigh-on-Sea or Southend. Stacks were also carried from the Kentish shore and the river Medway and surrounding creeks, but much less frequently than from Essex because of the differing nature of that county's agriculture. London's horse traffic began to decline about 1912 and the introduction of motor buses to replace horse drawn vehicles led to a marked decline in stack work, though it lingered into the 1920s and experienced a temporary revival in the carriage of baled straw from Colchester Hythe by barges during the later 1940s. Loading of the rectangular bales of compacted straw was quicker and perhaps easier than in earlier times but the stacks remained large and made passage-making cumbersome, even with the aid of auxiliary and fully powered barges. The barges engaged included the fine auxiliaries *Raybel*, *Beatrice Maud* and *Arcades*, owned by A. Sully of London and their motor barges *Phoenician* and *Convoy*.

To the author, the *Arcades* epitomised the best of sail and power in a barge. She was built as the *Olive Mary* by Wills and Packham at Sittingbourne, Kent, in 1921, during the post-war cargo boom which soon after collapsed. Like many sailing barges she suffered severe mishaps. In 1936, while still a sailing barge, she was towing into Yarmouth harbour, Norfolk, loaded with oil-seed cake when she was sunk in collision with a Scottish drifter. The *Arcades* was raised and was refitted as an auxiliary barge in the ownership of Alfred Sully and George Andrews, of the repairers. She was renamed at that time. During the Second World War she and similar auxiliary sailing barges were sent to the river Clyde, in Scotland, to carry Ministry of War transport cargoes. Some of the barges worked for a time to the islands of the outer Hebrides. All returned after the war to the south-east coast. The *Arcades* was unfortunately burned to the waterline off Sheerness, Kent, in June 1947 when bound to the paper mills at Ridham Dock, on the Swale, loaded with straw. Her remains were berthed at Sittingbourne for repair but this was reckoned too expensive for trading prospects.

The straw trade died out during the early 1950s and another aspect of barging ended.

6

A bargeman's life – from farm boy to skipper

Coasting bargemen sometimes came of seafaring stock but more frequently were from rural or urban areas bordering the coast where they might spend their working life. This was so for many in south-east England and the story of Felix Mallett is typical.

He first went to sea aged $15\frac{1}{2}$ in June 1897 as third hand in the Colchester owned sailing barge *Unique*. Like many before him Felix left the land to go afloat. He had worked since he was ten years old on farms at Wigborough, about eight miles from Colchester where he earned only three shillings per week. As third hand in a sailing barge he got ten shillings.

Mr. Littlebury, a corn merchant, was the principal owner of the *Unique* and also of the barge *Eureka*, both built at Maldon. The firm also managed the barge *Hyacinth* and the *Violet*; built to sail against each other at the instigation of E. H. Bentall, an agriculture engineering works owner of Heybridge and a wealthy eccentric. There were then only a few work-worn barges owned at Colchester Hythe. One owned by Thomas Wood bore his name. Shead had several, including the *Faith* and the *Prosperous* which frequently carried chalk and reputedly leaked so badly that the crew slept on the locker tops with one hand dangling over so as to be roused for pumping when the water touched it. Marriage, the

Colchester millers, had the well-formed *Fleur de Lys* and the bulkier *Maid of the Mill*.

Felix Mallett recalled the Hythe, Colchester's port, as a single quay, stretching from the present road bridge to the gas works (now demolished), about one quarter of its present length. A wooden jetty with a hand crane stood further down, opposite Distillery Lane and on the opposite bank the quay was shorter, quickly ending in saltings. Activity was dominated by ketch barges bringing coal for the gas works retorts and other barges unloading or loading freights for Owen Parry's oil mills along the quay. There were other businesses including Howe's barge yard above the road and railway bridges.

The crews of the Colchester barges worked for shares of the freight money, except for Marriage's barges, whose crews received £1 per week, with some additional payment for loading and other odd tasks. The crew's share was computed by dividing the freight money in half, for owner and crew. The skipper had two-thirds of the crew's half and the mate one third. The skipper paid for the third hand's food and for the 'huffler', if one was used. Returns depended on the freights which Felix Mallett recalled as 2 shillings and 6 pence per ton for linseed and 6 pence a quarter for wheat and barley. The *Unique* traded regularly to East Mills at Colchester with

Figure 44 Spritsail barges at the Hythe, Colchester, in 1901. This was the home port of Felix Mallett and of many other bargemen until the mid twentieth century

wheat. Her return freights to London were often stacks of hay, usually loaded at Hythe Quay, just below the road bridge and shipped to wharves at Vauxhall as horse fodder. Sometimes the barge worked elsewhere. One day in 1898, lying off Wrabness on the river Stour, they saw the new sailing barge *Edme* coming up river, fresh from the yard of her builders, J. and H. Cann of Harwich. She was bound to her home port of Mistley to load her first freight. Her owners were three of the Horlock family but it was said that her sails were paid for by the English Diastatic Malt Extract Company, after whom she was named in initials.

Soon after joining the *Unique*, Felix Mallett and others on board witnessed the capsizing of the sailing barge *Victoria* when she was racing in the lower Thames during a private match against the barge *Satanita* designed by A. White Junior, whose father was the builder of the *Victoria*. The race was arranged between them to test the worth of their designs and the owners of the barges *Vectis*, *Arrow* and *Conqueror* agreed to sail with them to make a more lively race. Added interest was that the owner of each barge was to steer and paid £5 into a prize fund to give £20 to the winning crew and £5 to the second. They started off from Gravesend on a Sunday morning, the first barge race ever held on that day, in a fresh south-west wind. The racers rounded the Mouse Light vessel, the *Satanita* first at 2 hours 18 minutes and the others following within a few minutes. On the beat back the *Victoria* was caught by a heavy squall near the Middle Oaze buoy and capsized, floating bottom up. Several of the crew were able to climb up the side as she went over and clung to the bottom but the owner, Henry Austen, the skipper and the mate were flung into the water. A tug acting as committee boat steamed to the rescue but the owner and the skipper

Figure 45 The view from the wheel. A spritsail barge 'up-Swin' in a fine sailing breeze. The mainsheet lower block, with the sheet belayed to its pin is hooked to the traveller on the wooden sheet horse. Sweeps are carried in irons above the wash of the lee side. The lee vang fall swings slack and a leeboard capstan is in the right foreground

were drowned. The barge was salvaged and refitted.

Felix Mallett's aptitude for his new way of life earned him the offer of the mate's berth in the Colchester owned barge *Eureka* in 1899. He was $17\frac{1}{2}$ years old and a mate's pay was 23 shillings per week. His work on board the *Eureka* included letting go and getting up the anchor with the windlass, raising and lowering the bowsprit and setting and stowing the jib, as well as the topsail, staysail and foresail, rigging the steering tackles if these were needed when carrying a deck stack, on which the skipper would stand and steer in fine weather. He helped the skipper row the barge when necessary during calms or in upriver waters and helped when the sails or the masts were lowered. The amount of unexpected labour experienced in a working sailing vessel was exemplified when the head chain of one leeboard of the *Eureka* broke. She was loaded with a stack of 40 loads of hay, which was about 10 ft above deck, about 25 ft wide and projected 2 or 3 ft outboard from each side. To get at the leeboard and effect a repair took a whole day, the barge having to be put ashore on the Maplin Sand, fortunately in fine weather.

Owen Parry's oil mills had regular trade and the crews of its barges were spared the periods of unpaid idleness which were the dread of sailing bargemen. At that time Owen Parry's mills were using imported cotton seed or groundnuts for their products in place of the earlier English-grown linseed or rape seed and this trade needed a fleet of sailing barges for transport of raw materials and products from and to the port of London. Much of the manufactured oil was shipped to the Union Oil Mills or to Younghusband, Barnes at Blackfriars, for use in varnish making. The oil was shipped in wooden casks which sometimes leaked and the coopers' remedy was to get some linseed from a press, apply it firmly to the leak and nail a lead tingle over it. Oil from cotton seed or coconuts tended to set in the barrel and had either to be steamed out or the hoops removed, leaving the contents standing as a lump, the barrel becoming a bundle of staves and hoops. Some oil cake was shipped from the mills but most of this was loaded into railway trucks.

Beckwith and Co. were prominent Colchester owners at that time with the sailing barges *Arnold Hirst*, *Jessie*, *Empress*, the steel built *Rathbale* and the *Pride of the Colne* which had her bottom sheathed on the blocks at Howe's Colchester yard. This was typical of the type of work carried out at local barge yards and involved placing the barge on level wooden transverse baulks which were well supported and had the upper edges about four feet above the bottom of the river. The sheathing was fastened by driving bolts up from below through a total of 4 in of plank, 6 in of floor and 2½ in of hold ceiling. Besides the difficulty of fitting the bottom sheathing planks in such conditions, the work of driving such fastenings from below in the confined space under the barge was desperately hard. This set of barge blocks was still in use into the early 1950s but has since disappeared.

Joseph Beckwith also owned the steam coasters *Esperando* and *Prompt*, of about 200 tons and a curious experimental vessel named *Tubular*, which had twin screws, then a notable exception in small craft – she was lost on passage to the river Humber – and the *Romley*, an old Lowestoft steam drifter. There were also in succession coasters named *Essex* and *Colchester*. Beckwith also had smaller steamers in the hoy trade; a survival of centuries, carrying goods of all kinds from London to east coast communities, returning with other freight. Four Colchester hoys are recorded in 1619, and in 1742

the weekly service was referred to in connection with an exemption of tolls.

Felix Mallett recalled the *Gem*, a 75 footer whose 7 ft draught was too great for regular working to Colchester's quays, so she traded mostly to Harwich and Mistley, on the river Stour. He served as a hand for four years in the 90 ft steam barge *Eagre*, which was built in Lincolnshire and worked a regular service from Colchester to London and return, from about 1900 until 1914, when the centuries-old hoy trade ended. George Gentry of Colchester was skipper when the *Eagre* loaded at Black Eagle wharf, in Wapping, below the pool of London, on Tuesdays, returning to Colchester and unloading, to load a fresh freight and then steam back to the Thames, being often able to make a second trip back to Colchester on a Friday, as the service was advertised as twice weekly, and in 1914 was stated to be three times a week: a great contrast to the sailing barge passage making.

Felix recalled that the *Eagre* left the Colne on Sunday night or Monday morning on alternate weeks, depending on the tide and often giving a friendly tow to a ketch barge. Her compound steam engine worked her up to 8 knots in smooth water and during the time Felix Mallett served in her she never missed a passage because of strong winds, but the fogs of November sometimes kept her anchored. Cargoes from Black Eagle wharf included a week's supply of Truman's beers, large quantities of groceries, machinery, large timber and many kinds of other goods consigned to Colchester. Then they were away, to call at Purfleet to load 20 or 30 barrels of paraffin oil and perhaps on to Silvertown for 20 tons of sugar, sometimes to Henley's cable works at North Woolwich to load cable for a local undertaking.

As the *Eagre* steamed up the Colne, sailing barges

struggling upstream were 'poked up the mud' to allow her to pass, but were occasionally rewarded with a tow and sometimes she arrived at Hythe quay with a string of six or so astern. One Sunday evening Mr Beckwith walked down to the quay after church as the *Eagre* arrived with a particularly long 'tail'. His only comment, peering through the dusk was to hail his skipper with 'Do you reckon the last one's round Rowhedge yet?'

The *Eagre*, the *Gem* and another steamer were not usually there to assist the sailing barges up the river Colne and they then relied on the services of the seven or eight hufflers working from the Hythe, who picked up the barges just above Alresford creek and often assisted by tracking them up with trace horses when above Wivenhoe and Rowhedge, where the river narrows. A long towline was made fast to the barge's bitts and every attempt was made to keep it clear of the water and mud. Barges also poked up with 20 ft long setting booms and sometimes hufflers on the river walls towed the barge themselves, using a light cotton line hoisted to the topmast head by the staysail halyard, to clear the bushes and trees. The Hales brothers, Charles and Daniel were well known Colne barge hufflers, rowing or towing down river in an old yacht's boat or a small punt on the last of the ebb. The larger ketch barges and schooners had to lie in Colne until the tides came round to springs, which occur about midday. There was then sufficient water for them to get alongside Hythe quays. Usually these craft were towed upriver by the small steam tugs *Seal* and *Walrus*, owned by Fieldgate of Brightlingsea, the local shipping agents who had various maritime interests. If bound to Hythe quay, sailing barges did not lower their gear (mast, topmast, mizzen, sails and rigging) to avoid windage when poking or tracking upriver against a strong wind. However, many barges bound under the

road and rail bridges above the Hythe to discharge at Marriage's East Mills would lower away near Rowhedge and poke all the way up.

After serving in the *Eagre* Felix Mallett became mate in the sailing barge *Queen* under skipper Fred Keeling. The *Queen* was the pride of Parry's fleet and was a notably fast barge with a good skipper. Felix recalled once lying windbound in the Colne when Parry's barge *King* got under weigh for London where she was bound to fetch an urgently needed cargo for the mills. 'If the *King* goes the *Queen* must', said Fred Keeling and they got under weigh. But the *Queen* was late for the tide at the Spitways, that ever shifting passage between the Buxey and the Gunfleet sands, off the Essex coast, constantly used by small craft bound to and from the rivers Colne and Blackwater, which was the short cut leading from the Wallett to the Swin channels on the route to the Thames and Medway. The *Queen* grounded there for a time and when she floated on the young flood it blew hard. However, Keeling decided they might as well carry on for the Thames as beat wearily back to the Colne, so the *Queen* struggled up Swin under half the mainsail, topsail, foresail and jib until off the Sheers light they could see the Mouse light vessel around the lee of the mainsail. Then they reckoned that the topsail could be lowered but, even so, the *Queen* threw spray everywhere. She anchored in the Yantlet channel, off the mouth of the river Medway, only $3\frac{1}{2}$ hours from the Spitway, a fast passage. The cargoes of the *Queen* and the other Parry barges were usually the raw materials and the products of her owner's oil mills, though sometimes other cargoes were carried. Felix Mallett's life as mate of a sailing barge on the Essex coast went on in the usual round of passages made and cargoes loaded and discharged. Hard work, anxious nights and

Figure 46 Felix Mallett in retirement proudly displays a painting of the *Queen*, his favourite barge

days in strong winds and Thames traffic, the rewards of fine days with the barge snoring up Swin under all sail, with a big white staysail set to the topmast head and the bowsprit end as a reaching jib, yacht fashion. Quiet nights at anchor waiting for the tide and the leeboards gently working in the current as the barge sheered to her anchor. But over all brooded the uncertainty of the life and its low income for a young man. Whatever the social background, those times were unquestionably the heyday of the Colne sailing barges and he recalled that almost every passage brought the interest of seeing one or two new barges, so rapidly were they coming from the yards.

Figure 47 Tracking a spritsail barge from the towpath at the Hythe, Colchester, in 1901. Charles and Daniel Hales, the local hufflers, are walking and hauling on a light line made fast to the barge's mast. The crew are poling with setting booms

The London river provided endless variety and its docks endless problems for the sailing barge crews, herded in the locks with dumb lighters and dock tugs to be released into the crowded waters of the docks whose sides were lined with ships from all parts of the world and which they had to warp against to await their turn to load

His most interesting recollection of that time was of a morning in Sea Reach when a fleet of sailing barges from Essex rivers met a large fleet of Kentish barges from the Medway, all bound up the Thames. There were so many that some were eight or nine abreast running up the lower river in a spectacle of sailing craft at work. There was occasional humour too. The hufflers Charles and Daniel Hales were tracking the *Queen* up the Colne above Rowhedge one day, with Daniel on the light track line and Charles helping. A puff made the barge sag off towards the lee mud. Daniel grasped a handy fence with one hand and tried to hold the barge on the straining line. 'Thass all right, Daniel has got her', Charles soothingly shouted to Fred Keeling, but at that moment the fence collapsed, taking Daniel with it, still clutching his handhold in a shower of splinters, while Fred Keeling and Felix jumped for the setting booms.

After several years as mate of Colchester sailing barges, sailing principally between there and London but also to the many ports, havens, riverside wharves and village hards between Harwich and the Thames and Medway, Felix Mallett's seamanship and reliability brought opportunity to become skipper of Owen Parry's sailing barge *Greta*, which had originally been owned by Hibbs, the Brightlingsea sailmaker who made and repaired sails for many barges. Parry's fleet then included the *King* and the *Queen*, both notable in barge racing, and the *Sirdar*, later a champion racing barge. They also had the *Vera, Victor* and the 130 ton *Millie* which was built at Brightlingsea by Douglas Stone for Jarvis, who had earlier been skipper of the *Unity* and then became warehouse foreman at the oil mill. He owned her in partnership with sailmaker Hibbs. She cost £1,109 and much of her rigging was made from that of yachts which were then extensively laid up and refitted on the Colne.

All the barges under Parry's black, yellow and black flag were smartly kept and received a biennial refit on the hard at Brightlingsea. The sails were unbent and carried to Hibbs' loft for overhaul. Then these were spread on the fields above Aldous's shipyard to be dressed with a mixture of various ingredients including horse fat. This mixture was applied with buckets, dipped hot from a copper. The resulting colour was darker than the later oil and red ochre dressing now familiar in the surviving pleasure barges. Hibbs' dressing never really completely dried and shone when wet with rain. The OO weight mainsails lasted about fifteen years in regular use and received a major overhaul after about eight years, though repairs were of course carried out if they were damaged. Meanwhile, the barge's hull was painted and the cabins and deckworks grained by professional yacht painters. When the barge left Brightlingsea hard she looked like new.

Besides the usual barge cargoes there were some unusual freights. Felix Mallett recalled some spars for the German Emperor's racing schooner *Meteor IV* being shipped from a yard at Brightlingsea which made them, to London for transhipment, on the deck of the *Greta*. The fore and main topmasts were solid but the 75 ft long main boom and other spars were of spruce, hollow cored. All were lashed on deck in cradles which were griped down. Fieldgate's steam tug *Walrus* took the *Greta* in tow for St Katharine's dock, where a German ship carried them to Kiel.

There was always considerable damage and loss of barges when these were trading under sail and the *Greta* did not escape. She lay in the Lower Hope, the second reach of the saltwater river Thames, anchored in company with the sailing barges *Victa, Surge* and *Nellie Parker*. The *Greta* was laden with wheat for Cranfields, the Ipswich millers. Soon after they got under weigh and off Cliff Creek on the Kentish side a sudden squall broke the *Greta*'s topmast in three places, which gave them a hard time securing the mess and getting the barge in a seaworthy condition to continue her passage.

One of Felix Mallett's worst experiences was during a severe gale on 28/29 December 1914. The *Greta* had made an uneventful passage down the Swin to the Spitway, the narrow channel between the Gunfleet and the Buxey sands, used for centuries by craft sailing from the rivers Colne and Blackwater or from Harwich, to and from the rivers Thames or Crouch. It is a convenient connecting channel between the coastal waters of the Swin and the alongshore channel of the Wallett. The *Greta* had a cargo of linseed below hatches and a deck cargo of pipes. At 4.30 in the evening they anchored near the Knoll buoy, in accordance with the wartime regulations requiring all sailing vessels in coastal waters to anchor at night, so their position was known to patrol vessels at darkness. As the wind was strong and easterly the naval trawler acting as guardship at the entrance to the rivers Colne and Blackwater allowed them to move to an anchorage inside the entrance to the Colne, in company with a dozen other barges. The *Greta* rode to 40 fathoms of chain cable. At 8 p.m. Felix and his mate Percy Green sensed that motion was steadily increasing and looking out found the wind had veered to a strong westerly gale which rapidly increased to almost hurricane force, raising a heavy sea which was accentuated by confusion with the earlier sea from the easterly weather. Bright moonlight showed a turmoil which was constantly blotted out by showers of rain, sleet and snow. The *Greta* started to drag, as did the other barges, including some large steel vessels of E. J. W. Goldsmith's fleet. Felix Mallett and his mate lashed the topsail with a secure stow and hove the mainsail brails in tightly. Below, the cabin lamp swung in pendulum-like arcs and the bowsprit soon had to be hove up to clear the anchor cable in her plunges. Felix's main worry was the deck cargo of pipes and they got tackles from the fo'c'sle to put additional gripes on them. By midnight the wind had shifted to the north and the ebb was sluicing out of the river. All the barges in Colne had dragged or were dragging and many were ashore. The *Greta* dragged across the river and grounded in the mouth of Blackstone Hole, on the St Osyth side. Many barges were blown ashore on the Brightlingsea side, along the saltings by the railway line and there was loss of deck cargoes and structural damage. Outside many barges were stranded, lost gear and suffered damage in the hurricane force winds.

In 1918 the coastal sailing barge trade slackened due to the ending of wartime shipping arrangements and Parry sold the *Greta* to the London and Rochester Trading Co., who had a large fleet of sailing barges based on the Medway, for £900, together with the *Millie* at £1,100. Felix Mallett stayed as skipper of the *Greta* until 1926, then returned to Parry's to skipper the barge *Victor*. He sailed in many sailing barge races at the annual matches of the Thames and the Medway on board the *Queen, Imperial, Alderman,* and in later years in the *Cabbie* and *Surrey,* yet his pride of achievement was reserved for the barge as a working craft and the feats of

seamanship in shoal waters which were commonplace for their crews. The Second World War brought the same restrictions prohibiting night sailing as in 1914–18. Added to this was the new danger of mines laid by enemy aircraft in the Thames approaches and off Harwich. Others were blown landward from the coastal sea lanes and many were seen floating by the bargemen and other shipping.

The sailing barges carried on as best possible, their crews given the small badge then worn by all merchant service sailors to denote they were on war service. Inconspicuous in a lapel but a most honourable device for men who had to take anything the enemy gave but had little or no defence of their own. With the onset of the blitz on London in the winter of 1940, their stays in the docks were very hazardous. Felix Mallett and his mate spent nights in air raid shelters near the docks, along with hundreds of unfortunate local residents whose homes were being destroyed each night by waves of bombers devastating docks and housing discriminately. The Millwall and the Surrey Commercial docks were badly damaged and the glow of fires silhouetted the masts and sails of several sailing barges moored amongst the hundreds of lighters crowding the docks as in peacetime and the dark bulks of merchant ships towering alongside.

Soon after, the *Victor* was ordered to the river Medway to join the many sailing barges employed in loading, storing and transhipping naval ammunition for ships in the river being serviced by the dockyards at Sheerness and at Chatham. The *Victor* loaded torpedoes and shells, transferring them to cruisers, destroyers and corvettes, making a strange contrast in vessels as she lay alongside. When loaded the barges usually laid on buoys off Upnor by day and were towed downstream by night to unload.

Figure 48 Spritsail barges beating down the river Thames about 1937. There are seven barges under sail in this photograph and one at anchor. This was one of the lower reaches of the river, lined with wharves and dock entrances but temporarily free of other shipping

During this work the barges had two crews, each serving a week on board then being allowed home for a week. Being shipmates with many tons of high explosive was a sobering experience but the bargemen seemed to prefer the relative quiet of the Medway to the hell of their trips for a freight from the London docks. However, the *Victor* had a narrow escape during a daylight raid on Chatham when a bomb fell between her and a lighter loaded with depth charges, which fortunately did not explode. The blast unshipped the *Victor's* cabin stove, disturbed her hatch covers and shrapnel damaged her mainsail.

I remember him at the wheel of his barge, coming up past the shipyard where I was an apprentice; a shortish, stocky man, in blue guernsey, jacket and oilskins and sea boots, a cloth cap jammed down on his head against the gusts of wind, which sent the topsail racketing when the mate ran forward and hauled on the clewline as the barge surged through Rowhedge reach, her deck and hatch cloths glistening with rain, Felix Mallett giving her wheel a spoke this way and that as the foresail and half brailed mainsail drew her at reduced speed to suit the flood tide, and an arrival at Colchester's quay from which he had sailed on his first passage.

The *Victor* was released to her owners from war service in 1946, along with the sailing barge *Chieftain*. They were to be towed to Brightlingsea for refitting but due to inept towing, a common fault with tug masters when dealing with small vessels, the *Chieftain* was towed under and sank. The *Victor* survived and was eventually towed round to Brightlingsea.

With the *Victor* on Brightlingsea hard for repairs, Felix Mallett was asked to become skipper of the owner's sailing barge *Alan*, lying on the Medway. He was 64 years old, had survived two wars and 48 years afloat and decided to retire at Christmas 1946. His many remaining years were spent at his home in Colchester. His thoughts were often on the barges and he retained contact with their decline and the surprising revival of them for pleasure sailing, which interested him considerably.

Felix Mallett died in 1982. He typified the best type of sailing barge skipper; consummate seamen in their own surroundings, conscientious for their craft and owners, ably managing their part of the barge's business and accounts. They were unassuming seafarers who have left the coast the poorer for their passing.

7

Yacht barges

Many owners of cruising yachts are interested in a craft offering spacious accommodation with inexpensive first cost and low subsequent expenses. Thus, at various periods of yachting history there have been surges of interest in conversions of commercial vessels or of surplus war craft to yacht use. The sailing barges which were once numerous in estuary and coastal trade on the east and south coasts of England led some British yachtsmen to buy barges which were occasionally offered for sale in good condition, and to have the interiors converted for commodious cruising. Sometimes the rig was altered in detail but usually this remained in working trim. Conversions of this type are still made, from the eighty or so hulls of these craft which are still seaworthy and in varying condition.

There was also interest in smaller barge yachts. At the end of the nineteenth century some British yachtsmen, led by the example of E. B. Tredwen, a noted sailing canoeist and canoe cruiser, became interested in small, flat bottomed craft having leeboards and a cutter or sloop rig, about 30 ft in length and designed for coastal cruising and, in some instances, also capable of short sea passages. This type of 'barge yacht' is now seldom seen but was fairly common on the south and east coasts of England into the 1940s and remains a practical form of cruiser.

It is impossible to define which was the first sailing barge to be converted for pleasure cruising. Probably the idea occurred to many from the occasional use of a freshly painted and clean swept barge by her owner and his family for short summer day trips and picnics, perhaps associated with the spectacle of a barge race. A few also may have taken their summer holiday on board, with hammocks slung in the hold. Clement Parker, the barge owning farmer of Bradwell-on-Sea, Essex, was fond of this form of holiday for his family and friends (fig. 49).

Cyril Ionides was a pioneer user of the spritsail barge as 'a floating home', and his book of that title, written with J. B. Atkins and published in 1918 described the acquisition of a sailing barge and her conversion for permanent living on board by a family who moored her at various places on the Essex rivers and creeks and occasionally made short cruises, always berthing close to a railway line so that Ionides could get to his office job in London. He gave up a house ashore to buy an ex-working barge and have her converted as a floating home which would, as he put it, enable him to educate his two sons at a public school by his not having to pay rent and rates. A romantic folly which one imagines he must often have regretted. However, the book well

Figure 49 Clement Parker, the Bradwell, Essex, barge owner and farmer at the wheel of one of his working spritsail barges on a pleasure trip with his family and friends, about 1900

Figure 50 Yacht barge *Thoma II*, designed and built by John Howard and Sons, Maldon, Essex, 1909. Dimensions 100 ft length overall 80 ft waterline × 18 ft 6 in × 7 ft 9 in depth, 4 ft 6 in draught

records something of the life of the bargemen and also of the distinctive dialects of parts of the Essex coast.

John Howard prepared the plans of several barge yachts, which were even more shapely than his stack barges. In 1909 he launched the barge yacht *Thoma II* built for Frank Callingham of Great Baddow, Essex. She was larger than an ordinary spritsail barge and had similarities to the fine ketch rigged barge *Record Reign*, which Howard had built in 1897. The *Thoma II* was 100 ft length overall, 80 ft length waterline × 18 ft 6 in beam × 7 ft 9 in depth. She drew 4 ft 6 in with lee-boards raised. She was yachtlike in appearance having a clipper stem, ample freeboard and fine ends, with a counter stern. The timber for her construction cost £345 and the oak had been seasoned for five years.

From forward, the accommodation comprised a fo'c'sle, with five cot berths, aft of this was a skipper's cabin to starboard and a galley opposite. A bathroom, a two-berth cabin, the saloon with tables to seat fifteen, the lounge and smoking room, a ladies boudoir and saloon, then an essential in any large cruising yacht, and a lobby with stairs to the deck. She carried three boats, including one motor launch.

The *Thoma II* was the pride of Maldon as she lay at the Town Quay ready for sea. The noted Mistley barge-man Jim Stone was her first skipper, with a crew of three. One of them, Lewis Waleking of Rowhedge, a yacht hand, remembered how, with her owner and his family on board, a brimming high water and an immaculate new big barge, Jim Stone merely ordered them to single up on the moorings, set the topsail and let go. He took the wheel as she glided out from the quay on her maiden passage down the Blackwater, with half Maldon looking on. She cruised extensively from the river Blackwater and on passage from Maldon to Guernsey in the

Figure 51 Sail plan of yacht barge *Thoma II*. Spritsail rig with gaff or mule mizzen

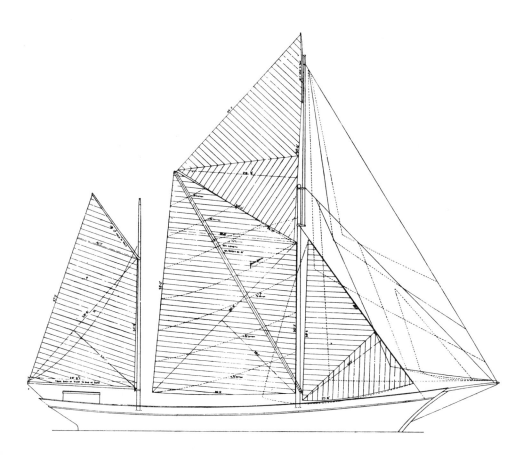

Channel Islands, in 1912, her rudder was damaged off Portland Bill. The owner immediately suggested signalling for a tug but Jim Stone and his crew managed to work her into Weymouth harbour under sail, a smart piece of seamanship. The *Thoma II* set 4,830 sq ft and her long sprit was a familiar sight on the east and south coasts. Mr. Callingham always had doubts as to the fitness of the barge rig for the *Thoma II* and he carried out some experiments which tended to make her look more of a yacht and less of a barge.

The outbreak of war in 1914 found the *Thoma II* at Oban, on the west coast of Scotland, where she was laid up. She was sailed home through the Caledonian Canal and down the east coast of Britain in 1919. That year Mr. Callingham commissioned naval architect James A. Smith to design a mule rig for her, with a sprit mainsail and a gaff mizzen (fig. 51) but the owner died before the work was completed. The suit of sails was made by Gowen and Co. of West Mersea, Essex and Mr. Callingham's sons had the rigging work completed. Under this rig the *Thoma II* could work along in heavy weather with the mainsail brailed up, leaving only the topsail and foresail set. She cruised from June to October as a mule. Her alternative boom and gaff rig is shown in fig. 52, complete with a large jackyard topsail which, because of the comparative shortness of the topsail yard, would require the luff of the sail to be laced to the topmast in contemporary yacht practice. In contrast the jackyard is of the usual length for a sail of this size. Afterwards the *Thoma II* was sold to Christopher Turnor, a member of the Royal Yacht Squadron, who thought she should be rigged as a boomsail barge and had a complete alternative rig made for her. She crossed the Bay of Biscay four times under his ownership, visiting the French and Spanish coasts and later the Mediterranean.

Figure 52 Sail plan of yacht barge *Thoma II* with gaff ketch rig having a jackyard topsail

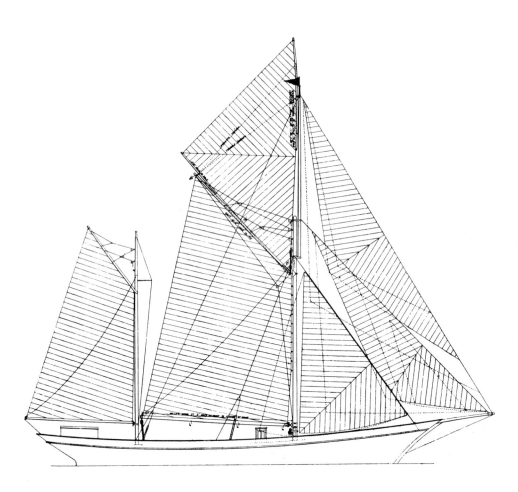

In 1921 an auxiliary motor was installed on deck aft. It drove an overside shaft and propeller and gave her a speed in still water of 4½ to 5 knots. By then she was manned by a skipper, a mate, four hands and a cook-steward. During a month's cruise in 1923/4 the *Thoma II* sailed to the French Riviera and back, via the Bay of Biscay and Gibraltar; the first barge yacht to make the voyage. She left Yarmouth, Isle of Wight on 20 July 1924 and arrived at Gibraltar on 26 July, enjoying a pleasant, uneventful passage across the Bay of Biscay. From 26 July she was cruising continuously in the Mediterranean until 3 February 1925, when she was hauled up on the slip at Leghorn, Italy, for hull cleaning. All the principal ports in Corsica, Sardinia and the Balearic Islands were visited, besides many of the French and Italian ports such as Genoa, Marseilles, Nice, etc. The *Thoma II*'s form, rig and particularly the leeboards caused astonishment at Riviera ports and she was remembered for years afterwards by the fishermen of St. Tropez as 'the yacht with wings'.

The *Thoma II* was laid up at Cannes from 5 February until 13 April 1925, when she changed ownership, and was purchased by C. Hardinge Tapp of Maldon, Essex. She sailed from Cannes bound for Southwick, Sussex, on 13 April. The homeward voyage was protracted as she called at Marseilles, Gibraltar, Cadiz and Lisbon. On 1 July, running before a strong west wind in the Bay of Biscay, she carried away the squaresail yard. The wind steadily increased to a hard gale and she hove-to, battened down, in the evening of 3 July. The *Thoma II* remained hove-to until 5 July and reportedly proved a good sea boat, not shipping any solid water and sustaining little damage. As a flat bottomed vessel she naturally made much leeway and was set away into the bight of the Bay, but fortunately the weather was clear. On 5 July

Figure 53 Scale model of the yacht barge *Cawana*, showing well formed hull with a counter stern, a gaff ketch rig with vangs to trim the main gaff

she sighted Belle Isle and anchored off Port Louis. Two days later she proceeded to L'Orient and docked. She left there on 10 July, being towed towards Ushant by the British steamship *Clan Ronald*, as her auxiliary engine was ineffective in a seaway. Soon after starting she cast off and made sail. The *Thoma II* passed signal point at midnight on 14 July and arrived at Plymouth on 16 July.

The *Thoma II* was re-engined at Burnham-on-Crouch in 1927 when two 36 bhp Kelvin engines were installed, with twin screws. She remained fully rigged and sailed from Brightlingsea in the ownership of Sir Matthew Thompson. She was refitted after the Second World War and raced in the 1950 Medway amateur barge match, besides cruising the east coast. Some years later she was unrigged and was converted to a motor yacht with more powerful engines, twin screws and a large deckhouse. Since this transition she has voyaged extensively between the Mediterranean and Norway and continues to be a useful and seaworthy yacht.

The 97 ft ketch *Cawana* was perhaps the best known of the several barge yachts designed and built by Gill and Sons of Rochester, Kent. She was laid down as a working barge but was sold in 1904 before completion to yachtsman R. Hill Dawe, who had a counter stern added and accommodation built into the hull. The *Cawana* was larger than most working barges; 97 ft length overall × 22 ft beam × 7 ft 6in depth. Her draught as a yacht was 4 ft 3 in. The ketch rig spread 5,272 sq ft and to aid stiffness on such a shallow draught, 40 tons of iron ballast was stowed in the bilge, hung from the floors so as not to touch the bottom planking. Construction arrangements followed English east coast sailing barge practice with 2½ in thick oak planking on frames spaced 18 in apart and having a 2½ in thick pitch pine ceiling. Floors were 6 in sides × 10 in moulded, oak.

The ketch rig had masts stepped in tabernacles and a gaff mainsail which was laced to a hollow boom. On deck a 16 ft sailing cutter and two 13 ft dinghies were carried in davits and a lighting engine and dynamo were housed in a small deckhouse. In contrast to the *Thoma II* she carried a crew of two, who must have had plenty to do handling and maintaining a barge yacht of this size. The accommodation was spacious. Her capacity for cruising can be gauged from the fresh water tank fitted in the counter which held three tons. A contemporary description of her accommodation conveys the

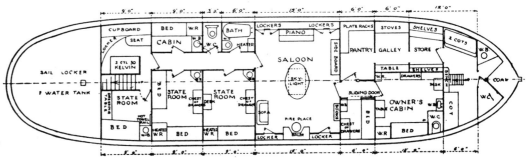

Figure 54 Accommodation plan of the yacht barge *Cawana*, typical of the spacious interiors of these craft

spaciousness:

'*Cawana* is equal to a nine-roomed house with the advantage of affording its inhabitants a constant change of scenery without the ruinous consequences of a removal. Right aft, in the counter, is a fresh water tank capable of holding three tons. The supply is by gravity to all taps. Hot water for baths is obtained by a Valor Perfection oil stove under a copper heater; and is therefore independent of cooking operations. The saloon stove burns anthracite night and day, and contains a small saddle boiler which provides hot water for central heating, the pipes of which pass through two linen lockers and a towel rail. The bath is fitted with gravity fresh water and hot water taps, a sea cock admitting salt water, and a semi-rotary pump clears the bath.

A large four burner Valor Perfection oil stove, with oven, provides for all cooked meals. The galley and pantry floors are marble tiled with wooden joints, giving a bright and clean appearance. Ample light and ventilation are afforded by means of cowls, skylights and portholes. The unlimited stowage space is ingeniously utilised without leaving any dark and musty corners. The generous floor space and head room everywhere make one almost forget one is afloat. This effect is best obtained in the saloon which extends the full width of the ship, the tiled fireplace, the large piano, the big Chesterfield and armchairs, the oval table round which any number of people can gather, the magnificent oak panelling and carvings – all these things take one miles from the sea, or from the unpleasant associations with the usual saloon of a cross-Channel steamer.

What could be more congenial than to lounge back in an armchair by the fire with a book, under the mellow light of a shaded electric reading lamp, with the smoke curling towards the skylight, oblivious of the rushing tide and howling wind outside? No noisy neighbours or rattle or smell of traffic; only the solid comfort and peace afforded by such a floating home.'

In 1908 two petrol motors were fitted, driving electric propulsion motors which turned the shafts of her twin screws. The motors were by the Pierce Arrow Co. of New York and the electrics by the Lancashire Dynamo and Motor Co. The *Cawana* was one of the largest craft of the time, except for submarines, to have that form of propulsion. The installation was removed in 1920, when she was owned by Major C. A. J. Younger. Two years later a 25 bhp Kelvin engine was installed and her rig had been reduced to a boomless, brailing mainsail, a foresail set to the stemhead and a gaff mizzen. A topsail was not carried and she was deliberately undercanvassed to the owner's desires.

In 1924 Major Younger presented the *Cawana* to the Portsmouth Sea Scouts for their use as a training vessel. By 1930 the *Cawana* had been sold to R. V. E. de B. Crawshay, was renamed *Mamgu* and became a motor yacht, at first with one engine and later with two. The leeboards were retained to aid steering when making a passage. The *Mamgu* remained in his ownership into the 1940s, being based on the Town Quay at Maldon, Essex, but she made few passages, her owner preferring to be on board in the Blackwater using his 29 ft motor cruiser *Bee*.

The 100 ft, counter sterned *Kia-ora* was another large barge yacht. She was designed and built in 1906 by J. R. Piper of Greenwich for T. R. Westray, who sailed from Seaview, on the east shore of the Isle of Wight. Her principal dimensions were 100 ft length overall and 21 ft beam. A more powerful craft than the same builder's

Haughty Belle, she had spacious accommodation for five in single cabins, two bathrooms and W.C.s, a large saloon, galley and pantry, a cabin for the skipper and a fo'c'sle for four hands, though she was usually worked with three all told. Despite her size she was, like many of Piper's barges, of rather shallow hull form and a coach roof was provided to obtain 7 ft headroom. This had a companion house at the after end. Her rig was as a mule with a sprit mainsail and a large gaff and boom mizzen. The rig's proportions were influenced by the ketch rig then fashionable in larger cruising yachts such as *Valdora*, *Julnar* and others, with which her owner would be familiar. Tan canvas was used for her suit of sails by Boulden, then a noted maker of sails for barges. Her owner cruised on the south and east coasts until 1914.

Sometimes well known sailing barges were converted to pleasure use. The *Haughty Belle* was designed by E. J. Goldsmith, a bargeowner of Grays, Essex, and was built in 1894 at Greenwich by J. R. Piper who had built several fast barges. She was unusual in having a counter stern of contemporary yacht proportions. Her dimensions were 92 ft length overall, 19 ft beam, 6 ft depth and 3 ft 9 in draught when in racing trim. The bottom profile was rockered and almost followed the sheer at side line. The forward and after form was fine and she had a steel keelson to attempt to preserve her shape. The *Haughty Belle* proved to be a fast barge and would turn easily. She won the 1894 Thames sailing barge match, sailed by skipper Harry Munns but in the Medway race, following, had to be withdrawn as the owners of the other barges entered would not sail against her on grounds that she was a yacht, an impression her white painted hull, white canvas and general trim did little to deny. However, immediately afterwards she loaded cargo and continued to trade until 1930. Her counter stern

was removed in 1902 as it was a nuisance in locks and docks, and her length was reduced to 83 ft. The forefoot was well rounded and emerged when she heeled in strong winds.

In 1933 the *Haughty Belle* was converted to a yacht for Captain A. C. Radford by Cooper of Conyer, Kent. The working rig was retained, with its gear. A wheelhouse was built abaft the existing wheel and a second wheel was fitted on the same spindle, allowing inside or outside steering. Cabin tops were built on the existing hatch coamings and cabins for five were arranged, with a spacious saloon, galley, toilets and access spaces, leaving the fo'c'sle for stores and the existing after cabin for the two hands. Two 15 bhp Kelvin engines were installed with deck controls. She achieved $4\frac{1}{2}$ knots under power. As a yacht the *Haughty Belle* sailed the south and east coasts and ventured west as far as Falmouth. She survived the Second World War but is no longer in service.

There was also a smaller size of barge yacht, intermediate between the full sized type and the little barge yachts under about 35 ft long. The 40 ft yacht barge *Boojum* was built at Greenwich, Kent, by George Hardee. She was presumably built as a speculation as she lay unfinished until purchased in January 1909 by Major General Sir A. W. L. Bayly. It is difficult to imagine for which trade this little barge was originally intended. As built she had a transom stern and the principal dimensions were 40 ft overall length, 11 ft 6 in beam and 4 ft 2 in moulded depth. Construction was of double-skin side planking with calico between the skins; oak frames, floors and beams; English elm chines and bottom planking laid with a diagonal inner skin and a fore and aft outer. The heels of the frames were connected to the floors with iron knees. She was fitted with steel plate leeboards.

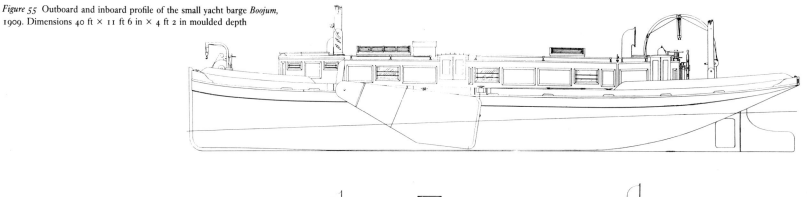

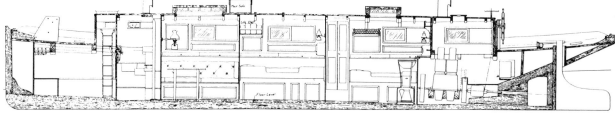

When bought for completion as a yacht the *Boojum* was removed to Eberhardt's barge yard at Greenhithe for completion and fitting out. A single cylinder Danish 'Dan' type engine was installed in the cockpit and drove a reversing and feathering propeller. The rig was a ketch with the masts stepped in steel tabernacles. The gaff mainsail and mizzen each had a boom and were roller reefed. The mizzen sheeted to a bumkin. The foresail and jib both set on Wykeham Martin furling gear. A topsail was not carried. Five tons of iron ballast aft gave her 3 ft draught in way of the propeller but forward she drew only 1 ft 3 in. The coamings were raised to provide full headroom and the accommodation was arranged

with three cabins, a saloon and a fo'c'sle for one hand, though the Baylys seem to have handled her alone or with friends. A 9 ft dinghy was carried in davits on one quarter. During the winter of 1909–10 the *Boojum* was altered at Felton's yard, Sandwich, Kent. A counter stern was added and a rudder post was fitted to enable the propeller and rudder to function efficiently. She emerged 47 ft 6 in overall. The cockpit was replaced by a small engine room. Shaft and bevel steering gear engaged with a quadrant on the rudder head. The following year a 14 bhp 'Dan' engine was installed, with deck controls. This enabled her to make headway in strong winds and against a tide, when on passage with sail set. As the bowsprit was more often topped up out of the way than in use, it was removed and a standing gaff sail with brails was substituted for the original mainsail. The mizzen was replaced by a brailing spritsail and a squaresail was added for running on passage. Later five brails were fitted to the mainsail. The *Boojum* cruised between Lowestoft on the east and Hayling Island on the south coasts, and across the North Sea

Figure 56 Rigging plan of the yacht barge *Boojum*

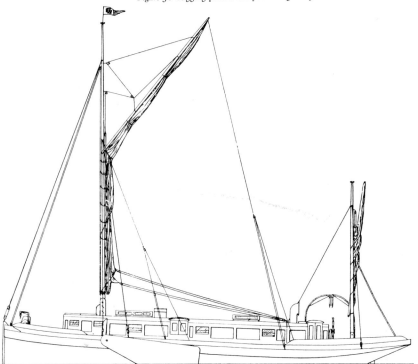

and the English Channel to the continental coast between Ijmuiden and Boulogne, including considerable estuary and inland waterway cruising. Her owner wrote of the rigging and deck arrangements:

'*Boojum* has a powerful winch (windlass) with gipsy wheel for chain and independent warping drum, also an anchor davit and chain compressor. With these and the aid of my wife . . . I have been able to deal with her ground tackle, which is heavy. My experience of barges is that they are rough on their anchors. *Boojum*, with her high cabin top, does a lot of sheering about; and she delights in dragging her anchors, of which she carries three, the heaviest (rarely used) being over a hundredweight (112 lbs). In addition she carries two chain cables, and for use in canals or rivers, four bank anchors of the Norfolk Broads pattern. Fenders are of the usual barge pattern and of coir with the addition of two rope fenders made of six inch hawser and each six feet long.

As the mainmast is stepped in a tabernacle above the level of the winch, it is necessary, when lowering or raising the mast, to ship in a socket in the fore side of the mast below the bolt on which the latter is pivoted, an iron stay about 8 ft long with a crutch at the top for the forestay to rest in. The mizzen is lowered by hand over the taffrail, and if not immediately required again is taken out and laid along the starboard side of the cabin top, where the two quants, two long ash boathooks, the squaresail yard and a 12 ft landing plank keep it company. For use when on the ground or alongside a wharf or other large vessel, a wooden ladder with seven rungs and also a short rope ladder are carried.

There is a small mast winch with two drums and on each davit is a small winch. The boats falls are thin

Figure 57 Deck and accommodation plan of the yacht
barge *Boojum*

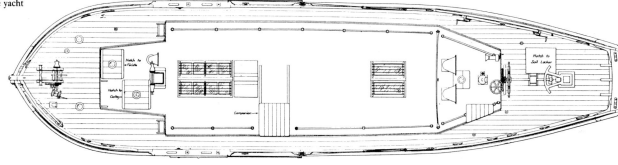

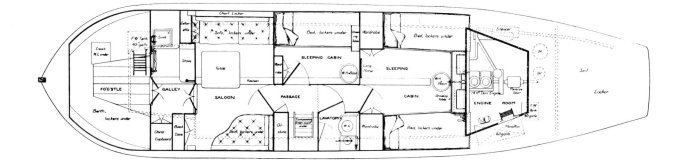

flexible wire wound on these davit winches. With their
aid it is easy for one person to hoist the 9 ft dinghy,
or put her in the water.'

The *Boojum* remained in the ownership of the Baylys
until 1939, being sailed by Lady Bayly after her
husband's death. Although unusual in appearance, she
was one of the most successful cruising yacht barges.

In 1933 the Sittingbourne Shipbuilding Co. of
Sittingbourne, Kent, who built and repaired sailing
barges, designed and built a 46 ft barge yacht. She
makes interesting comparison with the *Boojum*. Her
dimensions were 46 ft overall length × 12 ft 6 in beam
and 3 ft 6 in draught. The hull was of the usual flat
bottomed form with shaped ends and had a counter
stern which was rounded in deck plan. A small and
incongruous gammon knee was fitted at the stem head.
The rig was that of the spritsail barge but the mizzen

was proportionally larger to that carried by the full sized, working barges. The accommodation was arranged for four berths and there were also two canvas cots in the small fo'c'sle. An auxiliary engine drove a centreline propeller. The steering wheel was mounted on the forward side of the after cabin top coamings.

Other designers produced barge yachts. Linton Hope, ever an innovator with his small racing and cruising yachts and powered craft, designed the 69 ft *Mimosa III* in 1908 as a centreboard, ketch rigged craft intended to improve on the average yacht barge, particularly in ability to turn to windward in a seaway.

Hope and the owner sensibly decided to use steel construction to suit the hull form intended. Length overall was 68 ft 10 in. Waterline length 57 ft, beam 15 ft and hull draught 4 ft 5 in, increased with the centreplate lowered. Displacement was light at 34 tons. The above water profile was typical of cruising yachts of the time and the waterlines and buttocks were easy and fair. The centreplate was housed in a trunk which extended the full depth of the hull and formed a longitudinal partition bulkhead. She was built by W. Paaus at Roodevaart, Holland.

Accommodation was under a flush deck with skylights, bounded by low bulwarks. The gaff ketch rig was designed without a topmast or topsail but a longer masthead was arranged during construction and she was usually sailed with a topsail set. The *Mimosa III* was built with an auxiliary motor, which eased handling in anchorages and locks. Below deck, from forward, was the chain locker, a fo'c'sle for two or three hands, a galley, a spacious saloon, five single and one double cabins, ample alleyway space and a companionway leading to a roomy deckhouse with comfortable seats, a table and windows enabling those within to see everything

going on outside and a favourite place when at anchor. Altogether she was a practical cruiser for coastal and short sea voyaging and was the ultimate development of the moderate sized barge yacht. The *Mimosa III*'s rig might be improved by omitting the long masthead and topsail, as in the original sail plan, by giving the mainsail more peak and by substituting a bermudian mizzen of similar area. The single deep reef in the mainsail could be supplemented by two lower rows of reef points.

About 1910 the *Mimosa III* passed to the ownership of Wilson Marriage of the Colchester, Essex, family of millers, and was renamed *Raven*. She was well known on the Essex and Suffolk coasts in summer. By 1919 she was owned by J. Blott of Surbiton who was a keen east coast cruising man with a penchant for practical cruising yachts which later extended to a motor yacht on drifter lines and a motor bawley. The *Raven* was afterwards owned by Mrs. A. Schnapper and remained on the east coast.

The advantages of a modified English sailing barge hull for shallow draught power propulsion were recognised in the early 1920s, when several small coasters were designed and built to this hull form and arrangement. At least one motor yacht, the 90 ft *La Toquade* was also built on this principle, to the design of E. A. Stow of the noted Shoreham yachtbuilding firm, for Viscount Colville. He required a craft having the greatest possible comfort and accommodation on limited dimensions, which would enable passage of the continental canals, yet which would have fair seagoing qualities and be economical to run.

The dimensions of *La Toquade* were 90 ft length overall × 16 ft 7 in beam and 5 ft 6 in draught, to achieve adequate immersion of the propellers which is the most serious problem with motor barges. The hull had the

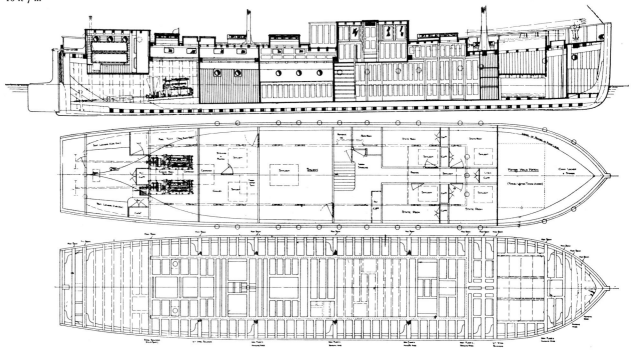

Figure 58 General arrangement and deck plan of the motor yacht barge *Toquade*. Designed by E. A. Stowe and built by B. Spiers Hallett and Co. (G. and T. Smith), Rye, Sussex, 1923. Dimensions 90 ft 9 in × 16 ft 7 in

bluff bow and amidships chine of the sailing barge but a finer run improved steering qualities and afforded a clear flow to the twin screws. She was built at Rye, Sussex, by G. and T. Smith who had built a number of ketch barges of around this size, besides fishing trawlers and other commercial sailing craft. The hull construction largely followed barge practice but three large keelsons were fitted over the floors and consequently the cabin soles were well above the bottom planking, needing a coachroof to achieve adequate headroom. The two engines were installed in a compact engine room. In 1927 these were replaced by two Gleniffer paraffin engines.

The outboard profile (fig. 59) shows the typical

uninspiring deckhouses of the time. A boomless gaff mainsail and mizzen were carried as steadying sails as nothing rolls so well as a light draught barge under power in a seaway. The usual spacious accommodation was arranged but had two unusual features; the crew of four lived aft in a deckhouse partially sunk below deck level and a motor car was carried in a small transverse hold forward, served by a derrick on the foremast. Altogether she was an interesting and practical, if rather ugly craft. The yacht was later renamed *Relic* and afterwards *Toquade* when owned by E. W. Janson who Registered her at Cape Town.

Between 1918 and 1939 several British yachtsmen bought Dutch leeboard yachts of various types and a few old fishing vessels of similar characteristics, though these cannot be regarded as sailing barges. However, a few of the Dutch Klipper type of sailing barge were converted

to yachts and some yachts were built which closely resembled the type. The Klipper was built in small numbers compared to the numerous Tjalk type of Dutch and German cargo carrying sailing barge. The Klipper was developed as a cargo carrier for the Dutch coastal trade, also being capable of working on some inland waterways, though many of the type had masts stepped on the keelson. Klippers also sailed to Germany and Belgium and, occasionally, across the North Sea to English ports. The gaff ketch rig was often arranged with topsails on main and mizzen masts and a jib topsail was carried for light weather. Pronounced flare in the forward sections, a snubbed style of clipper bow, a counter stern and a large rudder often with the area carried well above the light waterline to give maximum effect when heeled and sailing, were features of the Klipper type. The cargo hold was amidships and often a

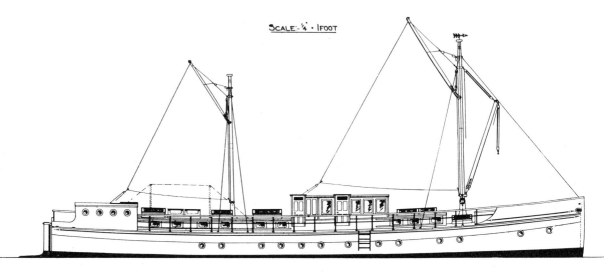

SCALE:- ¼ · 1FOOT

Figure 59 Outboard profile and sail plan of motor yacht barge *Toquade*

Figure 61 The spritsail barge *Vigilant* of Harwich converted to a yacht in 1934 for E. H. Clifford. She was built by W. H. Orvis and Co. at Ipswich in 1904 for owners at Mistley, Essex. Dimensions 84 ft × 20 ft 10 in × 8 ft 3 in depth. Sail area 3,272 sq ft. Note wheelhouse fitted when a yacht

Figure 60 Midship section of motor yacht barge *Toquade*

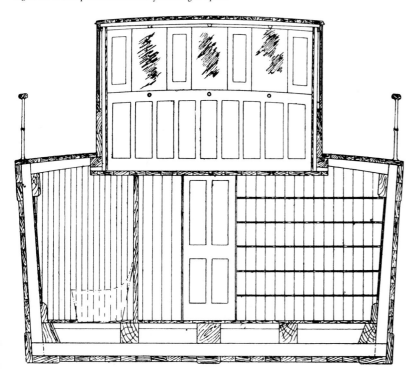

Figure 62 Profile and plan of accommodation arrangement of the Klipper yacht *Cluan*, 1930. Dimensions 70 ft length overall × 55 ft waterline × 16 ft 3 in × 4 ft draught. Auxiliary engine 60 bhp

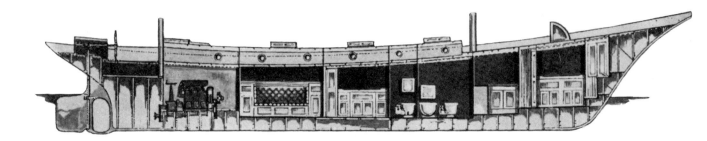

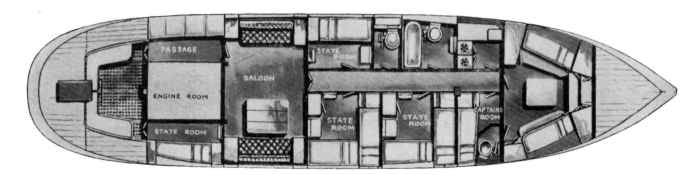

half-sunk deckhouse was arranged aft for the crew of two men and a boy. In the early twentieth century several Klipper yachts were built, at first for Dutch and Belgian owners but later some for British yachtsmen.

The Klipper yacht *Cluan* was designed and built by G. de Vries Lentsch of Nieuwendam, Holland, for Brig. Gen. D. Beale-Brown and was typical. The principal

dimensions of 70 ft length overall, 55 ft waterline length × 16 ft 3 in beam × 4 ft draught offered a roomy hull with a clipper bow and round counter stern. She had considerable sheer, a flat bottom and rounded bilges. Leeboards of the Dutch form were fitted. The gaff ketch rig of 1,850 sq ft had loose footed main and mizzen. Lazyjacks were provided to the mainsail, a sensible precaution with a long gaff and a small crew. Topsails were not carried. A 45 bhp auxiliary Gleniffer engine drove a centreline propeller. The rudder appeared small for her length and draught (fig. 62). Accommodation was generous. From forward there was a two berth fo'c'sle, a washplace and a galley and a single berth cabin, all arranged in the style of the time for a professional crew. There were two double berth and one single cabins and a saloon 16 ft × 9 ft panelled in oak. Abaft this was an engine room and a large cockpit with wheel steering.

Altogether the *Cluan* was a roomy and comfortable yacht for coastal cruising. Her steel construction offered long and reasonably trouble free life, with little chance of leaks. Several Klipper yachts of this size were built and proved efficient for pleasure sailing, though these might have improved if a chine had been introduced amidships to improve resistance to leeway and, incidentally to cheapen the construction; however, it was not a traditional feature of the type.

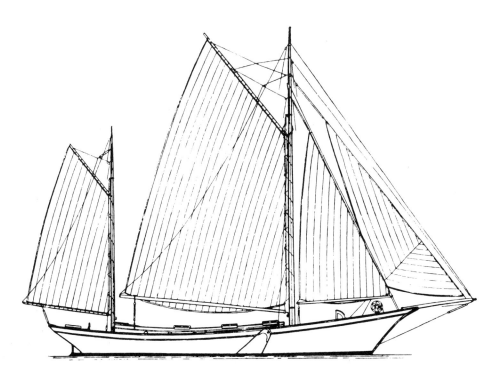

Figure 63 Sail plan of the ketch rigged Klipper yacht *Cluan*. Total sail area 1,850 sq ft

8

Barge yachts

The small barge yacht has for a century had a following. Although an insignificant minority in today's ever burgeoning sailing world, devotees of these shallow draught, leeboard cruisers praise the virtues of craft which are amongst the most individual a yachtsman can own. Small barge yachts are ideal for cruising in shallow waters which are not often rough, have the ability to take the mud comfortably, will float where other yachts of similar accommodation cannot go and have a subtle fascination for many.

However, a small barge yacht has defects compared with most small cruising yachts. These include low headroom, poor windward sailing ability, pounding in a head sea, a tendency for the hull, if planked, to strain and leak; the probability that bilge water will appear above the floorboards at times; a strong weather helm when pressed; the need to raise and lower leeboards when tacking; the noise of leeboards at night in a tideway, in a breeze or a jobble of sea (though this may be mitigated by wedging them tightly from the sides). Then there is the quick motion of a barge yacht and her restlessness at anchor, when she often tries to sail around it which can be as irritating as her habit of lying wind-rode when nearby yachts are tide rode. Add to all this that many small barge yachts are rather boxy craft and it is a wonder that anyone wants them, but to that eclectic few, the small barge has a usefulness and a cachet which outweighs all and ensures survival of the type.

The sailing barge, large or small, relies on hull form for power to carry sail. This is particularly true of small barge yachts which sail on their chines and whose directional stability is largely governed by the length of the chines, constancy of midship section shape and the fineness of the hull at the ends. The barge form has considerable initial stability and a righting moment which is usually adequate until the weather chine emerges, when it rapidly diminishes and is further diminished when the deck edge is immersed and capsize becomes possible or even probable. Beam depth of side are therefore crucial in the design of a small barge, as is the fullness and shape of the bow and stern. If too full in the ends and with too great a beam for her length, the small barge will be slow.

If is of course not possible or desirable to design a barge yacht on directly reduced dimensions of the typical 80 ft long sailing barges of the English south-east coast, the proportions of length/beam/depth would not be satisfactory. Beam and depth would need to be substantially increased in proportion to length, for the small barge. Barge yachts of 21 ft length have been built and have sailed satisfactorily but are generally considered too small for successful use. About 24 ft is a useful minimum length, with typical dimensions of 8 ft 6 in beam and 1 ft 6 in draught, carrying a sail area of about 300 sq ft.

Large yacht hulls should have slight rise of floor to enable them to be scrubbed on a hard if necessary, though most will need to be placed on blocks or be slipped to have the bottom maintained or repaired. The leeboards are often a source of anxiety in small barge yachts when sailing to windward in a fresh breeze, particularly if also facing a steep head sea. The strain on a leeboard and its hangings in these conditions is considerable. The barge's leeway puts severe pressure on the immersed part of the leeboard and when the barge yacht falls heavily in a trough of the sea, the pressure tends to wrench the board from its hangings. In such conditions the windward board should always be hauled up, as even in smooth water conditions considerable force may be exerted on it in fresh winds. Some small barge yachts have steel guides fitted close to the chine, horizontally, to retain the lee (or the weather) board close to the side when lowered. However, these are not considered good practice and could lead to serious hull damage if a board touched bottom when sailing in a tideway, for instance, when the retaining bar might be forced from the hull at its fastenings, causing leaks which would be difficult to stop quickly.

The use of steel plate leeboards which are usually about $\frac{3}{8}$–$\frac{9}{16}$ in (10–14 m/m) thick is usual in many small barge yachts, but well designed and well made wooden leeboards are better, provided these are weighted satisfactorily to overcome the natural buoyancy. Also, wooden boards may be shaped in the manner of Dutch leeboards to have a flat outer face and a curved inner one, for improved efficiency in diminishing leeway. This is an efficient method of using leeboards.

A few barge yachts, particularly those built by Frank Maynard at Chiswick, on the river Thames, had steel plate leeboards hung in cases built into the sides of the hull. This was structurally strong but caused problems in maintaining the insides of the cases. The arrangement also needs a slot in the bottom at the chines, which weakens the wooden construction at a vital place. Maynard was a versatile designer and builder who produced craft of many types and of good quality. He appears to have been the originator of this leeboard arrangement in Britain.

Rigs for the small barge yacht have varied from high peaked gunter lug mainsail and stemhead foresail sloop to a miniature spritsail barge rig, complete with a mizzen. However, the best rig for the barge yacht of about 35 ft and below is the gaff cutter. This allows flexibility of sail plan and adjustment of sail and hull balance in varied conditions on hulls which are unusually sensitive to adjustments of this kind.

All small barge yachts must be reefed before the wind becomes too strong. When the weather chine starts to emerge it is clearly time to reef. With the cutter rig a quick reduction in area may be made by lowering the staysail and this will relieve a small barge before it is time to put a reef in the mainsail and perhaps also think of changing the jib for a smaller one. Efficient reefing arrangements are necessary in the type and reef pendants should be kept rove. Alternatively, roller reefing on the mainsail, staysail and jibs is well worthwhile and with the present gears is an efficient method. The small displacement and shallow draught of the barge yacht cause her to lose way quickly and she must be kept going smartly when in stays, like a dinghy of older type. Coming to moorings in a fresh breeze needs careful judgement as she does not have a forefoot to hold her head up and it will blow away from the mooring as speed slackens.

E. B. Tredwen, a British sailing enthusiast, was pioneer of the small barge yacht. He not only designed them but sailed them vigorously on coastal cruises, proving that if handled competently these shallow craft could cruise coastwise despite the small displacement and lack of a ballast keel or much lateral plane. Tredwen

designed these small barges in various sizes from 21 ft × 7 ft up to 42 ft × 11 ft beam. The 29 ft *Nan* was perhaps the best known of these. She was intended to be moored on the drying foreshore off Southend, Essex, a flat and hard shore exposed to winds from the east to south-west, which can raise a considerable sea in the fetch across the mouth of the river Thames. The *Nan* was the twenty-first barge yacht Tredwen had designed and she reflected experience and refinement in form, construction and arrangement. None of these small

Figure 64 General arrangement of the 29 ft 6 in barge yacht *Nan*, designed by E. B. Tredwen, 1904. Typical of most small barge yachts

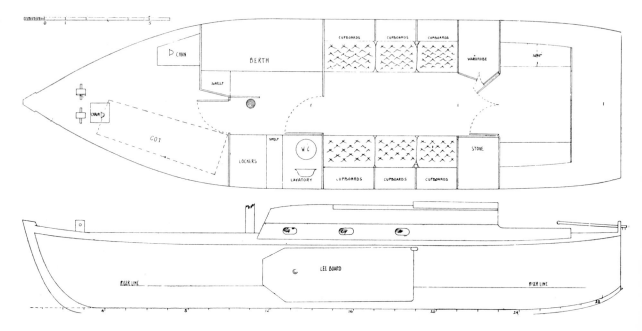

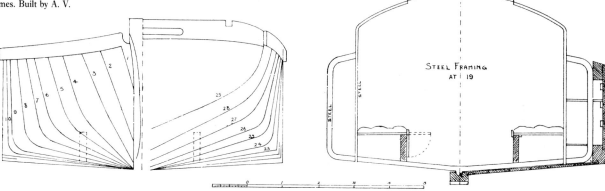

Figure 65 Body plan and midship section of barge yacht *Nan*. Note substantial chine and gunwhale and steel angle web frames. Built by A. V. Robertson, Woodbridge, Suffolk

barge yachts had then capsized or had trouble through being of that type. Several had made long passages. The 42 ft × 11 ft *Helen* sailed from the east coast to Inverness, in Scotland, experiencing much bad weather. The *Nan* cruised the east and south coasts in all weathers during the spring, summer and autumn.

These craft were designed with a shallow wooden keel and had slight rise of floor, a chine amidships and well shaped ends. A feature of the construction was a double skin bottom and heavy chines and gunwales which were rebated for the side and bottom planking. Four web frames and floors of steel angle provided the principal transverse strength, with intermediate wood frames and floors, and substantial longitudinal girders were worked into the form of bunk and locker fronts.

Tredwen believed in fitting steel plate leeboards and the manner of hanging these is controversial as he arranged them with a pivot bolt through the side planking at about mid-height of the side. This put considerable twisting force on the side planking, despite its being

reinforced with a chock and doublings. The steel plate leeboards are also prone to buckling, particularly in the lee side in shallow water over hard ground.

Although the outboard profile and the deck plan seem boxy and uninspiring, the *Nan* was a practical and much used cruiser with berths for four and ample locker space, galley, etc (figs. 64–65). The rig was unusual and as Tredwen was a tireless experimenter, it was frequently altered. As shown (fig. 66) the *Nan* was a sloop having a gunter lug mainsail with a batten across the sail just below the throat. The foresail tacked to the stem head and hoisted to the masthead. It was furled on a wooden roller. The mainsail was fitted with roller reefing and could be reduced from a full 300 sq ft to a close-reefed 165 sq ft in half a minute. The *Nan* would turn to windward under the foresail only or under the reefer mainsail. With foresail alone the leeboards were lowered as far as possible to bring the centre of lateral plane forward. Without the foresail set the boards were lowered half way.

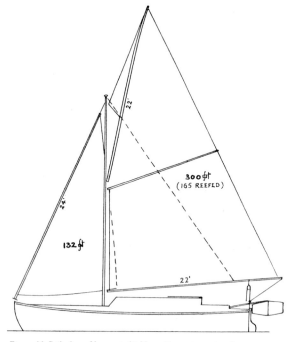

Figure 66 Sail plan of barge yacht *Nan* with gunter mainsail

Even small barge yachts need ample ground tackle. The *Nan* had two chain lockers and two chain pipes. On one side a 22 lb anchor was carried with 60 fathoms of $\frac{3}{16}$ in diameter chain cable and on the other a 32 lb anchor with 30 fathoms of $\frac{3}{8}$ in diameter chain. A spare anchor of 30 lbs weight was also carried. The cabin sole was on the inner face of the floors and despite a sizeable cabin top, only 4 ft 8 in headroom could be achieved. The dinghy was hoisted in horizontal stern davits across the transom, one of Tredwen's usual arrangements.

The *Nan* was the subject of an expensive misunderstanding in later years. She was for some time owned at West Mersea, Essex, where there has usually been at least one small barge kept. The *Nan* was left in charge of local waterman Charles Hewes. The owner decided to sell and told Charlie 'Anything you can get over £250 you may have for yourself'. Charlie, who was rather deaf, thought he said 'over £50' and muttered 'That 'ont be no trouble, Sir'. Soon after she was sold for £58 and Charlie approached the astonished owner with a handful of notes and a request for his £8 commission. The owner creditably smothered his anger and put the loss down to a good after dinner story!

The success of these small barge yachts designed by E. B. Tredwen inspired H. Wilmer, another amateur, to design a 25 footer for his own use. He closely followed the principles set by Tredwen for this 25 ft × 7 ft 4 in × 9 in hull draught gaff sloop. Her hull form had typical bow sections but the stern, particularly at the transom, was unusual. Afloat, she appeared more shapely than the plans suggest. The sail plan shows four rows of reefs in the mainsail and a roller furling foresail. Like most amateur designers, Wilmer was more concerned with drawing and describing odd details rather than the principal aspects of the design of hull and rig. However, the plans gave a good idea of the small barge yacht as a type.

Like Tredwen, Wilmer was originally a canoeist and sailed a canoe yawl before designing the *Venus* in 1895. He wrote of her:

'I eventually decided to build a boat after the type suggested by Mr. E. B. Tredwen, but with such modifications as special conditions and my artistic sense suggested. The Whitstable Shipping Co. undertook

Figure 67 Model of the sloop rigged barge yacht *Doreen*, designed by
E. B. Tredwen and J. Robinson. Built by J. W. Shuttlewood, Paglesham,
Essex. Dimensions 25 ft 6 in × 8 ft 4 in. Note roller furling headsail
and lifting rudder blade missing from model. The leeboards were of
steel plate

the construction of two boats from the same drawings,
the other being for Mr. T. D. F. Winser, the secretary
of the Royal Corinthian Yacht Club. They were
launched at Easter of 1896. The keel and stem is of
oak, the transom of elm. There are grown frames of
oak throughout, spaced about 14 in, with additional
heavy knees amidships. The sections as will be seen
by reference to the drawings, are 'square' for some
little distance fore and aft, and amidships, but close to
the bow and stern they are curved. The boats are
double-skinned throughout. Below the chine there is
an inner skin of $\frac{5}{8}$ in fir and an outer skin of oak of
the same scantling. Above the chine there are two half
inch skins of fir. The coamings are teak and the deck
and cabin top are covered with calico, dressed and
painted. The two boats differed considerably as
regards their internal fittings and rig. In *Venus* there is
a 15 gallon galvanised tank under the cockpit floor,
with a tap opening into the cabin. The cockpit floor is
lined with lead, the water running out through a pipe
in the transom above the waterline, and having a
weighted flap valve outside. It was found necessary to
bung up the pipe in the cockpit with a cork when
sailing in shallow water, as the action of the rudder
forced water up the pipe. When at moorings the cork
can be removed.

The sail area is very moderate; no ballast whatever
is carried. The boat draws about 9 in of water, and
displaces two tons. The mainsail has a hinged gaff,
which is convenient in an emergency, as the head of
the sail can be lowered entirely and still keep canvas
on. Four sets of reef points are fitted. When starting
out for a passage, we reeve either one or two reef
earings, and with a reef tackle permanently fitted
under the boom one or two reefs can be got down in

no time. The jib is of roller pattern and runs on a $\frac{5}{16}$ in galvanised rod instead of a flexible wire. . . . The roller jib has worked admirably all through the season, and we have never had a hitch with it. A wire forestay is carried in addition. There is good sitting accommodation under the cabin top and the berths are wide and give ample sleeping space.'

In July 1896 the *Venus* was shipped from Parkeston Quay, in Essex, for Denmark and a cruise by her owner accompanied by E. B. Tredwen. The *Venus* was discharged at Esbjerg, on the North Sea coast of Jutland and was rigged and provisioned for the cruise. She sailed south along the Jutland coast, inside the long islands of Fano, Romo and Sylt, in a channel about 6 miles wide; a rough passage in a two-reef breeze. The *Venus* averaged 4 knots for 60 miles of windward work to anchor off the head of Amrum. A sail to Tonning, on the Eider and then to Rendsberg, to enter the Kiel Ship Canal to Holtenau and the Baltic Sea; a passage made under sail, against the rules. The *Venus* cruised amongst the southern Danish islands, to Copenhagen, then up the Sound and across the Kattegat to the east coast of Jutland and the eastern entrance to the Lim Fjord, which gave passage across the top of the peninsular, via Aalborg and the attractive lakes and meers linked by channels, to emerge at Thybor Ron on the North Sea coast once again. The *Venus* then ran down to Esbjerg in 18 hours for the 94 miles.

Both her owner and Tredwen were well satisfied with the ability of the *Venus* during this cruise. She was shipped back to Parkeston where she was discharged and rigged. Then Wilmer sailed her single-handed to Burnham-on-Crouch, along the Essex coast, in 7 hours. During that time he had to heave-to to put one reef in

and also set the spinnaker three times. He regarded her as a good single-handed cruiser for coastal work.

Several other designers and builders produced small barge yachts. The 30 ft 6 in *Dione* is a good example of those built before 1939. She was designed and built by J. W. Shuttlewood and Son at Paglesham, on the Essex river Roach, in 1936. Dimensions are 30 ft 6 in length overall, 29 ft 6 in length waterline × 9 ft 1½ in beam and 3 ft 7 in depth moulded. Sail area of the gaff cutter rig is 470 sq ft.

John Howard was a notable builder of sailing barges, small yachts and fishing craft at his yard at Maldon, on the river Blackwater in Essex. He was a thorough designer and builder and a competent naval architect. In 1909 Howard and Sons built a barge yacht, to his design, for W. J. Tennant who kept her at Burnham-on-Crouch. The *Frances* was 48 ft long overall, 42 ft waterline length × 12 ft 5 in beam and 3 ft hull draught, excluding the leeboards. She was designed to accommodate the owner and four guests, two of whom might be ladies, who had their own cabin aft. The skipper and a boy lived in the fo'c'sle, in the fashion of the time.

The hull form of the *Frances* was well conceived and the rounded stem profile was typical of Howard's yacht work. Her entry and run were fine for a barge yacht hull and the counter stern was conventional at the time. A raised coach roof gave 6 ft headroom over the main cabin and part of the ladies' cabin. Construction was strong. The framing was 6 in × 6 in English oak and the skin planking, stem, sternpost, deadwood and keelsons were also oak. The keel was of English elm and the coachroof and deckwork of teak (fig. 71). She was copper fastened and was classed '+ 16 years A1' by Lloyd's Register of Shipping. The *Frances* had a miniature spritsail barge rig and sailed well on all points

Figure 68 Spritsail barge yacht *Frances* under sail

Figure 69 Lines of the spritsail barge yacht *Frances* designed and built by
John Howard and Sons, Maldon, Essex, 1910

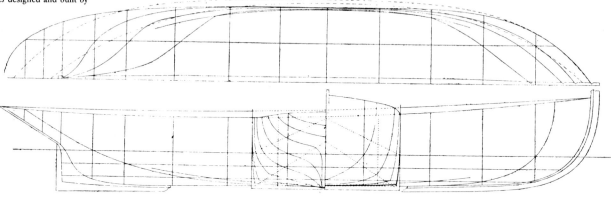

and was dry in a seaway (fig. 68). A contemporary description stated:

'. . . there is a great deal of living room. The standing berths are indicated by numerals and are five in number, there being two folding cots in the forecastle

for the hands. When ladies are carried, there being accommodation for two in the after cabin, the closing of a sliding door in the bulkhead at A A affords them complete privacy; at such times they have access to the deck from their cabin by way of the steerage ladder, which is then reserved for their use and at the

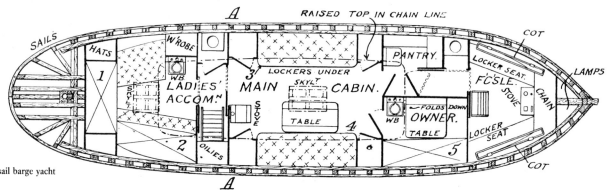

Figure 70 Accommodation arrangement of the spritsail barge yacht
Frances

foot of which is their own lavatory accommodation. A supply pipe for fresh water is led to the ladies' cabin from a 75 gallon main tank forward, filled through the deck. There are two W.C.s – one forward, the other aft – and each of them is shut off by at least two doors from all compartments with which it would otherwise communicate, there being ventilation, of course, to the outer air.

In the main cabin two broad sofas upholstered in red pegamoid (a waterproof material) serve by night as two of the standing beds.

The raised cabin top, indicated in the accommodation plan by chain lines, extends over the whole of the standing space, in the main cabin as well as over the steerage and far enough over the ladies' cabin, the pantry, and the owner's cabin to afford room for a tall person to stand upright in each. Owing to the rise of the sheer, there is good height under the deck in the forecastle. Primus stoves and a kitchener (stove) are

Figure 71 Structural midship section of barge yacht *Frances*

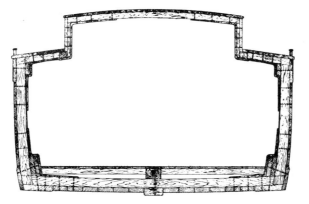

fitted in the forecastle, where cooking for seven persons can be carried out comfortably, and the after end of the vessel is heated by one of the London Warming and Heating Co.'s closed stoves burning anthracite. The main cabin, which is about 11 ft by 13 ft – as large as some shore-going rooms – is exceptional and could not be obtained in a vessel of 25 tons unless she were of the barge type; skylights and decklights so light up the interior as to leave no dark corner. Like all barges she lies comfortably upright when aground. Her high freeboard makes her a very dry vessel in a seaway and her underwater form and small draught make her extremely quick in stays.'

The 32 ft cutter rigged *Growler*, designed and built at Maldon, Essex, by John Howard in 1910 was amongst the best known and the prettiest of barge yachts. She was for many years owned by H. Alker Tripp, a Commissioner of London Police and an experienced yachtsman, cruising principally on the east and south coasts of England. Tripp wrote and illustrated four books and was an artist of ability. The *Growler* succeeded a yacht of deeper draught and enabled him to visit secluded anchorages and creeks, besides sailing the coastal seaways. Her 10 ft beam resulted in comfortable accommodation. He wrote of her in a coastal seaway, after leaving the entrance to Chichester Harbour bound for the Isle of Wight on the ebb,

' . . . the yacht sailed down the harbour and out of it, in the steep, breaking seas that are always knocked up when the wind and tide are at feud. The bar was a mass of white broken water . . . By this time, the whole ebb tide was sweeping towards Selsey Bill, and was determined to carry the yacht there also. With the

Figure 72 A barge yacht, in foreground, and a ketch barge in the river Deben, Suffolk, about 1910. The yawl rigged barge yacht has low freeboard, a counter stern and long coachroof. She is of more yacht-like appearance than many and the leeboards are just discernible. The gaff mainsail has a stiffening batten and the mizzen is similarly fitted

wind dead foul, the poor thing earned incredibly little on each patient board. It was a regular tussle. We stood as close inshore as we dared at the end of each landward tack, so as to cheat the tide; and the lead was kept going. So we won our way gradually along towards the Winner at the mouth of Langston Harbour; but there the sands stretch farther off shore and we were driven out again into the full run of the tide. The green seas were coming on board, the spray flew in sheets and the wind shrilled. The clouds that scudded above were low and gloomy, and the evening was drawing on. It was just a case for patience and perseverance, and plenty of both. We had to sail ten miles to gain one. Windward work on a lee going tide is a thing that shows up a barge at her very worst.

But this crawl alongshore could not last. We had to "jump off" for the Island some time or other – and then. Out in the deep fairway from Spithead, the east-going stream simply seized her and carried her by the beam away and away towards the Nab Tower. How it swept her! She was pointed hopefully towards her objective at first, then at Culver Cliff, and so on. But she was slashing through the water all the time; and, as she began to close the shore down by Culver, she was again out of the strength of the tide. Then, gradually, she made good again; in the late twilight she crept northward once more. The great headland of Culver, piled high in the gloom, was passed. Lights were twinkling ashore, and the Warner Lightship and the Nab Tower were flashing. The wind had taken off with nightfall, and she worked her way warily up the edge of the St Helens Sands to the Drumhead. As the tide made again, she crept up the narrow channel, guided by the fairway lights, into Bembridge.'

A typical barge yacht passage in contrary conditions.

Some barge yachts were also built in Holland as cutter rigged variants of the klipper type, often having rounded rather than flared bows. The *Harelda II* was designed and built at Nieuwendam by G. De Vries Lentsch in 1922 for a Belgian owner and proved a practical cruiser. The steel hull was 58 ft 3 in length overall, 53 ft waterline length × 15 ft beam and 3 ft 6 in draught. She had a plumb stem and a steeply raked counter stern. The cutter rig of 1,700 sq ft had the mast stepped well into the hull. The sails were made by F. Zeilinga and the loose footed mainsail was laced to the mast, which is an efficient method provided it is tautened after reefing. The staysail foot was extended by a boom and the jib was set on a fairly long bowsprit which could be topped up when in port. The rig needed a pair of running backstays. The anchors were stowed in hawse pipes and the chain cables were handled by a compact, geared windlass of typical Dutch pattern. Leeboard winches and wheel steering eased work on deck and a low coachroof provided 7 ft headroom throughout the accommodation and had a fast runabout stowed on chocks to port. The accommodation plan (fig. 73) was unusually spacious for three and a crew of two. In practice there were often more on board in the owner's party and a professional crew of three was carried. A 54 bhp auxiliary engine by Ailsa Craig drove a centreline propeller and gave the *Harelda II* a speed of 7 knots in smooth water, though as with all barge types this dropped radically in a seaway.

By 1927 the yacht had been sold to Captain Richard Hennessy, a thoroughly practical yacht owner with wide experience of many types of yacht. He sailed the *Ivernia*, as she was now renamed, on the south and east coasts of England and on the Norfolk Broads for two years. She

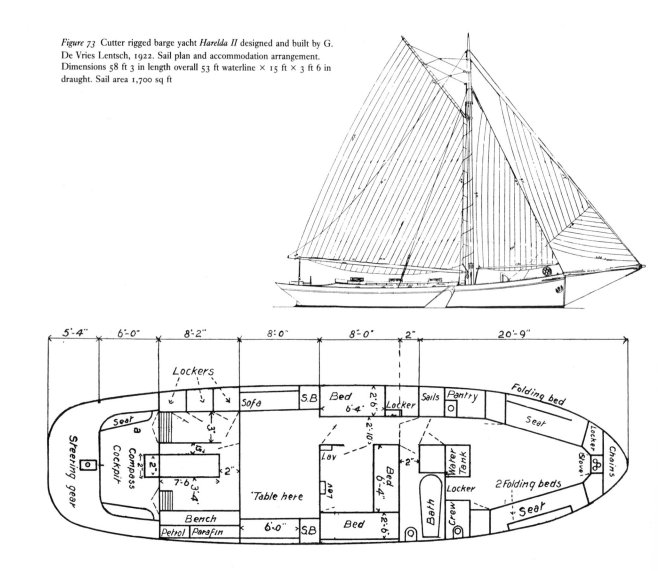

Figure 73 Cutter rigged barge yacht *Harelda II* designed and built by G. De Vries Lentsch, 1922. Sail plan and accommodation arrangement. Dimensions 58 ft 3 in length overall 53 ft waterline × 15 ft × 3 ft 6 in draught. Sail area 1,700 sq ft

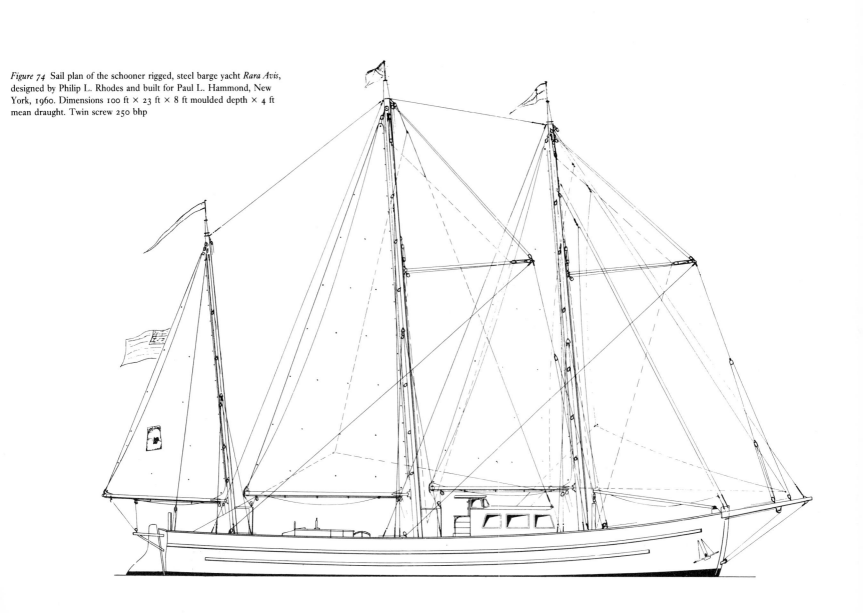

Figure 74 Sail plan of the schooner rigged, steel barge yacht *Rara Avis*, designed by Philip L. Rhodes and built for Paul L. Hammond, New York, 1960. Dimensions 100 ft × 23 ft × 8 ft moulded depth × 4 ft mean draught. Twin screw 250 bhp

Figure 75 Lines of the American barge yacht *Rara Avis*

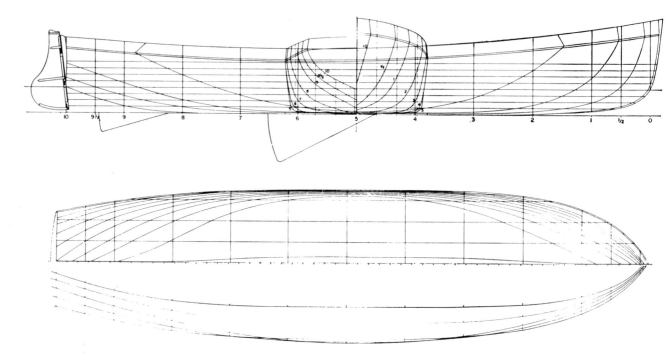

was later owned by Vice Admiral Sir Edward Heaton-Ellis. As a weatherly and roomy compromise the *Harelda II* is amongst the most interesting of the middle size of barge yachts.

The 99 ft steel huller *Rara Avis* was perhaps the largest barge yacht. She was designed in 1956 by Philip L. Rhodes, a noted American yacht designer, for American yachtsman Paul Hammond. She was rigged as a three masted Bermudian schooner and was conceived to

be capable of ocean passagemaking as well as coastal seafaring, with shallow draught for lying in shallow anchorages. A study of her lines (fig. 75) suggests that her form may have been influenced by the lines of the spritsail barge *Giralda* which was designed and built by J. R. Piper of Greenwich, on the river Thames and was a notably fast sailing barge which won the Thames barge match seven times and the Medway race four times. Her lines and sail plan appeared in Uffa Fox's book *Uffa*

Fox's Second Book, published in 1935. The sailing bargemen of south-east England would readily accept the hull form of the *Rara Avis* but her bow was finer than that of a working barge and the small bilge radius worked into this design would be considered unnecessary and promising a loss of weatherliness compared to the usual chine form. It must also have caused annoyance to the shell platers of Gebr. de Klerk, her Netherlands builders.

The *Rara Avis* was 94 ft 6 in waterline length × 23 ft beam with a hull draught of 4 ft, extended by a large centreboard amidships and a smaller one aft which could be lowered to aid steering at sea. These were sensibly selected instead of the usual leeboards, which are dangerous in severe sea conditions. The designed displacement was 160 tons. Although ocean sailing was contemplated, the barge hull form, with its limited range of stability, is not really suitable for comfortable deep sea sailing, but the *Rara Avis* has made at least two trans-atlantic passages.

Scantlings were of commercial standards and three transverse watertight bulkheads were arranged and oil fuel and fresh water were carried in double bottom tanks. The rig totalled 3,500 sq ft which approximates to that carried in the spritsail rig of an English sailing barge. The Bermudian foresail, main and mizzen were loose footed and the staysail and jib were set on furling gears. The bowsprit was short and well steeved. It was supported by two bobstays. A yard was crossed on the fore and main masts and from these a pair of triangular running sails could be set, also fitted with roller furling gears. The comparatively small area of the rudder appears inadequate in relation to the underwater profile and the hull form and shallow draught. Two steering positions were arranged; one aft which was enclosed by a bulwark and intended for use when under sail. Another forward was raised to bridge height abaft the deckhouse. This had a shelter and was used for steering

Figure 76 Deck plan of the schooner barge yacht *Rara Avis*. Note bulwark around wheel

1. ENTRANCE NAV. CABIN & ENG. ROOM
2. ENTRANCE ADMIRAL'S CABIN
3. ENTRANCE CREW'S QUARTERS & GALLEY
4. ENTRANCE DECKHOUSE & STATEROOMS
5. EMERGENCY EXIT ENGINE ROOM

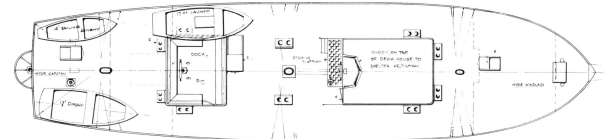

Figure 77 Accommodation plan of the *Rara Avis*. Note the two centreplate cases, amidships and aft

PLAN DECKHOUSE

under power or when in confined waters. The unobstructed deck is shown and three boats were carried in davits with plenty of room to spare. Two bower anchors were carried in hawse pipes and were handled by a hydraulic windlass. As with the conversion of several sailing barges to power, twin screws were fitted, driven by two 120 hp diesel engines but with the refinement of controllable pitch propellers.

Below deck the *Rara Avis* was perhaps the most spacious and comfortable barge yacht with arrangements for an owner's party of five and cabins for skipper and engineer and a fo'c'sle for two hands. A large dining room and lounge was carried the breadth of the vessel abaft the spacious galley dividing the crew's quarters from the other accommodation. A cabin was provided aft for the navigator, though why he had to be so isolated is

difficult to imagine unless it was that the kick and groan of the rudder in a seaway would keep him awake! For her first two seasons the *Rara Avis* cruised in the Mediterranean and the Aegean. Afterwards she crossed the Atlantic to the West Indies, making the almost 2,400 miles passage from the Cape Verde Islands to Martinique in 11 days. Later she was based on Long Island Sound and cruised southern New England waters. Later she returned to Europe and a few years ago I saw her under the French flag and in use as some form of youth training vessel.

Phil Bolger, the Gloucester, Massachusetts yacht and boat designer who has produced some of the most imaginative craft of recent times has designed several barge yachts. One of the most graceful is a clipper bowed, three masted for American owners. She was intended to have the amenities of a small house, except for space for a car. The hull has shapely ends and a 'square' midship section with a very small bilge radius. The transom is not flared in the manner of the English spritsail barges but the bow has considerable flare, which might aid in keeping spray clear in a seaway. The rudder has a small skeg immediately forward of its leading edge, to give improved steering under sail and power and there are two short fin keels just aft of amidships. These will assist directional stability under power with leeboards raised, or when running under sail.

The schooner rig has a single headsail set to a short bowsprit and a mizzen which is fully battened lugsail sheeted to a bumkin. The gaff foresail and mainsail have a type of sprit boom favoured by the designer. All masts are stepped in tabernacles. The leeboards are worked by winches and are of wood. The deck and accommodation arrangements are spacious. Steering is by a wheel in a cockpit just aft of amidships. Construction of the hull is a glass reinforced plastic shell with a plastic foam core sandwiched between two skins. Transverse strength is assured by structural bulkheads. Altogether she is an ingenious interpretation of the barge yacht as a shoal draught cruiser and the more interesting as Phil Bolger has designed several other successful craft of this type with rigs varying from yawl to fully battened lugger.

So the barge yacht lives on and appears likely to continue to attract owners and designers into the twenty-first century.

PART TWO

Other English barges

9

The keels of Yorkshire and Lincolnshire

The British industrial age of the late eighteenth and the nineteenth centuries was coupled with an expansion of agriculture to feed a quickly growing population and this demanded rapid movement of goods and produce. Ports and distribution of foodstuffs and goods increased in capacity and traffic, and inland waterways were constructed or rivers adapted, to bring waterborne commerce to many northern and midland cities and towns. A network of canals and canalised rivers served the industrial West Riding of Yorkshire, the vales of the East and the North Ridings of Yorkshire and the counties of Lincolnshire and Nottinghamshire. Keels and sloops were cargo sailing craft which then offered the cheapest and reasonably quick means of transport of bulk goods and the river Humber and the port of Hull formed a natural entrepot and outlet for this busy hinterland.

Canal builders were active years before. The Aire and Calder Navigation Canal was opened as early as 1699. It was 32 miles long and had 10 locks. Yorkshire commerce was seriously affected when the 5 mile canal between Haddlesley and Selby was cut to make inland Knottingley and Selby centres of shipping and small craft construction; connections and traditions retained into modern times. The Barnsley Canal was opened in 1799 and created a large trade in keel-borne coal. The Knottingley and Goole Canal was opened in 1826 and led to the small riverside village of Goole quickly becoming a busy port with extensive docks and ship-building yards by the embanked river Humber. Keels had to be of shallow draught and of restricted length and beam to use the shallow, narrow and locked waterways of Yorkshire and Lincolnshire but be sufficiently able to stand the strong winds and tides of the Humber estuary. A few made occasional coastal passages, sometimes to Yarmouth or Lowestoft, in Norfolk and Suffolk and some to Scarborough on the north coast of Yorkshire. There are a few recorded instances of keels voyaging to the river Thames.

Many early keels were clench planked on sawn frames but by the nineteenth century almost all were carvel planked of oak, with bottoms of Baltic softwood and decks of American Georgia Pine. The box-like form of keels and sloops gave maximum cargo capacity and as no cargo carrying craft could sail against the tides of the Humber, their fullness did not impair sailing efficiency. The hulls were particularly full forward but the stern shape, from just forward of the hold after bulkhead to the sternpost was usually well formed and the craft sailed remarkably well considering their shape. It is surprising that the need for capacity and weatherliness in

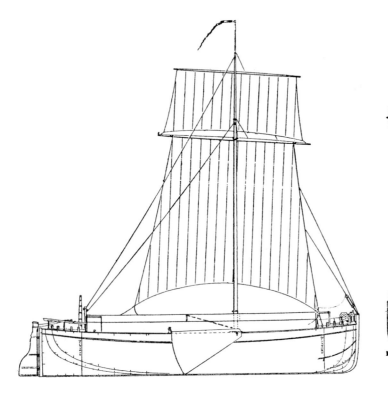

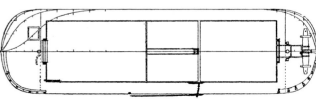

Figure 78 Lines, sail plan and general arrangement of a typical keel of a size used to trade to Sheffield. Dimensions 60 ft × 15 ft 3 in beam

the narrow waterways did not result in constructing them with a chine amidships, like the sailing barges of the Thames and its estuary. The short forward and after decks connected with narrow side decks outside the high coamings of the main hatch. There were generally 18 hatch covers with tarpaulins over them, battened down and wedged for watertightness. A loaded keel had water at deck level amidships and only about 18 in of freeboard at each end. Keels built to work on the Aire and Calder Navigation Canal differed from others in having a transom stern and more shape in the bow.

The dimensions of typical keels were usually between 55 and 65 ft length × 15 ft beam and 8 ft depth. Capacity was 110–130 tons. Size was governed by the dimensions of the locks encountered in their trade routes and types of keels were commonly referred to as of 'Sheffield', 'Manvers', 'Driffield', 'Barnsley' size, etc.

The keel builders constructed them in the manner of

wooden shipbuilders, rather than boatbuilders; a natural method in view of the heavy construction of the keels. The building berths were usually covered by a roof and nearby was a mould loft, where the lines were laid down and faired, and templates and moulds were made. There was usually also a sawpit or later a sawmill, a wood stockyard, a sparmaker's shop, a quay for fitting out alongside, a joiner's shop, a sail loft for making and repairing sails and making up rigging, a store and in some yards a ropewalk was in use.

The English elm keel was often 6 in sided × 9 in moulded and stem and sternpost were also, surprisingly, of English elm. The sawn frames and floors were of English oak, erected on the keel and ribbanded fair. Then the 3 in oak binding strakes were fitted at the sheer, acting as thicker chafing strakes in the years of hard use ahead. Afterwards the 2 in thick hull planking was spiled off and fitted. The oak deck beams and carlings followed and the hatch coamings, about 3 in thick, before the deck shelves or gunwales were placed inside the frames. A knee was fitted to each beam to resist pressure in locks or when alongside. Five thicker planks formed a bilge stringer or thickening in the wood ceiling which lined the hold. The transverse bulkheads were fitted and the deck planking laid. Hatch beams were fitted about 10 ft from the mast beam which supported the fore and after on which the inner end of the hatch covers rested. The fore and afters acted as guides when the mast was lowered. Heads of the side timbers were carried up above the sheer to form stanchions for the wooden rail around the stern. The keel's name and port of registry were cut into this. Bow boards supported fairleads, deflected spray and carried a single decorative design or 'featherings'; the white rose of York being common. Launching was end-on or broadside to the river or canal. The hull was tarred except for the sheerstrake which was varnished. Coamings and hatches were usually painted in bright colours.

The foregoing construction applied to most keels but sloops differed in some details. These wooden keels and sloops were more strongly constructed than the spritsail barges of the English south-east coast and had an inherently stronger hull form and consequently usually a longer life. Iron and then steel construction were introduced for keels and sloops during the late nineteenth century and proved efficient, though a wooden sloop was built by Clapsons at Barton-on-Humber as late as 1935.

Oak leeboards 12–13 ft long × 6 ft broad were hung near the mainbeam and were slung by a toggle at the forward end, via a strong chain, to the traveller on the coamings. The leeboards were $3\frac{1}{2}$ in thick at the forward end tapering to about 2 in aft. A timber head near the after end of the hold was used as the 'leeboard stanchion'. This carried an iron or steel sheave with a wire rope or chain which was fastened to the after end of the leeboard. The leeboard tail chain was shackled to a block which had a wire fall rove through it. The forward end of this was shackled to the stanchion at the forward end of the rail and the other end led to a vertical roller on which it was wound by hand, raising or lowering the leeboard. A small vertical roller was fitted under the stern rail for the fall of the leeboard purchase.

Two tillers were carried. The longer shipped over the head of the mainpiece and was curved and ornamented. This was used when under sail but was changed for a short tiller for lock work, allowing it to be put hard over for clearance or sharp turns. Two stocked anchors were also carried, each having 30 fathoms of chain cable for use on the rivers Humber and Trent. These were not used in the canals. Other equipment included a long sweep, two long boathooks, a cargo derrick, two setting booms or 'stowers' each about 20 ft long with a double-pronged iron end. Bass rope warps were used for mooring or towing and a water cask was carried in chocks on the starboard side of the after deck. A heavy handspike windlass worked in stout chocks forward and handled the anchor cables and mooring warps. Side navigation lights were carried on light boards and a riding light and a stern lamp were provided. A sounding pole was indispensible in these craft and a foghorn was provided as some protection from the serious dangers when anchored in the Humber in fog. For some reason keels and sloops did not usually carry a compass, which would have been useful in the open waters of the Humber.

The keels boat was about 12 ft × 4 ft 6 in and was known as a 'cob' or 'coggy boat' (perhaps a variant of 'Cock boat', an earlier term for a ship's small boat and much used in the north of England for any small boat). This was towed astern, was clinker planked with a full shaped bow but had a fine run and in the manner of all sailing bargemen, was usually sculled with one oar, rather than rowed. George F. Holmes, a Hull engineer, and accomplished canoe sailor and designer was noted as a designer of good cob boats at the end of the nineteenth century and early twentieth century.

The skipper lived in the after cabin, often with his wife and children. This cabin was usually about 6 ft × 5 ft, with a double berth opening off on one side through sliding doors, usually on the starboard side, in the customary seafaring tradition. The bunk to port was used for any children and had a coal bunker under. If there were bunks to port and starboard there were also seat lockers on each side. A folding table lowered to provide places for two to eat. All cooking was done on a small coal stove. There were drawers and cupboards and

a ladder led to a hatch to the deck. There was also a trapdoor through the bulkhead into the hold but the purpose of this is obscure. Water was kept in a cask on deck and was filled whenever possible. At Hull water could be obtained from a 'steam keel' waterboat which served shipping.

If on board, the skipper's wife usually helped handle the keel and washed and scrubbed, cooked and brought up the family in cramped conditions and often for long periods. The children attended school as best they could while the keel was unloaded or loaded, or was waiting a cargo. Some never went to school.

The mate lived in the fo'c'sle, which also housed stores and was known as the 'caddy', probably a corruption of cuddy. He had a bunk and a stove with an oven and shared the space with shelves and lockers for blocks and gear, ropes, paints, navigation lights, pump gear, handspikes, rigging equipment, tools, a spare anchor, kedge, chain cable, the topsail and possibly the top-gallant, when these were unbent.

The keel's long masthead flag or 'vane' was usually red. At regattas, launchings, a keelman's wedding or other occasions the keel hoisted a 15 ft long burgee which was about 5 ft wide and had a union jack in the hoist followed by her name. The burgee was given to the keel's owner after launch by the builder and was afterwards carefully kept in a locker.

The rig and its rigging were carefully arranged and supervised by the skipper and if he were also the owner, his wife might oversee the completion of the after cabin, which would be their home for long periods.

A cash deposit was paid on placing the order for the keel or sloop and the balance was paid on completion; a simple statement but full of meaning, with the bearded skipper signing the contract with care and perhaps a tremble from a toil-worn hand, counting the gold sovereigns from a leather bag. An old keel was sometimes accepted by the builder as part payment, to be refitted and afterwards sold. Amounts credited by a builder constructing a new keel for an owner offering his old in part exchange might vary from £200 for a useful craft to as little as £30 or so. Sometimes the agreement included deferred payment on completion until the keel was earning and the debt repayments could start. Stage payments were often arranged for construction, payable on signature of contract, when planking was completed, and on delivery. Most keel skippers owned their own craft by the mid-nineteenth century, in contrast to the comparatively small number of coasting or river sailing spritsail barges owned by their owners in the south-east.

The keel skipper had to find his own cargo through agents and there was rivalry for cargoes, occasionally leading to disputes, fights and stealthy manoeuvring at night to be first alongside to load. In keels not owned by the skipper, earnings were divided by a system termed 'thirds'. The keel owner paid for her maintenance, equipment and insurance and received one third of her returns on cargo. The skipper had the remaining two thirds, but had to pay the wages of the mate, towage, food, loading and unloading charges. It was a system suited to the times of cheeseparing economy, established business customs and direct cash payments. The skipper paid the balance and accounted to the owner on his return to the office. When a keel carried gravel the cargo returns were divided equally between the owner and skipper, for obscure reasons.

Keels, sloops, ketches and lighters were insured by the Keel and Lighter Owners Mutual Insurance and Protection Society Ltd, established at Hull in 1874 as a non-profitmaking organisation. Craft were covered for their assessed value, which was then between £25 and £800 and included £10 for leeboards, £7 for the boat and £12 for sails, which seems inadequate for those items. The *Tiger* of Hull was built by Parkinson Groves in 1874 was 53 ft × 14 ft 10 in beam and 7 ft depth. She carried 90 tons and in 1899 was insured for £150. Insurance premiums were often paid at four-monthly intervals and early in the twentieth century this period might cost £3.

The keelman's favourite dress was a navy blue guernsey, dark corduroy trousers and a blue serge coat in cold weather. A cloth cap or a cheesecutter was worn and in rain or rough conditions, sticky black oilskins and leather boots.

The lore of the keels and sloops was passed down the generations. Many of the crews were religious and some superstitious.

Larger keels had a mast of Norway fir about 55 ft long, stepped just forward of amidships in a tabernacle, locally known as a 'luchet'. An average keel mast was about 45 ft long and the luchet was fastened to the mainbeam across the keel at deck level, and to the keelson. The mast was of parallel section to the hounds, which carried the slings of the mainyard, then it tapered to the truck. The mast could be lowered into a depression in the centre of the hatches, while the heel remained in the luchet. A retaining bolt was passed through the luchet when the mast was erect. In light winds a keel might set the mainsail and a topsail. In stronger winds the topsail was handed. In very strong winds one or two reefs were taken in the mainsail. The effective area of the mainsail could be reduced by the truss line on the after side, lying like an inverted letter Y. The lifting part led through a sheave in the mast and

Figure 79 A keel with mainsail and a topsail set to a fair wind. This unusual rig for a craft trading on rivers and canals survived into the 1930s. Note the keel's bluff bows

then to a winch aft. A useful arrangement in confined waters.

A forestay, topmast stay and a shifting backstay were fitted on each side of the mast, set up or slacked off by hand winches. The main course or mainsail was a simple square sail, hoisted in slings. Above it a square topsail could also be set and some keels also carried a topgallant, to catch wind above trees, river banks and buildings. The mainsail was white, untreated canvas, as was the topsail. When not in use the sails were furled on the yards and were covered with a canvas sail coat. A keel main course might last fifteen years with careful use. The mainsail was about 27 to 39 ft from the centre of the foot gore to the centre of the headrope. The sails were often dressed with a mixture of horse fat and red ochre. The topsail was of lighter canvas and the head earings were spliced to it and led through holes at the yardarms. The head of the sail was held to the yard with robands. The topsail was carried in light or moderate winds or in stronger when the wind was favourable. When not in use it was lowered and stowed in the fo'c'sle. In 1905 a new mainsail and topsail cost £15 to £19, which was low even for the times. A complete rig for a keel then cost under £180.

The sails of a keel were controlled by the braces and sheets. The mainsail tye led through the mast sheaves and ended in a block. The halyard led through this and through another block shackled to the after coaming (headledge) and the fall led to a roller. The topsail halyard was led through another sheave in the masthead.

The mainsail was of heavy cotton or flax canvas with gores at the foot and on each side. It was roped all round and the earings for hauling the head out on the yardarms were spliced to the sail. A bridle was spliced to the footrope as a trussline to shorten the sail or to spill wind from it. The mainyard had a sheave at each end through which the earings were rove and set up. Then the head of the sail was laced to the mast with robands. There were braces to trim the yard which was hoisted by

Figure 80 Scale model of a Yorkshire keel showing the typical hull form, rig and arrangement. The protrusion of the lower stem is not exaggerated

a halyard working through one large and two small sheaves in the mast and was held to it by a hemp rope parrel with wooden balls on it to allow it to move freely when hoisting or lowering. Small wooden blocks were shackled to the yard to take the topsail sheets. There were two shrouds on each side and these and the backstays led to the hounds just above the main halyard sheave. The shrouds were set up with deadeyes and lanyards and led to chainplates on the hull. The wire rope backstays had a wooden deadeye spliced to the lower end which had three holes in it.

The forestay led to the stay fall purchase blocks which were shackled inside the stemhead. The wire purchase was led to a forward roller. The after coaming had a pair of wooden winch posts to support the main and topsail rollers which were of wood. The main brace was made fast to a wooden cleat on each post and the truss halyards to a smaller one. The mainsheets were led to sheet rollers port and starboard on the after end of the coamings. These were formed with two iron stanchions curved inboard at the top with a wooden roller between them. This had gears at the forward end and at the after end a ratchet with more gears and a handle. These winches had a ratio of about 2 to 1.

The wire mainsheets were led from the roller, across the hatches, through a fairlead sheave on the coaming and through a block on the gunwale to lead to the clew of the mainsail.

The tack rollers were supported by an iron frame fastened to the foredeck and to the fore coaming. The rollers were arranged longitudinally and the tack chain led from the roller, through a bushed hole in the 'tack timber' and then to the clew (or tack) of the mainsail. 'Mast rollers' at the forward end of the hatch were used to raise or lower the mast and also for warping the keel.

When tacking a keel the helm was put down until the luff of the sail came aback, then the pawl of the sheet roller was lifted and the leeboard of the new lee side was lowered. The mate let go the tack and took in the slack on the other tack roller. The lee brace was held and the bowline was left made fast until the skipper gave the order to let go and for the new tack line to be set taut on the roller. The skipper hauled the weather brace and got the sheet in, putting the helm to leeward slightly to meet her tendency to fall off before gathering way. The bowline was hauled taut and the keel settled on another tack.

When possible, keels sailed in the canals but had to be towed by the crew or by horses in contrary winds. The keelmen termed this 'head wind racks'. A man owning towing horses was locally known as a 'horse marine'. He had his meals on board the keel when towing and walked backwards before the horse to see that the towline did not foul and pull the horse into the canal. A horse might take eight hours to tow a keel ten miles and was fed with a nosebag as he toiled along. After the day's work the horse had to walk home carrying the horse marine on his back – a hard life.

In calms, on the rivers, keels were rowed with sweeps to maintain steerage way but the fierce tides did most of the work, sometimes reaching 5 or 6 knots. If the keel was sailing in a fresh wind her speed with a fair tide might be 9 to 10 knots over the ground.

The anchors, cable and windlass were much used. Keels often 'dredged' with the tide, stern first, keeping the crown of the anchor just touching the bottom and sheering the keel with the helm. Tides in the Humber are so strong that at anchor on spring tides a keel had to be 'steered' to prevent her from coming broadside-on and being swept under by the tide, if deep loaded. As Humber tides may run at 5 knots on the flood and 7 on the ebb, such caution was prudent. Dog leg type anchors were used for mooring to the banks of canals or rivers.

A keel could be capsized if caught broadside-on in a squall, under sail, deep loaded. The coggy boat was kept ready at such times in case it was necessary to abandon ship suddenly.

The keel *Marley Hill* foundered off Whitton Ness in the Humber and was quickly buried in the sand by the strong tides. Some years afterwards she was revealed by the river's scour, was raised, re-rigged and resumed trading under sail. The rivers Humber and Trent are subject to a bore known as the Aegir or Eagre, which occurs as a tidal flood on a spring tide in calm weather, when it can be heard about ten minutes before the smooth, rushing wave arrives to set craft back sharply on their cables and mooring ropes. Occasionally it causes collisions and the capsize of small boats.

Hufflers were sometimes taken by keels to aid the passage of a difficult part of a river and were locally termed 'purchasemen', possibly from the additional hauling power or 'purchase' they could provide. Light keels were often flooded in the hold to reduce air-draught to pass a fixed bridge, depending on the water level. Up to about 20 tons might be let in by a seacock. If a keel leaked badly the skipper might lash a saucepan to a boathook and fill it with wetted sawdust, to be worked over the area, if it could be reached. It was hoped the sawdust would be drawn into the seams as a stopgap caulk. This was known as a 'branmash'. The keels were generally smartly kept and laid up for two weeks each year for refitting and repainting. A severe winter brought thick ice on the waterways and keels and sloops were often trapped for long periods.

Although power towage of lighters had little effect on

the keel trade for many years, a steam tug demonstrated the possibilities by towing four keels loaded with 3164 quarters of grain from York to Hull in 10 hours. By the early 1900s sailing was declining in favour of steam and horse towage, saving time and speeding delivery. There were 150 keels working in 1906 but this had dropped to 70 six years later and by 1935 a keel under sail was a rarity. Motor road transport, towage and steel motor barges all contributed considerably to the decline of the keels and sloops, a process accelerated by changing trades. From 1905 until 1935 the decline was continuous. Ten years later the sails had vanished from the Humber and its feeder waterways. A few keels remained under sail until 1945, some being rigged for a topsail, but all were increasingly towed. One of the last to sail was the *Nav* of Hull, owned by Farley and Co. She sailed between Hull and Gainsborough, on the river Trent until 1941 under skipper Albert Barass. Need for quick transport and reliable delivery dates during the Second World War led to a grant being made for

owners to install engines in sailing craft and most keels and sloops were converted with low powered diesel engines. Most of their crews were sorry to lose their sailing traditions but preferred the new independence over winds and tides, the comfort of an enclosed wheelhouse and improved regularity of trips to the hard slog with canvas and stower.

The Humber keel trust was founded in 1952 at Hull to acquire and preserve a sailing keel and took over the *Mayday* from Joseph Rank of Hull. She had been built by Richard Dunston at Thorne in 1900 and had principally carried grain and flour. The hull was refitted and a start was made on re-rigging but she was confined to towed work from 1955–1957, after which she was laid up at Goole, where she remains.

In 1970 the Humber Keel and Sloop Preservation Society was formed to acquire and restore a keel, and the steel *Comrade*, built at New Holland, Lincolnshire in 1923 was purchased and restoration work commenced.

10

Sloops and Billy Boys
The Sloops

The sloops were a fore and aft rigged version of the square rigged keels, having the same bulky hull form and dimensions but setting a gaff mainsail and a foresail and also sometimes a jib set on a bowsprit. The sloops were usually owned in Lincolnshire, principally at Barton-on-Humber, New Holland and South Ferriby. These craft traded to many of the places served by the keels but they rarely entered canals, preferring more open waters. They also traded coastwise.

Although the hull form of the sloops was similar to that of the keels, the sloops were not restricted in dimensions by considerations of navigation lock sizes as were many keels. The sloop rig with its boom was not convenient for canal work and the type was devised for other waters. Nevertheless, the similarity of hull form between keels and sloops was considerable. To illustrate this, the sloop *Fanny* succeeding the earlier *John and Elizabeth*, ran as a weekly market boat between Butterwick and Hull and to Owston Ferry, Keadby and Crowle Wharf during the 1920s and early 1930s. She was built in 1877 as a keel and was converted as a sloop when sold to William Caldicott in 1920. She was further altered to a motor barge in 1935 and foundered off Hull three years later, after working for 71 years. In contrast, in 1908 Scarr of Beverley launched the *Hope* as a sloop, but she was later re-rigged as a keel.

Until about the 1880s sloops carried a larger rig than in later years. The mainsail was larger and the boom protruded beyond the sternpost. These sloops frequently had a fidded topmast and set a topsail. A bowsprit was housed between heavy bitts and was run in when in dock or confined waters. The jib was set on a running stay shackled to the traveller and a jib topsail was also often carried, hanked to a topmast stay. The mast was stepped in a tabernacle, locally known as a luchet. These older sloops had a small cargo hatch forward of the mast and the larger abaft it. The bulwarks were continuous. Later, bulwark arrangements varied. Some extended from the stem to the forward shroud, others for this length and also from the sternpost, forward to the after end of the leeboards, leaving a clear opening amidships for loading and discharge of cargo. Others had only a rail, capping stanchions, around the after deck.

A typical sloop of the turn of the century is shown in fig. 81. Her principal dimensions were 68 ft × 17 ft 3 in × 8 ft 3 in depth. The hull was built in steel with rivetted connections. She was owned by John Deheer and could carry about 170 tons. The sloop sail plan had the mast stepped well forward to suit the hull form, which needed leeboards hung well forward to balance it

129

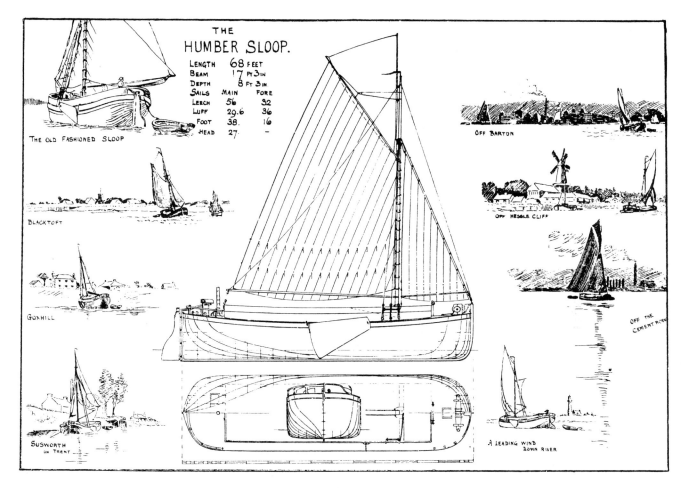

THE
HUMBER SLOOP.

LENGTH	68 FEET	
BEAM	17 FT 3 IN	
DEPTH	8 FT 3 IN	
SAILS	MAIN	FORE
LEECH	56	32
LUFF	29.6	36
FOOT	38.	16
HEAD	27.	-

THE OLD FASHIONED SLOOP

BLACKTOFT

GOXHILL

SUSWORTH ON TRENT

OFF BARTON

OFF HESSLE CLIFF

OFF THE CEMENT WORKS

A LEADING WIND DOWN RIVER

Figure 81 Lines, sail plan and general arrangement of a Humber sloop.
Dimensions 68 ft × 17 ft 3 in × 8 ft 3 in depth moulded. Drawn by
George Holmes

Figure 82 The Humber sloop *Esme*. Note staysail boom

and aid turning under sail and also to leave the main hatch opening clear aft. Many later sloops had a continuous hatch from forward to aft, as did the keels, and the halyard and topping lift winches were fitted abreast the mast, by the shrouds; an arrangement which facilitated loading and unloading with improved quayside cargo gear.

A 68 ft sloop typically had a mainsail 29 ft 6 in on the luff, 38 ft on the foot, head 27 ft and leech 56 ft. The staysail was 36 ft luff, 16 ft foot and 32 ft leech. There were two rows of reef points in the mainsail and the staysail of some sloops was fitted with a light boom sheeted to a horse on deck. However, in most it was caught to the lee rigging with a bowline and had to be handled at each tack. The clew was held aback on the bowline until the head was well through the wind. Then the bowline was let go and was again made fast to the lee forward shrouds as she settled on the new tack.

Unlike the keels, a sloop's sails were usually tanned and did not have a sail coat. In sloops, the powerful mast rollers were fitted against the headledge and were used for raising and lowering the mast, which was a heavy spar. The mainsail throat and peak halyards were led to rollers abreast the mast, above the coamings and the topsail halyard was led to a smaller roller fitted above one of these. The falls of the purchases used to hoist the leeboards were worked by rollers fitted vertically on the after rails.

Some sloops sported a little 'chokker pole' topmast when the long topmast was laid ashore, as many no doubt were in winter. Sloops could beat to windward light and in smooth water, slowly, but could not be pinched under any conditions. Most sailed best when trimmed slightly by the head. When turning to windward in smooth water with a fair tide both leeboards were often left down to save time in tacking. In strong winds the sloops had to reef well down in the squally Humber and if they missed stays, had to be gybed round quickly. Some skippers streamed the mainsheet astern while gybing, to avoid it fouling the crew and generally gybing in a breeze was dreaded by the sloop men.

Sloops sometimes got into trouble in the Humber or alongshore, on passage to the Wash or elsewhere. The *Dora* foundered off Barton Haven during a gale in September 1935, when loaded with 60 tons of chalk from quarries at South Ferriby Sluice for Barnby. Her foresail was blown away and the crew tried to anchor but she dragged and was swept continuously by the short sharp seas of the Humber. The crew abandoned her in the boat but the other sloops *Sunbeam* and *Brilliant Star,* owned by the same company, stood by the *Dora* and the crew of the *Brilliant Star* managed to get a rope fast and began to tow her, under sail, out of the deep water channel, but the *Dora* foundered half a mile from the shallows on the Barton Sand. The *Brilliant Star* was a powerful sloop built of iron. She could carry 90 tons, set a mainsail, foresail, jib and a topsail and voyaged principally from Hull to Wells, Snettisham and King's Lynn, in north Norfolk and to Spalding in Lincolnshire, often with cattle cake. She was sailed by a skipper, a mate and a third hand/cook.

The usual crew for a sloop was a skipper and two youths but many were sailed by two men and some by a man and a boy, though the mainsail was heavy work for them. Wages and conditions were poor but owners would usually provide a 'sub' when bad weather or a long wait for a cargo caused hardship. Like the keels, some sloops were owned by their skippers or were partly owned by them in conjunction with local shareholders. Many were built for companies to carry their raw materials or products. In most sloops the crew lived in the after cabin and the fo'c'sle was used as a store for gear and sails. However, if there was a three handed crew, the boy usually slept there.

Besides carrying ordinary cargoes many sloops at various times worked in the sand and gravel trade. They sailed to a bank of sand or gravel such as that off Paull in the Humber where fine sand was found, or to Spurn Point, Howden Dyke and Swainfleet Beach where there was good gravel. In the river Trent, sloops dredged at Cliff End and at Blacktoft at its mouth. Sometimes the sloop was grounded and the crew loaded with shovels. Others dredged sand and gravel with a leather bag having an iron 'A' frame at its mouth. This was towed by a warp led through a block on the boom and hauled by a hand winch.

The sloops *Ocean Spray, Rose, Rising Hope* and *Thistle* often brought cargoes for the maltings at Barton Haven, where a regatta race for sloops was still held in the 1920s, usually on August bank holiday. Races had been held before 1914 at various times. After the war sloop races were revived and as many as 25 vessels started off Barton Flats heading for the Middle light vessel off Grimsby, if the tide was ebbing during the morning. If not, they turned the Upper Whitton as the mark before sailing back. The race was held on a Saturday, often in August and was open for sloops built of wood, iron or steel. Wooden sloops received a 30 minute allowance and started ahead of the others as they were reckoned slower than those with metal hulls. A racing crew of five was carried and the entry fee was ten shillings. The skippers drew for places and anchored in line with the best berth to windward. There was a two gun start from the committee boat and then anchors and sails were got up. A sloop race might last from 3 to 5 hours depending on the wind and tide. The winner received a medal and a side of bacon. Afterwards he shipped a metal cock at his masthead for the next 12 months.

The sloop *Alva S* won the 1926 event and the *Saxby* the following year. Six sloops raced in 1928 when the *Faxfleet* won, sailed by Harry Hodgson a noted waterman. The last sloop regatta was held in 1929.

The Stamp family owned three 62 ft wooden sloops in general cargo trade between Hull and Barton on Humber. These were the *Ever Ready, Rising Hope* and *Rosalie Stamp,* an old fashioned keel with a main hatch abaft the mast and a small fore hatch. Loading and discharge was by derrick and a hand worked dolly winch; sometimes the cargo was loaded or unloaded by hand, if it was of sufficiently light individual items. One of Stamp's sloops often left Hull and took the flood up to Barton and another sailed from Barton that high water. They continued trading into the early 1940s.

Sloop construction continued into the 1930s. Many of these later sloops were built at Hessle, Thorn and Beverley in Yorkshire and at Gainsborough in Lincolnshire. There were about 70 sloops sailing in 1933 and many had been built between 1924 and 1929. As many as 17 were launched in 1926 and in 1931–2 the Trent Navigation Co. ordered 6 sloops. In 1935 Clapsons of Barton on Humber, built the *Peggy,* the last wooden sloop to be launched.

Many sloops continued to sail until 1939 but numbers of them were then unrigged and converted into lighters or had engines installed. However, several worked under sail throughout the Second World War.

Earles Cement Co. of Hull owned 8 sloops including the *Britannia, Miss Madeline* and *Swinefleet,* carrying clay across the Humber from New Holland and up the river Hull to their works at Wilmington. Before mechanised loading the crews had to fill the sloop's hold with shovels, and shifting 160 tons of clay was an unbelievably tiring task and one ill-rewarded at 1s 3d per ton freight money, as it took four tides to make the trip from the pits to the works and back to Barton. The return trip was always made with an empty hold. On entering the river Hull the mast was lowered and the sloop drove up with the anchor on the ground and the crew poling the sloop along. The crews worked on a system of thirds shares but when Earles put engines in the sloops in about 1943, the crews could work regular hours without relying on wind and tide and received a weekly wage. However, the reaction to the new comforts and improved pay were mixed with some regret at the passing of their old way of life afloat.

James Barraclough of Hull owned several sloops including the *Annie Maud* of Barton. The firm's craft were often unloading at Victoria Pier, Hull, smoke wisping from the cabin stovepipe, the mainsail swung out clear of the hatch and the coggy boat bumping gently alongside while the skipper stood on deck watching the dock workers unload and keeping tally. Barraclough's *Sprite* was the last sloop to trade under sail. She was unrigged in 1950 to become a lighter, like the *Nan* which just preceded her. With them commercial sail ended on the Yorkshire and Lincolnshire waterways.

The Billy Boys

A variant of the keel and sloop types was the 'Billy Boy' coaster, which may have antedated the smaller river and canal carriers by descent from the chubby-hulled Dutch, Fries and also English Bilanders and Hoekers, though no one can be sure of this lineage. This theory is strengthened by the schooner *Newcastle Pilot* of Blakeney, Norfolk, which was taken as a prize from the Dutch in 1812 and which was lengthened by 15 or 20 feet afterwards. Her hull form was that of a typical pointed stern Billy Boy.

The Billy Boy was in use at the end of the eighteenth century to carry cargo coastwise in an area generally extending from Scarborough in Yorkshire, in the north to Southampton in the south, though these arbitrary limits were exceeded, certainly to the Tweed and to Portland, and probably further. Billy Boys also occasionally sailed across the North Sea to the nearer continental countries and also possibly ventured into the Baltic at times.

The hulls of many early Billy Boys clearly resembled those of the sloops of Lincolnshire and Yorkshire. The hull was deeper for coastal seafaring and the leeboards were usually retained. It is believed that most of the Billy Boys at the end of the eighteenth and early in the nineteenth centuries were rigged as sloops. These craft carried a large gaff and boom mainsail, a forestaysail, a jib set to a traveller on a long bowsprit which was often 'fitted' or fixed. A gaff topsail was set with its luff on hoops to the topmast, which was fiddled and a squaresail was often carried, set from a yard for running and reaching on a passage and sometimes a square topsail

was set above that. A few also set a triangular rafee topgallant above that, but this was exceptional. A good example of this type of Billy Boy was drawn by E. W. Cooke at Shoreham, Sussex, in 1830. Probably later, many Billy Boys were rigged as ketches but retained the same hull form and usually, but not always, the leeboards. The lines of a typical Billy Boy, the *Aimwell*, are given in fig. 83. She was built in 1883 at Winteringham, Lincolnshire by Routh and Waddingham and was rigged as a ketch. The *Aimwell* was 84 ft Registered length × 17 ft beam and drew 7 ft 6 in loaded. The lines are typical of the type, as are the general arrangements below and above deck. Although the bow is full, the stern sections are relatively fine and suggest that she would sail reasonably well despite her bulk. The lines may be compared with those of a Kuff or some types of Galliot from the German North Sea and Baltic coasts.

Billy Boys were built at many places over several counties of eastern England, from the river Tweed in south-east Scotland to as far south as Fingringhoe, on the river Colne in Essex. Most were built in Lincolnshire or Yorkshire, on the rivers Trent and Humber and the associated waterways. Others were launched in Norfolk and Suffolk.

In 1855 the ketch rigged Billy Boy *Excelsior* of 59 Registered Tons was built in the rural village of Fingringhoe, near Colchester in Essex for owners at Goole, Yorkshire. In contrast, the similar sized Billy Boy *Bernard*, also Registered at Goole, was built at Knottingley, a small town in inland Yorkshire where small ships were built into the late twentieth century,

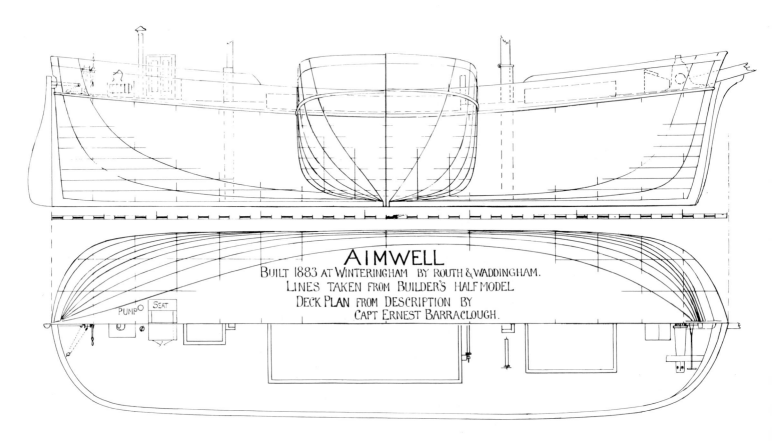

AIMWELL
BUILT 1883 AT WINTERINGHAM BY ROUTH & WADDINGHAM.
LINES TAKEN FROM BUILDER'S HALF MODEL
DECK PLAN FROM DESCRIPTION BY
CAPT ERNEST BARRACLOUGH.

PUMP   SEAT

Figure 83 The Billy Boy *Aimwell*. Lines, outboard profile and deck arrangement. Built by Routh and Waddingham at Winteringham, Lincolnshire in 1883. The full bow merges into a clean run and despite the hull's typical general fullness, she would have sailed well

Figure 84 A Billy Boy with a rig of yawl proportions. Photographed on the river Thames before 1914

many miles from salt water on the Aire and Calder Navigation Canal. The *Bernard* was launched there in 1904 for owners in Leeds, an inland city with canal links, emphasising the connections between commerce and small shipowning in Yorkshire and Lincolnshire. In Suffolk, William Bayley the Ipswich shipbuilder, launched several Billy Boys until the mid nineteenth century and others were built at Woodbridge on the river Deben, at Snape on the Alde and at Southwold, a small coastal town where Billy Boys often unloaded coal.

Many were built at Goole and at Hull, on the river Humber, some at the fishing port of Grimsby, on the Lincolnshire side of the river and others at Burton Stather on the river Trent. Some were constructed at other inland towns such as Mexborough and even at Leeds, where the small Billy Boy *Brilliant*, Registered at Goole, was built in 1841. She survived in trade for 80 years.

Like many coastal cargo carriers the Billy Boys were affected by the revolution in the transport of goods wrought by the spread of railways. By the 1840s this had seriously changed the opportunity for cargoes in the midlands and north and forced many owners to seek different freights and make longer passages with them, coastwise along the east and south coasts of England. They faced competition from ketches, schooners and brigs and some ventured towards the west, in the English Channel, loading stone at Portland and carrying clay from Devon and Cornwall to Poole and elsewhere.

This led to some increase in size of new Billy Boys which were built to load perhaps 120 tons of cargo and the ketch rig was adopted to maintain the size of the mainsail and its gear for a small crew. The Billy Boy crews referred to the ketches as 'dickie rigged'; the dickie being the mizzen. These craft also carried, besides the mainsail, forestaysail and mizzen, one, two or sometimes even three jibs, set on a standing or a running bowsprit, as well as a jib topsail. The outer jib halyard was sometimes led over at a shallow angle to a block on the topmast iron (fig. 86). Some craft also set a square topsail and a topgallant. A very few also reputedly set studding sails to the square topsail when off the wind on a long passage. These Billy Boy ketches carrying square topsails and topgallants were known as 'Jackass Schooners'. The 74 ton *Abeona* built in 1865 and the Blakeney-owned *Bluejacket*, built in 1860 were the last of the type so rigged. Some Billy Boy ketches were rigged with a small mizzen of yawl proportions. One photographed off Gravesend, in the Thames, is shown in fig. 84.

The Billy Boy had a reputation for slowness. The classic story regarding this was of the ship's boy idling on deck with a fishing line trailing astern. When reprimanded by the skipper for slacking, the cheeky lad responded with 'All right, skipper. I'll chuck another line ower and stop the old B..... altogether'. However, they were doubtless not all that slow and were generally seaworthy little ships with small hatches and stout bulwarks, which made them good to be aboard in strong winds and big seas, but were a disadvantage in loading or discharge.

A Billy Boy carried a crew of perhaps two men and a boy if a sloop, or perhaps two or three men and a skipper if a ketch. They were generally adequately fed, despite the boy's cooking, if poorly paid, but usually made some extra money by helping to load and unload cargo.

Their length varied between 60 and 80 ft and the hulls had considerable flat of bottom, were deep for their length and were bluff bowed and full lined above the load waterline, but were relatively fine below and usually had a well formed run to the rounded stern and vertical sternpost. Even so, it is difficult to understand how they got to windward when light. The hulls of many were clinker planked and were amongst the largest craft so constructed. Others were carvel and all had substantial sawn frames and floors. Other Billy Boys were built of steel and a few of iron. Some were built with restricted beam and draught to suit certain canal locks and as a consequence were poor sea boats. The *Evening Star*, built at Mexborough, Yorkshire in 1873 was reputedly the last Billy Boy to be clinker planked. She was run down and sunk in the Lynn Channel before 1914.

Except in the few Billy Boys having a counter stern, the rudder was hung, exposed on the sternpost and was consequently vulnerable in locks and docks, or at close quarters with other craft. A few larger Billy Boys had wheel steering but in most a long tiller came inboard through a port in the high bulwarks. Billy Boys frequently used their anchors and unlike most other coasting sailing craft, carried them at cat heads on each bow for easier handling. Many smaller Billy Boys had a handspike windlass but larger ones often had a hand cranked windlass with brakes.

The hulls were often black tarred but had a coloured or varnished wale strake. Despite her bulky hull and general lack of windward ability, the Billy Boy traded on a shallow, shoal strewn coast subject to strong tides and much bad weather. When beached for discharge their hulls often suffered pounding when settling or getting off. Many cutter and ketch rigged Billy Boys had the masts stepped in tabernacles but others, particularly those rigged as ketches, had theirs stepped through the deck to land on the keelson.

Billy Boys handled under sail like other coasting craft

Figure 85 Ketch rigged Billy Boy *Star of Hope* of Goole. Painted with the port leeboard raised. Hull clinker planked as was common into the late nineteenth century. Built at Stainforth, Yorkshire, 1862

of the same rig. They would heave-to with a reefed mizzen and fore-staysail. Some of the larger schooner rigged Billy Boys set a large square sail on the foremast when off the wind, resembling in cut those carried by the smacks and schooners and cutters of the 1840s. The squaresail was often slung from a jackstay leading to the deck from the topmast cap iron.

The skippers of many were also part owners, the other shares often being held by local shopkeepers or small industrialists. Other Billy Boys were owned by mills and maltings or other enterprises whose cargoes they might carry frequently but not exclusively.

Generally the men who built and manned the keels and sloops and to some extent also the Billy Boys, were a cheerful lot despite their poor circumstances and the demanding labour. Certainly they were alive to innovation in the equipping and handling of their bulky craft and displayed little concern for tradition. Some Billy Boy skippers had carrier pigeons on board which were released if they were near home but were delayed by tide or adverse weather.

The Billy Boys produced many fine sailors, some of whom were in later life mates and masters of square rigged seagoing ships and steamships. For instance, Captain Woodget, master of the *Cutty Sark* at one time, started his sea life in a Norfolk Billy Boy. Usually boys were shipped at 11 or 12 years of age and had quickly to learn to cook, to splice a rope and to steer in fine weather. They also learned to reef and help heave on the windlass and the cargo winch, to scrape and paint and keep the craft clean. It was a hard life with little pay, but boys who could not stand it were soon put ashore as there were plenty of others waiting.

Billy Boys traded to many small harbours and sometimes discharged on open beaches such as Cromer in Norfolk and Aldeburgh in Suffolk. Coals were taken to places as diverse as Bridlington harbour in Yorkshire and Blythborough in rural Suffolk. Others ventured further south with cattle food or grain, to the rivers Deben and Stour in Suffolk, the Essex Colne and Blackwater, to the Thames and Medway, and again others sailed to south coast ports, to Holland, Belgium, Germany and France. Besides the numbers of Billy Boys owned in Lincolnshire and Yorkshire, many others were sailing from East Anglian ports. The ketch rigged Billy Boy *Bluejacket* of Wells, north Norfolk, was built at Walsoken on the river Nene, Norfolk, in 1860 as a 57 tonner with owners at Blakeney, where she ended as a hulk in the 1930s. Like many of her kind the *Bluejacket* did not carry leeboards and although her hull was relatively fine and fair in form below the waterline, she carried much weather helm in a breeze and needed relieving tackles rigged to the tiller for the helmsman to keep control.

The *Garson* of Ipswich was a ketch rigged Billy Boy built at Great Yarmouth, Norfolk in 1864 and one of the largest at 75 Registered Tons. After many years trading on the east coast she was converted to the club house ship of the Erith Yacht Club on the Thames.

Messrs Anderson of Howden Dyke, Yorkshire, owned the Billy Boys *Nitro*, *Sulpho*, *Hydro* and *Phospho* which for some years shipped fertiliser to the small ports of the Wash and returned with various cargoes. The cutter rigged *Hydro* was typical of her type, having only a few inches of freeboard amidships when loaded, but carrying a good spread of canvas.

In 1900 there were 25 Billy Boys owned at Barton on Humber, including the *Mary Maria* (Capt. Thompson), the *Jehovah Jireh* (Capt. Barley), *Dekar* (Capt. Oldridge), *Mary Ellen* (Capt. Gladhill), *Edwin Austin* (Capt. Thompson), *Fuchsia* (Capt. Winship), *Marmaduke* (Capt.

Figure 86 Scale model of a typical Billy Boy ketch showing the deep hull with its prominent forefoot, leeboards and small rudder. The rig is of modest area. Note the arrangement of jib halyard and lacing tautening the luff at the head of the jib to the topmast stay

Tompson), *Elizabeth* (Capt. Thompson), *Celestina* (Capt. Winship), *Stirling* (Capt. Barraclough), *Gamaliel* (Capt. Barraclough), *Zephyr* (Capt. Seddon), *Day Spring* (Capt. Dinsdale), *Woodlark* (Capt. Chapman), *Mavis* (Capt. Aaron), *Sandringham* (Capt. Grimboldby), *Mary Eliza* (Capt. Gledhill), *Spray* (Capt. Gell), *Spencer* (Capt. Dinsdale), *Corinilla* (Capt. Barraclough), *John and Lily* (Capt. Barraclough), *Sarah* (Capt. Sweeting), *John* (Capt. Hamilton), *Aimwell* (Capt. J. Barraclough), and *Mary* (Capt. Gledhill). John Barraclough was skipper of the *Aimwell* for many years. In January 1894 she and five other small sailing vessels lay weatherbound in White Fleet Roads, in the Humber. To proceed upriver seemed impossible in the conditions. However, after two days the *Aimwell* was missing but the other skippers were not unduly worried, thinking her skipper had risked the passage. The bad weather persisted for a week and then a vessel was sighted coming in from sea. It was the *Aimwell*. As she approached the still anchored vessels they hailed her, thinking she had dragged anchor and been forced offshore. However, she had been to London, loaded another cargo and then sailed back. Barraclough capped it by leading the other vessels upriver. The 50 ton, ketch rigged Billy Boy *Jehovan Jireh* had a particularly deep hull. She was built at Grimsby in Lincolnshire in 1886 and often traded along the Yorkshire coast. In 1901 she went ashore near Flamborough Head but was got off with minor damage. By 1907 she was owned at Hoylake, Lancashire and had been Registered at Liverpool.

Barton-upon-Humber's last two Billy Boys ended their days in 1923 when the *New Eagle* was wrecked on Barton Ness and the *Evelyn* was broken up. The quays of Barton are now silent and deserted, the little harbour has silted and like so many other small ports, its busy

Figure 87 The Billy Boy ketch *Mavis* of Hull at sea loaded. The main topmast is housed and the staysail has a boomed foot. The mizzen has one reef and a storm jib is stowed at the bowsprit end

days of shipping and seamen are distant memories.

By the 1880s the Billy Boy was in decline, though some similar craft were built at intervals into the early 1900s. These faced competition from the shallow draught and sometimes larger ketch barges, which could usually outsail them. The larger spritsail barges were also beginning to be of similar size and needed an even smaller crew, besides having large hatches for faster loading or discharge.

A few Billy Boys attempted to keep pace with the changes. The *Opal* of Harwich, Essex, was built at Port Downie in 1866 with a schooner rig, then was re-rigged as a ketch and was finally rigged with a sprit mainsail. The smaller *Director*, built at Barugh Locks in 1825 was

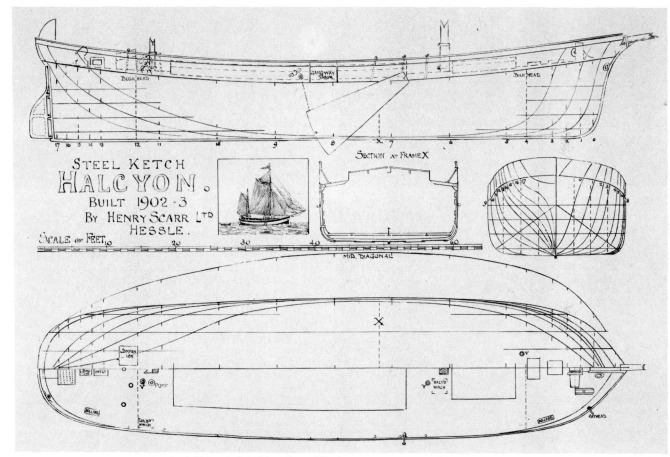

STEEL KETCH
HALCYON.
BUILT 1902-3
BY HENRY SCARR LTD
HESSLE.
SCALE OF FEET

SECTION AT FRAME X

MID. DIAGONAL

Figure 88 Steel Billy Boy ketch *Halcyon*, built by Henry Scarr of Hessle, Yorkshire in 1902. Lines, outboard profile, deck arrangement and structural section. The hull form and arrangements are similar to those of the Dutch Klipper type. See Figure 62

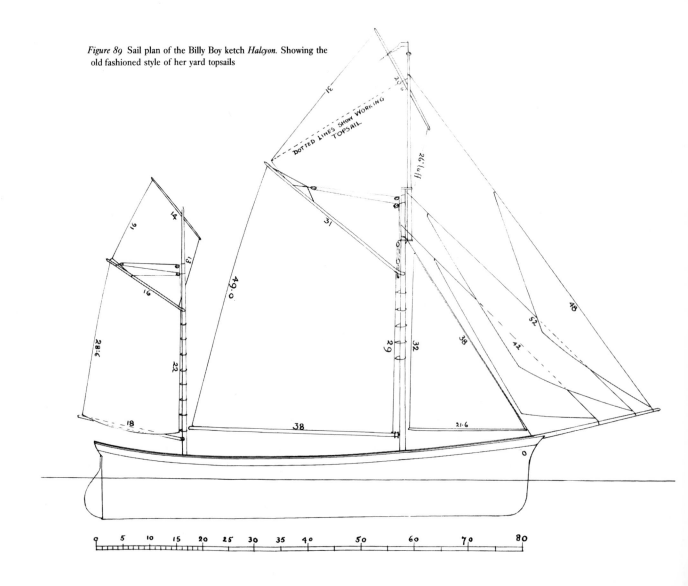

Figure 89 Sail plan of the Billy Boy ketch *Halcyon*. Showing the old fashioned style of her yard topsails

also re-rigged with a spritsail and survived until the First World War. But by 1914 there were few Billy Boys still sailing. The ketches *Bounty of Providence*, *Gills* and *Evening Star* and the sloop rigged *Lily* were amongst the last wooden Billy Boys in trade and sailed until 1918, being laid up when the freight rates dropped.

Iron and steel superseded wood, even in the Billy Boys. By the 1890s several larger ones were built including the sloops *Industry*, *Sarah* and *Brilliant Star*, which was wrecked at Wells, north Norfolk, before 1914. Four large metal hulled Billy Boys were built. The steel *Sarah* at Hull in 1899, the iron hulled *Mavis* at Beverley in 1896, the larger, steel *Halcyon* of 63 Registered Tons at Hessle by H. Scarr in 1903 and the *Bernard* of steel at Knottingley in 1904, the last Billy Boy to be launched. These were well built vessels, comparable with the contemporary ketch barges. The *Halcyon* was one of the largest Billy Boys, being 83 ft 4 in Registered length × 20 ft beam × 7 ft 10 in draught. These four craft participated in the remarkably profitable cross-Channel trade to France during the First World War when freights of coal and coke were bringing up to £5 per ton instead of the 5s 6d rate of 1913. After 1920 or so these were the only Billy Boys active, trading mostly to King's Lynn from the Humber with wheat, oil cake, malt and fertilisers. The *Bernard* was run down and sunk and the *Sarah* was unrigged to become a lighter. The *Halcyon* was fitted with an auxiliary engine and was sold to the Bristol Channel. By 1950 she was a full powered motor vessel owned at Campbeltown on the west coast of Scotland.

The steel hulled *Mavis* was one of the best remembered Billy Boys built at Beverley, another of Yorkshire's inland shipbuilding towns, noted for its trawlers.

Launched in 1896 the hull of the *Mavis* resembled the shapely coasting ketches in many respects and had a counter stern (fig. 87) but her bow had the fullness above water and the characteristics of the keels and sloops, with the addition of deep bulwarks and hawse pipes for the anchor cables. The main and mizzen masts were stepped in tabernacles and the boat, which was carried on the hatch at sea, was hoisted on board by tackles from the mastheads. The *Mavis* was a long-lived vessel. Originally owned at Barton on Humber, she voyaged to many places on the east and south coasts, and to the continent. By 1907 she was owned in Hull and in 1919 she was again owned at Barton. The *Mavis* traded mainly between Hull and King's Lynn and made occasional trips to London, Grimsby and Lincoln and to Wells and other small ports in Norfolk and Suffolk until 1939. In the 1920s and 1930s her skipper was John Grey and a small auxiliary engine of 36 hp was installed in an engine room bulkheaded off from the aft end of the hold. At that time she had a shorter bowsprit which could still be topped up in docks but she had by then lost her topmast.

The *Mavis* was fitted with a wheelhouse in 1938 and the following year was converted to a tank barge for the carriage of gas oil at Shoreham, Sussex, where she worked into the 1950s, rarely if ever leaving the harbour limits. By 1962 she had been re-converted to carry dry cargo and her clipper bow had been altered to a straight stem and a wheelhouse, with a deck cabin abaft it, had been added. The *Mavis* continued to trade for a few further years from the river Medway, resembling a counter sterned and deep hulled version of the many contemporary converted spritsail barges.

11

The Solent barges

The Isle of Wight and the coast of Hampshire, which is divided from it by the broad, tide ridden channel of the Solent and Spithead form a natural trading ground for small vessels carrying cargo to and from the many small and two large ports between Poole, in Dorset, to the west and Chichester harbour, bordering Hampshire and West Sussex in the east.

Local waters can be rough, particularly with a spring tide against a strong breeze and local craft had to be seaworthy even if their voyages might be short. Cargoes were carried from the major merchant port of Southampton at the head of long and broad Southampton Water, with its deep channel, and the naval port of Portsmouth. However, many freights were carried to or from small ports and watersides in the area including Cowes, Ryde, Bembridge, Newport, Wootten Bridge and Yarmouth on the Isle of Wight; Poole in Dorset and Christchurch, Lymington, Itchen, Bursledon, Hamble, Hythe, Ashlett, Fareham, Porchester, Gosport, Langston and Emsworth in Hampshire and Bosham, Birdham and Itchenor in West Sussex. Besides these, other island cargoes were unloaded occasionally at places such as Fishbourne, on Wootten Creek, on the beaches of Ventnor, Sandown, Shanklin, Freshwater and Totland in fine weather and in the sheltered Newtown River

creeks. On the mainland the barges occasionally visited places like Hurst Castle, Keyhaven, Ower and Tonner lakes, Exbury, Bucklers Hard, Beaulieu, Marchwood, Eling up the Test, Netley on Southampton Water, Warsash on the Hamble, and Lee on the coast towards Portsmouth, where in the harbour creeks, they traded to hards and wharves at Gosport, Priddys Hard, Bedhampton, Fareham and Porchester. There was an occasional cargo for Southsea beach, usually building materials or roadstone and the tiny and remarkably isolated village of Langstone on the lagoon-like harbour of that name, so close to the eastern end of Portsmouth and Southsea yet so far removed in atmosphere. Just to the east, the many creeks of Chichester Harbour floated cargoes to and from the villages of Hayling and West Wittering, besides the slightly larger local places already mentioned.

The trade in the area varied from grain and coal, bricks, tiles, stone for building and roadmaking, sand, timber, and shingle, to manufactured foodstuffs, household goods, retail supplies, potatoes and anything which could be moved by water in a small craft and at a profit.

Although a definite type of small cargo vessel was devised for the Solent area in the form of usually round bottomed ketches, much trade was carried on there by

COWES BOAT &c. coming out of the Harbour.

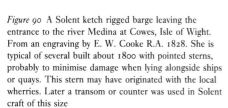

Figure 90 A Solent ketch rigged barge leaving the entrance to the river Medina at Cowes, Isle of Wight. From an engraving by E. W. Cooke R.A. 1828. She is typical of several built about 1800 with pointed sterns, probably to minimise damage when lying alongside ships or quays. This stern may have originated with the local wherries. Later a transom or counter was used in Solent craft of this size

spritsail barges of the east coast type, some of which were owned and a few built locally, some ketch barges and a few schooner and square rigged barges in the coal trade to Portsmouth. There were in addition several small individual craft under varied rigs.

There was no recognised centre of barge ownership in the Solent but such craft were working from Southampton and Portsmouth in the eighteenth century and undoubtedly in various forms much earlier. E. W. Cooke drew a ketch rigged example fetching out past the castle at the west entrance of the river Medina at Cowes in 1827 (fig. 90). She had most of the characteristics of the local ketches some 70 years later with a full hull form which had a pointed stern and clinker planking like the much slimmer and smaller local wherries, used for carrying passengers and light goods in the same waters. Open wooden rails forward and aft were another feature of these craft into the mid nineteenth century. Most of them do not appear to have carried leeboards but in many other ways these early Solent ketches much resembled the east coast Billy Boys.

The *Bee* of Cowes built there in 1801, reputedly by Hansen, was of this type and was trading until 1926 in the ownership of Shepard Brothers of Newport, Isle of Wight, a firm specialising in the carriage of island cargoes for many years, who owned wharves at Newport and Cowes. The *Bee* carried a great variety of cargoes which may have included oak for building wooden warships at Beaulieu in Nelson's time, to gravel to extend the berths at J. Samuel Whites for building larger destroyers in the First World War. It is probable that these small ketches superseded earlier and smaller sloop and cutter rigged craft and others which were rigged with a sprit mainsail. The Sloop Inn at Wootten Bridge probably commemorates the type and it is known that

small, pointed sterned shallow barges rigged with a sprit mainsail, a foresail and sometimes also a mizzen carried timber and other goods to and from Newport in the 1890s. The *Bee* shows a hull form finer than that drawn by Cooke (who was a most accurate artist) but her size, plumb stern, slightly raked sternpost, flat sheer and rig with its loose footed mainsail have the same characteristics. The *Bee*'s dimensions were 51 ft length overall × 10 ft beam and 6 ft depth of hold. Her probable average loaded draught was about 5 ft aft. The midship section shows a well rounded bilge and it is likely that her ends were fine, helping her to sail reasonably well without leeboards and accounting for her small Registered Tonnage of 27.

The deck arrangements included a single cargo hatch, a handspike windlass, bowsprit bitts, a hatch to the forepeak store and one to the small cabin aft where the crew of two lived for short periods. The mainsheet horse was unusually short at the width of the after coaming of the hatch and the staysail sheets were worked at each tack, which was unusual in barge practice. In contrast to Cooke's drawing the *Bee* had planked bulwarks. She was tiller steered. Her rig has the mainmast well forward and the mizzen is relatively large and a useful sail in most conditions. She was a characterful little vessel and a familiar sight in and out of the Medina until 1926.

It is possible that the *Bee* may have originally been clinker planked and was replanked carvel in later years, as was done with fishing vessels in other places. Later Solent ketches were built with carvel planking, which came into general use for local fishing craft at least by the 1850s. The liability to damage when lying alongside in exposed places like Ryde Pier may have been a further factor in the change as craft unloading or loading there could be exposed to violent wave action.

Figure 91 Solent ketches anchored in the river Itchen awaiting cargoes, about 1910. The nearer has a standing gaff mainsail with brails, which some adopted at the end of the nineteenth century. She also had lee-boards and may be the *Fortis*, built at Emsworth in 1904

Some of these ketches did not carry a topmast but set a yard topsail to a pole masthead. Some had white painted quarter boards shipped on the bulwarks to give some protection to the helmsman against going overboard when heeled in a breeze. All carried sweeps for use in a calm, when the mate might also tow with the boat while the skipper helped to keep her moving with the tide with a long stroke at a sweep.

Unloading and loading was sometimes carried out with the aid of a large diameter 'gin block' slung on a cargo gaff hoisted up the mast and steadied by guys.

The ketch *Arrow*, also owned by Shepard Brothers, was built at Cowes in 1875 and has the transom stern and finer hull form of the later local ketches. Her plans are shown in figs. 92 and 93. Her builders were Hansen and Sons, at East Cowes. Her Registered Tonnage was 20. The *Arrow*'s dimensions were 50 ft length overall × 14 ft 6 in beam and average draughts were 4 ft 2 in aft and 3 ft 6 in forward. The slack sheer, rounded bow profile, plumb but shapely transom and well formed body sections had considerable resemblance to the hulls of local fishing boats, which were fast and weatherly little craft on limited draught, and the waterlines and after buttocks of the *Arrow* suggest a craft which would sail well within the limitations of small draught and a gaff ketch rig.

The deck arrangements were similar to the *Bee* but the staysail worked on a curved horse and the tiller was awkwardly placed above the raised hatch to the after cabin. The rig, also, is similar to that of the *Bee* but with the mainmast even further forward. However, it seems to have suited the trade and the small crew of two, which was the usual complement. In later years a few of these Cowes ketches had engines installed but some were still working under sail into the early 1930s, though without topmasts, but facing increasing competition from fully powered motor barges which still operate the Solent cargo carrying services.

The *Arrow* was the last to trade under sail and was laid up in 1938. Some of the later ketches of this type were fitted with leeboards and some had a boomless, brailing mainsail with a standing gaff. As would be expected in an area so concerned with the building, maintaining and manning of yachts, the Solent ketches were often smartly kept and well sailed. There is no evidence that these craft made voyages to the Channel Islands and France but it is probable that some did, particularly up to the late nineteenth century.

Few small barges for local trade appear to have been built at or sailed from Poole, an ancient Dorset port on the many creeks forming Poole Harbour. The fine ketch barges *Princess May* and *Alexandra* were built there for Frederick Griffin who lived inland at Salisbury in Wiltshire. The *Alexandra* was launched in 1891 and was of 86 Registered Tons. She was built by J. Allan and Sons, who built many yachts, Poole fishing boats and similar craft. They had a reputation as sound designers, as did the other contemporary Poole yards, and this was reflected in the well shaped hulls of these ketches.

The *Alexandra* had Registered dimensions of 85 ft × 20 ft 2 in × 8 ft 4 in depth. The *Princess May* built at the same yard in 1894 was also of 86 Registered Tons. Both had a pleasing sheer, some flare forward, a deep, seaworthy hull and the mainmast stepped well aft. They were designed and built to suit conditions in the English Channel and as a result were perhaps more seaworthy than their counterparts built on the east coast in Kent, Essex and Suffolk. Leeboards were carried when built. The mainsail had roller reefing gear, an inner and outer jib was set on the bowsprit and a jib topsail was also set.

Figure 92 Profile and deck arrangement of the ketch *Arrow* owned by
Shepard Brothers of Newport, Isle of Wight

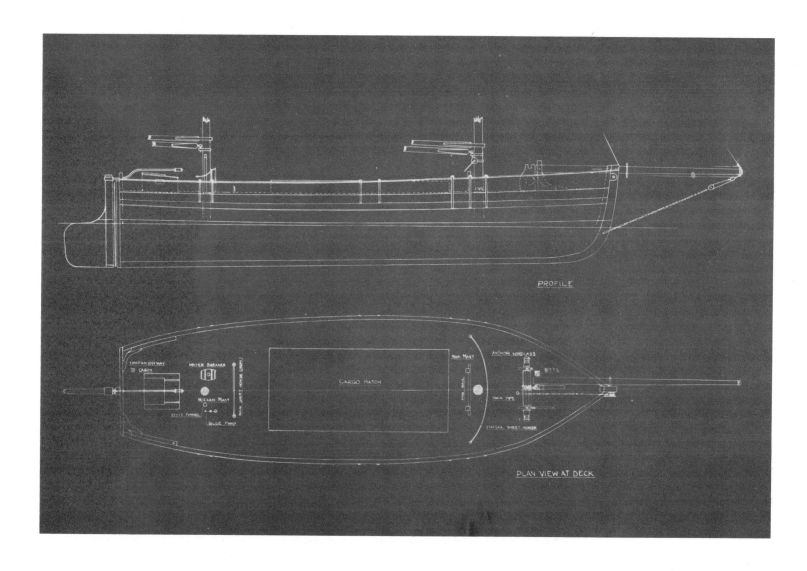

Figure 93 Sail plan of the ketch *Arrow*

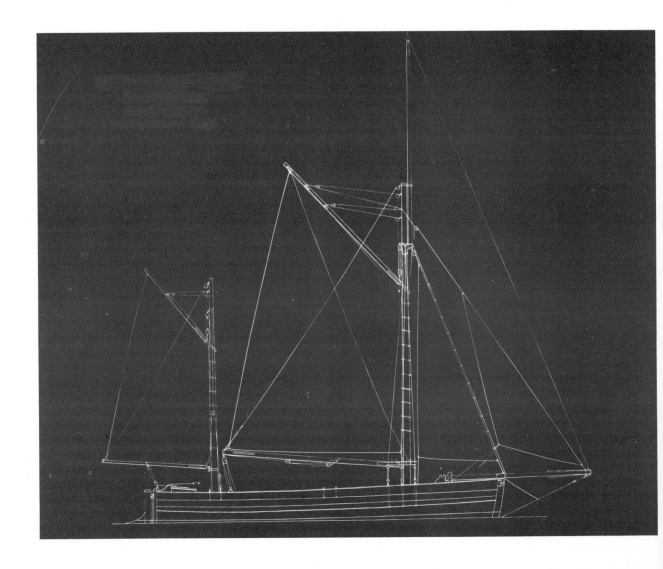

Figure 94 Lines of the ketch *Tally Ho* of Cowes. Built by F. Hawke, Stonehouse, Plymouth in 1912 for Croucher and Co. Newport, Isle of Wight. Plan drawn to sheer at side. Dimensions 62 ft 4 in × 17 ft 8 in × 6 ft 3 in. Note counter stern. The *Tally Ho* was converted to a motor barge in 1950

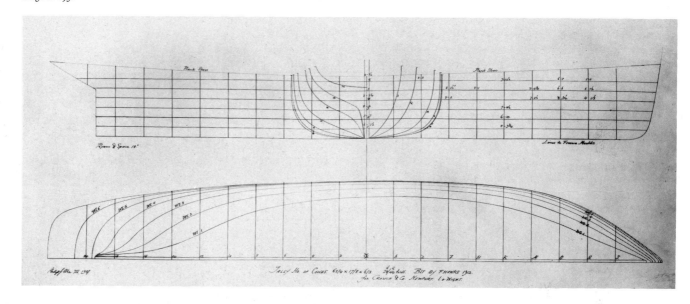

A small gammon knee set off the slightly raked stem and a shapely counter stern with rounded quarters and well raked bulwarks gave them an almost yacht-like appearance above water, complemented by the unusually tall mizzen mast and large mizzen.

The *Alexandra* and the *Princess May* traded coastwise and across the English Channel to France, the Channel Islands and Belgium with grain, stone, cattle foods, coal and bricks as the principal cargoes. By 1907 the *Alexandra* was owned at Shotton, on the river Dee in Flint, north-west England and afterwards by F. Nicholls of Whitstable, Kent. She was later sold to become a yacht by the 1930s and sailed under the burgee of the Hamble River Sailing Club for some years, apparently without leeboards. The *Princess May* was owned by

William Whitmore of Harwich, Essex, in later years. These were probably the finest ketch barges ever built for sea work.

Ketch barges owned in various places traded to Southampton into the 1920s. A regular visitor in the mid nineteenth century was the barge *Forerunner*, Registered at Arundel in Sussex and built at Littlehampton in 1862 by J. and W. B. Harvey who were the most prolific builders of large sailing barges for various owners and also for their own use in the coasting trade. The *Forerunner* sailed under their flag for a time before she was sold to other coasting owners.

Portsmouth saw numbers of ketch barges and also spritsail craft well into the twentieth century. Ash was a Portsmouth coal merchant who at one time owned the

Figure 95 The Cowes ketch *Excel* (in foreground) alongside the quay at Bosham, Sussex. The 38 ton *Excel* was built at Cowes in 1884. When this photograph was taken in 1907 she was owned by Harry Martin of Bosham. She has the full hull form and transom stern typical of her type. The unidentified ketch astern has a cargo gaff rigged on the mainmast with a gin block and purchase to discharge cargo by hand.

unusual 185 ton barquentine barge *Thorney Island*, which had a raised quarterdeck. She was built by William Foster who came from Southwick, near Shoreham in Sussex and established a yard at Emsworth, a Hampshire fishing village on Chichester Harbour, where he first built a ship in 1861. In 1871 he launched the flat bottomed brigantine rigged barge *Thorney Island* for his own account, afterwards selling her to Ash. She was later owned at Portsmouth by John Crampton but ended as a hulk at Emsworth, like so many other craft built at that village of innovative small craft builders.

William Foster may also have built the schooner rigged barge *Annie Florence* of 130 tons in 1878, possibly for his ownership at first. She was 96 ft 6 in × 23 ft 1 in × 8 ft 8 in depth. Launched as a brigantine, she was re-rigged as a ketch in 1881 when owned at Portsmouth by John Crampton. However, it is possible that she was built by Joseph Apps, who took over Foster's yard when he retired. John Crampton of Town Quay, Portsmouth, was an owner of sailing barges and small ships. His principal interest was in supplying coal for naval bunkering and also for industrial and domestic use. He owned a small fleet of colliers of various types and a yard at Landport which repaired them and occasionally built a vessel.

Crampton was possibly influenced by the large Smeed Dean and Co. barges from Kent, also in the coal trade, as in 1879 his yard launched the 279 ton flat bottomed *Enterprise*, variously described as barque or brigantine rigged. She may not have been the success he hoped and like many large barges, was soon sold. She was later a brigantine and her fate subsequent to 1893 is unknown. Crampton's yard had built the 169 ton brigantine *Albion* in 1875, the 101 ton *Camellia* in 1876 and the 372 ton barquentine *Dahlia* in 1878. These may

have been flat bottomed, barge hulled craft but this is uncertain. Crampton also owned several small ketches for local cargo carrying. These included four flat bottomed leeboard barges: the *Emerald* and the *Ruby*, built at Landport in 1877 and the *Pearl* and the *Diamond* built at Portsmouth in 1878 and 1879. The *Ruby* was of 36, the *Pearl* 42, and the *Diamond* 47 Gross Registered Tons. These barges were deep in proportion to their beam and length. A chine was worked amidships and the bow was fairly bluff, but the run was fine, with a deep tuck and a small, shapely transom. They were loftily rigged and had a long topmast and a running bowsprit. Leeboards were fitted and they sailed more smartly than the Cowes ketches, which they resembled in deck and hold arrangements. This quartet were often to be seen in Langstone and Chichester Harbours.

The 29 ton ketch *Fortis* was built at Emsworth by Apps in 1904 for local owners and sailed in the trade to Birdham Mills on Chichester harbour. Her dimensions were 60 ft length overall, 54 ft waterline length × 16 ft beam and 5 ft 6 in draught aft when light. Her displacement was about 45 tons unladen. Registered Tonnage was 29. She remained in ownership of the mills into the 1920s until sold to Cowes. The *Fortis* became a yacht in 1939 and in 1945 her owner, whose home she was, had her re-rigged with a standing gaff mainsail without a boom and able to be brailed up. A topsail of the shape of that of a spritsail barge was set above it and the gaff mizzen and staysail and jib were retained forming a handy rig for short handed sailing. The small ketches were frequently at Bosham Quay in Chichester Harbour and worked to the village hards on its many creeks besides using the canal from Birdham to Chichester until the beginning of the twentieth century.

Besides that carried by local craft there was consider-

Figure 96 An unidentified coasting spritsail barge in Southampton Water, well loaded. About 1925

Figure 97 Spritsail barges at Ashlett Mill at the head of Ashlett Creek off Southampton Water. The coasting barge *Glencoe* was built at Rochester, Kent in 1905 and was owned by James Little of Strood, Kent. She frequently worked down the Channel and into the Solent

able cargo traffic into the Solent area ports by round bottomed ketches and schooners, brigantines and larger sailing ships and steam vessels. There were also many cargoes carried by flat bottomed ketch, schooner and spritsail rigged barges owned on the east coast. This lasted into the mid-twentieth century with the mule rigged barge *Cambria*, sailed by the irrepressible Bob Roberts, in the cement trade to the river Medina, Isle of Wight. Cargoes of many kinds were shipped in and out by these craft, whose shallow draught and small crews enabled them to compete successfully with larger round bottomed and deeper vessels, needing more water and more men. Figure 97 shows a scene typical of this work with the spritsail barge *Glencoe* ready to unload at Ashlett Mill, on the west shore of Southampton Water, with another spritsail barge to the right. The *Glencoe* was built at Rochester, Kent, in 1905 for James Little of Strood, who owned several barges which often traded on the English Channel coasts. I remember the *Glencoe* in the ballast trade to the Essex river Colne in the 1940s. Here she awaits discharge and shows the marked sheer and long bowsprit of the Channel barge, a large vessel for spritsail rig under sea conditions. The spritsail barge commended itself early to Solent owners and several were bought by them and others were built locally. The 41 ton *Enterprise* built at Cowes for owners at Rochester, Kent, in 1879 was an early example and there were others, many built for the London sailing barge owners E. J. and W. Goldsmith in 1898–99 in two classes, which included the *Gloria, Calluna, Decima, Lorna, Siesta* and *Esterel* of from 57–67 Registered Tons and the *Briton, Saxon, Spartan, Trojan, Norman* and *Grecian* of 80 to 82 Registered Tons. For reasons now difficult to establish, these barges, built at the noted Southampton yacht yard of J. and G. Fay and Co., had radiused bilge plates, which was a more expensive construction than the usual chine, and made these barges less weatherly than the chine hulled craft, but slightly improved their performance off the wind. These were long lived craft and some were still trading under power in the 1960s.

12

West Country sailing barges – 1 Cornwall

Small sailing barges evolved in the western counties of Devon and Cornwall to serve various local trades including the carriage of agricultural products and fertilisers, building and roadmaking materials and lightering cargoes from ships lying in local deepwater harbours to small ports alongshore or in the hinterland. The principal areas of ownership and use were at Plymouth, the large Devon naval port and Falmouth in Cornwall, a port of call for sailing merchant ships for many years. Both ports have a spread of rivers and creeks radiating from them. Sailing barges were also used to a lesser extent in the rivers Taw and Torridge in north Devon and from Salcombe and on the Teign in south Devon.

At Plymouth the rivers Tamar, Tavy, St Germans, Plym and their many associated creeks formed a system of tidal waterways serving many small towns and villages in a wide hinterland. Falmouth had similar rivers and creeks radiating from the Carrick Roads, the deep water anchorage. These include the river Fal, Truro river, Penrhyn river, Tresillian river and the Percuil river. Just to the south of the entrance to Falmouth is the Helford river, also once a centre of barge trade. These watery arms served a hinterland concerned principally with mining and agriculture. The Taw and Torridge estuary at the confluence of those rivers was less complex but

had the old ports of Bideford, Barnstaple and Appledore to attract trade. In south Devon sailing barges were also owned at Salcombe estuary and the river Teign.

The sailing barges of these localities must be considered together as their building and often ownership at various times was spread over the region. They have been overlooked in most studies of similar craft, perhaps because of the relative isolation of their home waters and also because there were no large numbers of defined sizes and types of craft or a homogeneous tradition of hull form and rig. Most were cutter rigged, some sloops and others ketches. There were two broad and ill defined divisions of craft used principally but not exclusively in rivers and creeks and those which also voyaged coastwise for short distances. The larger barges, although also working the sheltered waters, were principally employed to carry cargo coastwise, usually between the Fal and the Helford rivers in the west and the river Teign in the east, trading at various times to the many rivers, creeks and small ports between and in some cases making longer passages such as to Lyme Bay, the Bristol Channel ports and in at least one case to the Thames.

The carriage of various goods and some bulk cargoes about the Fal estuary and river system and along the

Figure 98 The cutter rigged Cornish cargo smack or coastal barge *Mystery* of Truro. Lines, structural section, deck arrangement and inboard profile. Dimensions 58 ft 7 in × 17 ft 2 in × 7 ft draught loaded. Note combined windlass and cargo winch

158

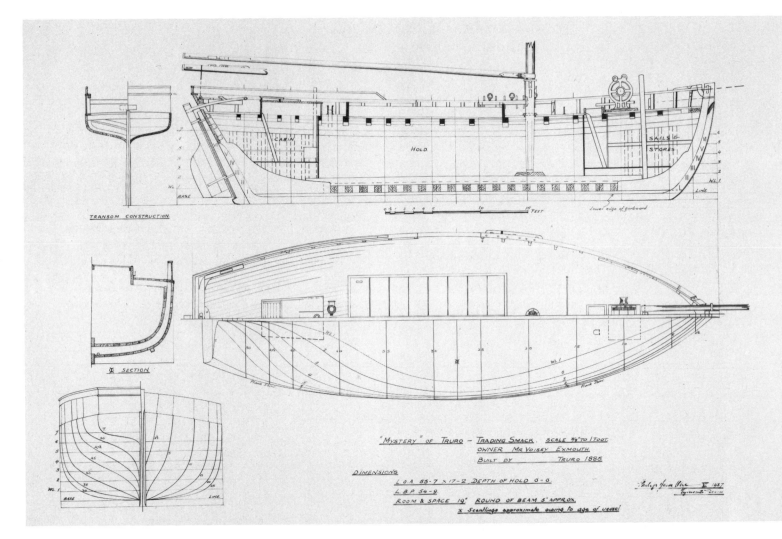

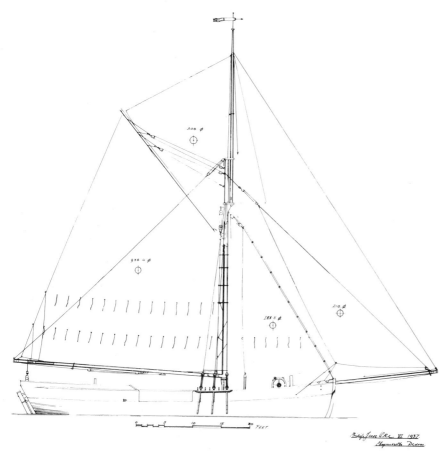

Figure 99 Sail plan and outboard profile of the barge *Mystery* of Truro.
Cutter rig with boom length reduced from the original. Total sail area
1640 sq ft. The bulwarks were removable in way of the hatch and
quarter boards were shipped on the bulwarks aft. A bobstay was not
fitted

adjoining coast was by small cutter rigged barges which
although usually referred to as smacks or sloops in official Registers, were also known simply as barges to the
men who built, owned and sailed them.

There were two basic uses, which led to them being
regarded as either 'inside' barges or 'outside' barges.
Inside barges traded within Falmouth Bay and the rivers
and creeks running inland from it. Outside barges were
generally larger and might sail fifty or so miles coastwise
from Falmouth, along the Cornish and Devon coasts.
Although of shallow draught for handiness in confined
waters and ability to load at farm wharves, these west
country sailing barges did not have leeboards and almost
all were round bilged, though the hulls were usually flat
bottomed. Typically the hull was planked in English oak
from sheer to bilge and had English elm bottom planking on oak frames and floors. The keel, stem, sternpost
and deadwoods were also oak and the pine deck was laid
on oak beams. The rig was unremarkable and craft of
both types often carried a topmast and jib headed topsail
and also often a jib topsail.

The area of water inside Pendennis Head at the west
side of the entrance to Falmouth and St Anthony Point
on the east, included a west arm forming Falmouth harbour proper and leading into the Penrhyn river, and a
large area of deep water leading north to south and
known as the Carrick Roads, the principal anchorage for
merchant shipping.

Just inside St Anthony Point the Percuil river runs off
to the north-east and on the west side of the Carrick
Roads are the creeks of Mylor and Restronguet and on
the east side St Just creek or pool. The river Fal leads
from the head of the Carrick Roads as a narrow channel
which is known as King Harry Reach, having two short
creeks on its west bank. At the end of the reach it

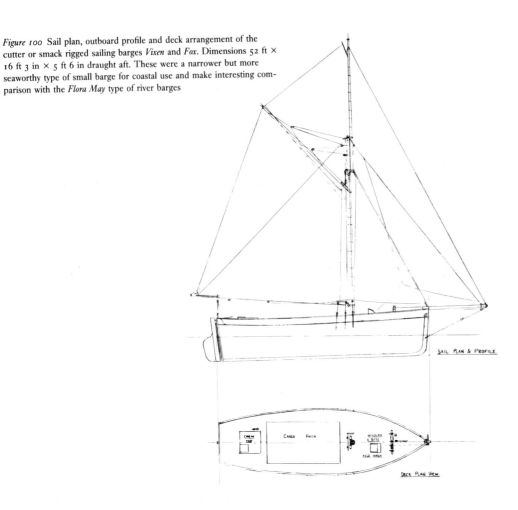

Figure 100 Sail plan, outboard profile and deck arrangement of the cutter or smack rigged sailing barges *Vixen* and *Fox*. Dimensions 52 ft × 16 ft 3 in × 5 ft 6 in draught aft. These were a narrower but more seaworthy type of small barge for coastal use and make interesting comparison with the *Flora May* type of river barges

SAIL PLAN & PROFILE.

CARGO HATCH

CREW CAB

WINDLASS & BITTS

DECK PLAN VIEW.

divides into the Fal, which continues north-east towards Ruan and the other branch which runs north-west as the Truro river. This divides at Malpas to continue as the Truro river to the county town of Cornwall and the other arm northwards as the Tresillian river. All these waterways had quays at the small towns, villages and farms on their shores, which were often densely wooded. A few miles south-west of the entrance to Falmouth harbour is the Helford river which runs inland from east to west and has a number of creeks but a less densely populated hinterland than the Fal complex of waterways, which itself was a mainly rural and thinly populated area. This spread of waterways reaching far inland made water transport vital in the days before the introduction of motor road transport.

The English industrial revolution brought an increase in the Cornish population particularly in the mining areas which were not self-sufficient in food. This encouraged a change to arable farming to supply a growing local market but the Cornish soil is naturally too acid for crops and limestone was not readily available, so a substitute was found by dredging sand from the bottom off Falmouth and St Mawes and also by digging it from local beaches. The inside barges were first evolved for this trade and the *Charlotte* and *Truro* were recorded as engaged in it in 1816 and others probably earlier. The Falmouth regatta of 1840 included a race for 'Dredging Barges' and six started.

In the troubled times of the Napoleonic wars even these rural watermen were not free from the press gang. The barge *Mary and Eleanor*, owned by the Scoble family of Coombe, on one of the creeks off King Harry Reach, was bound up river with a cargo of newly dredged sand. Scoble and his grandson were usually her sole crew. The old skipper saw with anxiety a naval gig overhauling them, obviously manned by 'the press', no doubt seeking his young hand. With quick thinking he threw overboard some loose gear on deck and the protests of the astonished grandson were silenced by a blow on the head with a sweep, felling him senseless to the deck. The naval boat ran alongside to be met with an apparently enraged skipper shouting, 'Here, take him, he's crazed and no use to me!' The officer of the press gang stared at the sprawling, slumped boy and told his crew to shove off.

Sand dredging was carried out under sail, presumably with 'A' framed dredges having a hoeing edge and a close meshed 'bag' or net to contain the sand, towed on a bass warp in the manner of oyster dredges, which were used in the Carrick Roads by local rowing skiffs and small sailing cutters. The deadweight of sand in a dredge would be hard work to raise and even harder to get on deck. The inside barges also found other work. In 1852 the *Wave, Union* and *Mary* were advertised as maintaining a daily passenger and goods service between Truro and Falmouth. In later years many barges lightered cargo from ships in Falmouth Bay to Truro or St Mawes and the *Betty, Sprightly* and *Tregottman* survived in this work into the early twentieth century and were referred to locally as 'Old salters', perhaps from their being salted in the sides in an attempt to preserve the hull timber.

The bulk carriage of cargoes up to perhaps 20 tons led to some barges being built with an open hold amidships and short forward and after decks. As the variety of goods and trade increased, many half decked barges were built to suit particular trades. The *Bessie, Maggie, Marion* and *Sunbeam* were built near Truro to carry grain and timber from ships discharging at Falmouth and elsewhere to the flour and saw mills of Truro and Perran Wharf. All had the mast stepped in a tabernacle to allow passage under the old road bridge at Devoran. The *Graham* and the *Topsy* were built to carry beer from Carne's Falmouth brewery to Truro and the *Clipper, Daisy* and *Jessie* were some of the barges working up to Devoran with tin ore and ballast. The half decked barges *Swift* and *Louisa* occasionally carried timber, besides many other cargoes, and the similar *Sweet May* was wrecked in 1927 bound into the Fal from the coastal quarry loading berth at Porthoustock on the coast south-west of the mouth of Falmouth harbour, with a freight of roadstone.

Inhabitants of many local villages and farms sent produce such as vegetables, fruit and poultry to Falmouth, Truro and St Mawes, and sometimes to adjacent coastal towns in 'Tonnage boats', 18 ft clinker planked open boats rigged with a standing lug main and a mizzen. The foremast was stepped 'in the eyes of the boat'. In calms the tonnage boats could be rowed by two men, each pulling an oar. The helmsman stood aft at the tiller and also 'sheaved' at a third oar, facing forward. Origin of the name 'Tonnage boat' is obscure; perhaps they were rated as 'One ton' for customs purposes. Early in the nineteenth century the *Dove, Judy* and *Ripple* were working between St Mawes and Falmouth and by the mid nineteenth century the *R.J.W.* and the *Wave* were worked by the Kelways from Pill, and J. Allen of Truro sailed the *Daisy.* The Tonnage boats also raced at Falmouth regatta and in 1853 four from that port and one from St Mawes competed.

A further type of craft known as a lighter was built, mainly as open craft displacing 15–20 tons and relying on the tide and a sweep for propulsion, though in the local regattas the lighters raced under a rig of a standing lugsail, helped on by two sweeps. Setting booms or poles were also used in shallow water. The usual work was to lighter cargo for Truro from ships discharging in the Fal, which by the mid nineteenth century began to silt in its upper reaches. Several lighters were built between 1850 and 1885, mainly on the Truro river, by Charles Dyer of Sunny Corner and also by Scoble and Davis of Malpas. As the demand for agricultural lime increased, suppliers had to look further than the locally dredged or beach-dug substitutes. The barges were required to voyage coastwise, notably to Plymouth, about 50 miles distant to the east of the Fal, to load local limestone which had been burnt in kilns. This could be a rough trip for a small barge, particularly in the prevailing south-west winds which make that coast a dangerous lee shore for these deep laden craft. So the fully decked and more seaworthy outside barges were developed and the *Mary* of Devoran was typical.

In 1875 John and Hugh Stephens, who built several schooners and ketches at sites by the Fal, launched the two sailing barges *Mary* and *Gleaner*. The 49 ft 4 in *Mary* was typical of the larger outside barges owned on the Fal and was probably built at Penpol Pill or creek on the west side of the river. She was designed by Charles George, who also supervised her construction. She was reputedly built from timber remaining after construction of some schooners and as there were no further orders for larger craft Stephens decided to build a barge, possibly for the stone trade from Porthallow but also to be capable of trading to Plymouth if necessary.

The *Mary*'s lines show a shapely little cargo carrier having 17 ft 6 in beam and a depth of 5 ft 7½ in. The long straight keel was slightly raked and the raked stem and sternpost were typical of the type. The hull sections, waterlines and buttocks were sweet and fair, suggesting she was possibly designed by draughting rather than by

the west country method usual into the mid twentieth century of carving a half model, usually having an exceptionally fine bow and a sharp tuck. The rise of floor of the bottom sections suggests a potentially smart sailer and the small rudder indicates her handiness.

The *Mary*'s modest draught of 6 ft 9 in aft was dictated by the need to load from the beach or at a quayside berth which dried out at Porthallow. There was limited depth of water at Devoran Quay for discharge and the *Mary* had to be capable of berthing there at neap tides, besides being able to work up the many other shallow creeks then used to load or discharge cargo in south Cornwall.

When built the *Mary* was rigged as a pole masted cutter with a gaff mainsail, a foresail and a jib set to a traveller on a running bowsprit; a handy rig for a crew of a man and a youth. However, the *Mary*'s boy, Charles Trebilcock, worried her skipper, his father, to carry a topsail like the larger Plymouth owned barges and eventually the father allowed him to cut a sheave hole in the masthead to allow reeving a halyard to set a long yarded topsail, which added speed off the wind and caught a breeze above the trees and hillsides of the confined waters she frequently sailed.

From forward the hull was typically divided into a fo'c'sle store, a cargo hold amidships and a small cabin aft with berths for three, a cupboard for food, a coal stove and a small hatch to the deck over which the long tiller projected. The large cargo had two fore and afters and a supplementary cross beam, with hatch boards and tarpaulin covers. To suit the frequent loading aground on beaches and in creeks the bulwarks were made portable on each side in way of the cargo hatch, to ease the work of handling cargo. An iron framed hand crank winch stood on the foredeck just forward of the mast

Figure 101 Small sailing barge *Mary* of Truro on the hard of St Just in Roseland, on the river Fal, 1926

and had a barrel and warping ends for whipping cargo and assisting in mooring and warping the barge and probably a rope messenger from it assisted with getting the anchor cable in strong winds or when kedging off a lee shore beach. A double barrel winch was clamped to the mast just above the hatch and served for halliards and for cargo work.

Ownership of these barges was frequently in several shares and the *Mary*'s original owners numbered ten or more. It is interesting that each were from a different locality, all hoping to produce freights for the barge or influence others to do so.

From her launch in 1875 until 1955 the *Mary* worked about the rivers, creeks and coast between the Lizard peninsular and the river Tamar, above Plymouth. The largest cargo carried was 64 tons, and 45–50 tons was a usual load. The outside barges worked to many small ports, villages and isolated quays, beaches and hards between the Lizard and Plymouth and typical cargoes included stone to St Just, Porth Navas and Gweek on the Helford river; cattle food to St Mawes; bricks from local brickworks far up the Fal; lightering timber from Gweek to load ships off the mouth of the Helford river; carrying limestone from the river Tamar to Truro and many cargoes of stone from the quarries at Porthoustock to Truro and Tresillian quay for road making and maintenance, one of the last trades worked by these barges. The crew of these barges were usually away for the week but in later years, when bicycles became fashionable, they cycled home whenever possible, leaving the barge locked up and moored at some quiet quay, to puff their way back up the hills the next morning.

The *Mary* was a stiff barge, even when light, and she was relatively fast. She once sailed from Plymouth Sound to the approaches to Pendennis Point in four

Figure 102 Small sloop rigged Fal barge with foresail lowered. In Gillam Creek, 1927

hours, in a fresh north-west wind. She reputedly sailed to Falmouth, from east Cornwall, in company with a steamer capable of 8 knots and occasionally drew ahead of her in the puffs. In later years the *Mary* was given a new mast and the topsail was set from a chain jackstay from the head of a fidded topmast. In 1926 a 13 hp auxiliary motor was installed and she achieved 5 knots under power. She continued in the usual trades until 1946 when she was sold to Harris and Lamey of Appledore, on the north Devon coast, making her longest and most adventurous passage 'around the land' to be refitted at Appledore as a motor barge for the gravel trade in the Taw and Torridge estuaries. Afterwards she carried stone for the sea walls on the rivers Severn and Wye and by 1952 was used to dredge coal waste from the docks at Newport, in south Wales. She returned to the stone trade and finally became a mooring barge at the Berkeley atomic power station project in the Bristol Channel. In 1958 the *Mary* was laid up at Sharpness in Gloucestershire, aged and scarred but still afloat.

Dozens of the Fal barges traded until 1914. The primitive harbours of Portloe and Coverack saw them discharging and some of the small barges ventured to Looe, and beyond to the Tamar and its creeks, usually for limestone as fertiliser. But most of their passages ended at rural quays and hards on the lovely Fal or at the Helford river, where Merthen quay frequently had the chubby cutters alongside unloading or loading and where John Tyacke owned the small ketch rigged market boat *Rob Roy* and from where the little *Industry* sailed. The stone trade from Porthoustock quarries, on the east side of the Lizard peninsular frequently brought the barges down the Fal with a fair, offshore breeze in the morning and, after loading under the shoots, they returned in evening with a breeze off the sea; the cycle of fair weather sailing which can obtain for several days in the English summer. On calm mornings the barges were rowed downriver with sweeps and were poled along in the shallows until the breeze made. Like all seafarers, the bargemen welcomed the installation of auxiliary motors to relieve this drudgery.

Just inside the eastern side of the entrance to the Carrick Roads the Percuil river reaches far into the Roseland peninsular, with the small town of St Mawes at its entrance and the village of Percuil sited well inland at the sharp bend in the river where there is deep water and sheltered anchorage. This, coupled with a large and shelving hard made a centre for trade of sailing barges, ketches, schooners and other craft. With 6 ft of water at low water springs and up to 24 ft at high water this became a busy place with vessels grounded on the hard loading or discharging into carts alongside.

The larger outside sailing barges varied in size. The *Ocean Belle* was built at Malpas by T. Coad in 1862 and was the smallest to venture beyond the Fal at 31 ft × 12 ft 11 in × 5 ft 10 in depth. The *Mystery*, built at Sunny Corner in 1885 by C. Dyer was largest at 54 ft 7 in × 16 ft 7 in × 6 ft 11 in depth. Perhaps the *Ann* built at Flushing by her owner in 1872 was typical at 44 ft 6 in length × 12 ft 10 in beam and 6 ft 5 in depth. Many of these outside barges were of relatively light displacement and had fine bows and sterns. They needed to be reefed early in strong winds. In 1827 three of them were beating back to the Fal against a strong westerly wind which backed and freshened. The barges made such heavy weather of it that a passing revenue cutter stood by and escorted them into the Fal.

Some outside barges occasionally voyaged across the English channel to the French port of Roscoff for onions and broccoli. Others sailed round Lands End and up the Bristol Channel to load coal cargoes. These included the little *Ocean Belle* of Malpas, which foundered off Newport, Monmouthshire in 1866. But carrying limestone remained the main trade for the larger Fal barges and as demand for it decreased with the fluctuations of Cornish agriculture and depressions in trade, the larger barges were forced to seek cargoes in competition with the more seaworthy schooners and ketches, and the barges' limited capacity and seaworthiness restricted their share of short coastal freights. However, in the first half of the twentieth century road construction in Cornwall led to considerable carriage of quarried stone from Porthoustock, particularly to a wharf at Tresillian, on the river of that name miles inland. Porthoustock was an exposed loading berth and untenable in easterly winds. Many surviving outside barges worked in this trade, joined by old sailing barges bought from Plymouth and other south Devon owners. Of these the *Dorothy*, *Magpie* and *Sweet May* were lost off Porthoustock at various times.

The roadstone work lasted into the early 1950s and was fairly active during the 1940s when the *J.N.R.*, *Silex*, *Shamrock* and *Sirdar* were still sailing, helped by auxiliary motors which were particularly appreciated working up the creeks. When these were laid up the Fal sailing barges were finished.

13

West Country sailing barges – 2 Devon

After the Napoleonic wars the Tamar valley area grew in population and the expanding industries included quarrying, agriculture, naval dockyards and defence works. The expansion of Plymouth and adjacent Devonport dockyards during the period approximately 1885–1918 brought further growth in population, house building and construction of dockyard and defence establishments coupled with a general increase of trade and a need for the movement of goods in the area. Much of this in later years was carried by railways but the sailing barges retained a share of the trade, which remained significant until about 1920.

The Plymouth area barges, coupled with those from Salcombe and other Devon rivers were more numerous than those from nearby Cornwall and were generally better managed and more profitable to their owners. The Devon craft were also of more varied type, depending on their trade and the builder.

The principal early trade of the Tamar barges was carrying limestone from quarries near the river Plym up to St Germans or Lynher river and the creeks off the Hamoaze. The stone was taken upriver after burning in kilns to produce agricultural lime for use on the acid soil of the fields of the hinterland and was also sent elsewhere by barge along the coasts of Devon and Cornwall.

Other cargoes included blue evlan building stone, farm produce, granite, bricks, various ores, grain, hay, straw, manure, timber, roadstone and even arsenic. Much of this trade was from one quay to another, often from the city of Plymouth but also to and from rural watersides and village hards. Many cargoes were taken for transhipment to or from larger vessels lying in the deep water anchorage. Some cargoes were taken 20 miles inland to places like Calstock and Cotehele Quay, up the Tamar.

These barges had to be of moderate draught and be able to be sailed by a crew of two or three. Maximum cargo space had to be obtained on the dimensions and building and maintenance had to be inexpensive. Most were rigged as sloops, some as cutters, with or without a topsail. These craft, primarily for use in the rivers and creeks with an occasional coastal passage, were distinct from the larger cutter and ketch rigged barges sometimes referred to as 'smacks' in official records, which were more frequently engaged in trade along the coast, as well as the river work. These carried cargo to and from small ports and havens alongshore including Salcombe, the Yealm, the Dart, the Exe, the Teign, Looe, Falmouth, Fowey, Charlestown, the Helford river, and occasionally to further places such as Weymouth,

Figure 103 The barge *Silex* of Plymouth in Falmouth harbour 1927.
Typical of the Plymouth barges which made limited coastal passages,
usually to the rivers Fal, Helford, Yealm, Dart and to Salcombe

Bridport, Lyme Regis, Southampton and in one case, reputedly to London. Many of this larger type were owned and built at Plymouth.

The smaller Tamar barges usually had the mast stepped in a tabernacle to lower when passing bridges and the forestay was set up by a purchase to the stem head. The sloop rig set a gaff mainsail with a long boom and gaff and a short luff. The staysail set to the stem head. Those rigged as cutters had a running bowsprit on which a jib was set flying to a traveller. Some, including the larger, coastal passagemaking barges, many of which were rigged as ketches, carried a fidded topmast and set a topsail. A spare staysail, a storm jib and perhaps a balloon staysail or jib were also often carried. Surprisingly none appear to have had leeboards and consequently their windward ability was usually indifferent.

The river barges were variously referred to as 'sloops' or 'Blue evlan barges' on the Tamar because many were owned by local quarries and carried cut stone from quarries at Forder, Notter or Landsaker. Many barge crews were from villages and hamlets on the banks of the river Plym, to the east of Plymouth, to which this shallow river gave its name. Craft built and owned in that area were called 'Laira' barges but were almost identical to the Tamar craft. The barges existed during the eighteenth century when their bulky hulls carried stone for construction of the dockyard and other works. Probably they existed in various forms long before that.

Some barges were owned by breweries, by general merchants and by small shipowners also having schooners and ketches, such as Eastcotts. However, most were owned by syndicates of local small business people, often publicans and grocers, occasionally by their skippers, who almost always had the responsibility of finding freights, even if the barge was owned by others.

Many barges were built from seasoned timber surplus to the building of schooners and ketches by yards specialising in these craft, but also building the occasional barge of either type, or a fishing smack. However, many barges were designed and built at small yards which made their building and repair a major part of their activities. Plymouth builders of the barges included Moore at Friary Slip, Sutton Pool and Hawke Brothers of Stonehouse, whose yard was active into the 1930s and built many. A few were launched at Saltash and Calstock on the river Tamar and at Beere Ferrers on the river Tavy. At Calstock, above Plymouth, Brooming and later Goss built a number of barges. Craft by all of them were long lived. Most were designed by carving a hull half model from which the lines were lifted by transverse offset measurements taken on stations at each waterline. However, some, including Fred Hawke, draughted plans, and craft from that yard were notably well built and sailed well. Many Plymouth built barges had the full bow and fine run of the 'cods head and mackerel tail' tradition of hull form, but Hawke seemed able to achieve a more subtle shape within the limitations of restricted dimensions.

Plymouth built barges included the *Yealm* built in 1878, the 39 ton *Emma* of 1878 and later sold to the Fal; *Industry*, built at Calstock in 1880; *Mayblossom* of 34 tons 1889; *Gwendoline* of 1894; *Triumph* of 30 tons built by Hawke in 1898 and the 34 ton *P.H.E.* launched in 1900. Fred Hawke was the major partner in the Stonehouse yard and was an experienced and thorough builder of barges and other small vessels. His barges had the reputation for being strongly built and fast sailers. One of his apprentices, the late Fred Dan, recalled the taut way Hawke Brothers yard was run, with apprentices often doing the work of men but always closely supervised by Fred Hawke's quick eye which allowed

Figure 104 Lines of the Tamar barge *Flora May*, built by Frederick Hawke of Stonehouse, Plymouth in 1897. Typical of the well formed and soundly built craft from this yard, she would have sailed well, within the limitations of type and draught

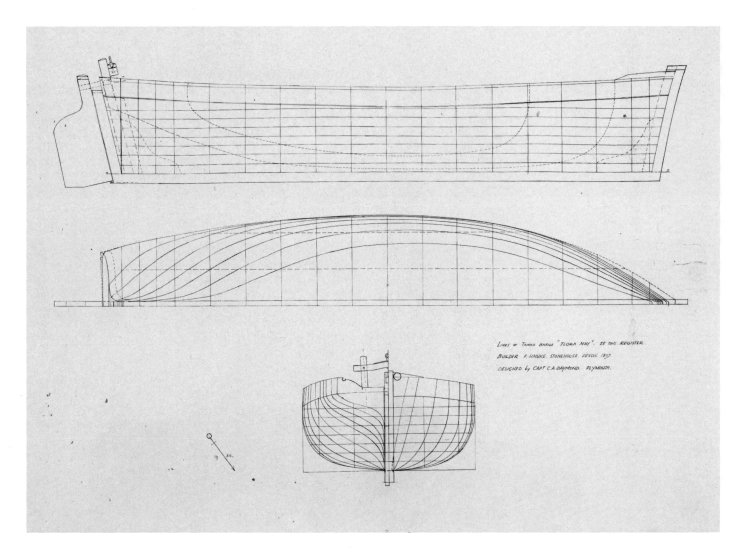

LINES OF TAMAR BARGE "FLORA MAY". 28 TONS REGISTER.
BUILDER. F. HAWKE. STONEHOUSE. DEVON. 1897.
DESIGNED by CAPT C.A. DAYMOND. PLYMOUTH.

Figure 105 Deck plan and inboard profile of the barge *Flora May*. Note the rudder blade projecting below the keel when afloat. The length of tiller, the handspike windlass and the cargo winch to starboard

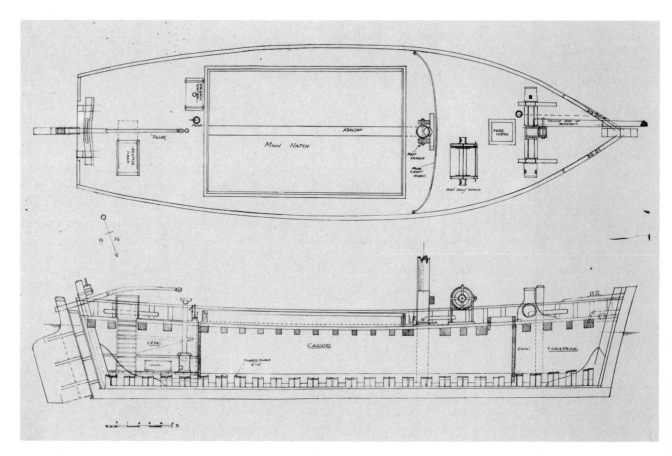

nothing but sound timber and well fitting members to go into his vessels. Sometimes he shrewdly bought old wooden naval vessels to be broken up and the large scantling timber from these was converted to prime material for smaller craft.

The 50 ft 6 in long *Flora May* was typical of Hawke's barges. She was designed and built in 1897 for her owner/skipper C. A. Daymond, who discussed his requirements in detail with Fred Hawke. The builder draughted the lines, basic construction and sail plans and made a half model, as was his custom, to incorporate the owner's ideas in tangible form and satisfy his interest in the new craft. Several smaller barges were afterwards built to the same design.

The *Flora May*'s keel was 47 ft long. Her beam was 15 ft 6 in and depth of hold 5 ft 6 in. Loaded with 50 tons she drew 5 ft 6 in forward and 6 ft 6 in aft and then had only 2 in freeboard amidships in still water: a typical condition. The hull had well rounded sections and a fine entry and run ending in a small and raked transom. As in several of Hawke's designs the stem had a slightly concave shape. The lines, fig. 104, show a hull which would slip along well in the smooth waters these craft usually sailed. From forward she was arranged with a forepeak store entered from a deck hatch, a cargo hold and a small cabin aft having two bunks and a coal stove. This was entered by a hatch under the long tiller. The rectangular main hatch left only narrow side decks between the mast and the forward bulkhead of the crew's cabin.

Construction was heavy for long life and avoidance of structural movement when loading and discharging aground. The keel was of English elm, sided 9 in and moulded 12 in, with a similar sized oak keelson on top of the transverse floors, to resist hogging. Hawke considered that the elm resisted rot better than oak in the local river water, which is surprising as this wood will rot quickly in purely fresh water rivers and the *Flora May* would spend much time well upstream in rivers and creeks and in harbours, subject to a mixture of fresh and salt water.

The frames were 6 in sided × 8 in moulded, fitted double, in pairs with only 8 in between their faces. The bottom planking was elm, 2½ in thick at the bilge with side planking of 2 in oak up to the sheerstrake, which

was 2½ in thick English oak. Deck beams were oak, 8 in square. The hatch and mast beams were 10 in square and the deck planking was 2½ in thick pitch pine. Fastenings were galvanised iron bolts and wooden treenails, which Hawke preferred as hull fastenings because these wore down evenly with the surface of the hull planking as it chafed in service. The 18 in high bulwarks were planked on oak stanchions set through the covering board and bolted to the heads of the frames. Like most Stonehouse-built barges the *Flora May* had a mainsheet horse of 8 in square oak, bolted across stout bitts on the inside of the transom, allowing the tiller to work between them. A water breaker stood on deck abaft the main hatch coaming close to the deck pump which was within reach of the helmsman. A hand-spike windlass handled the chain cable or warps for mooring alongside. An iron dolly winch for whipping cargo stood to starboard, immediately forward of the mast which could lower in a wood tabernacle when negotiating low bridges in creeks and to reach some upriver berths. The lowering was accomplished with a double purchase tackle of two iron blocks with chain falls, which was shackled to the lower end of the forestay.

The cutter rig did not usually set a topsail but nevertheless had a rakish appearance (fig. 106). The 40 ft boom was 8½ in diameter and the 30 ft long gaff, with its inefficient angle of lead for the peak halyards which was dictated by the short masthead, made the mainsail hard work to set and stow for the crew of two. With two reefs down it remained a sizeable area and even snugged down to this and a jib, the barge would need watching in a breeze during a coastwise passage. All spars were of pitch pine, then obtainable in long lengths and the mainmast was particularly heavy, being 12 in diameter at

Figure 106 Outboard profile and sail plan of the barge *Flora May* in loaded condition. Note sail area and unstayed bowsprit, short masthead to clear ship's yards and rigging and warehouses, when alongside. The long gaff sets at an inefficient angle. The boom length was 40 ft

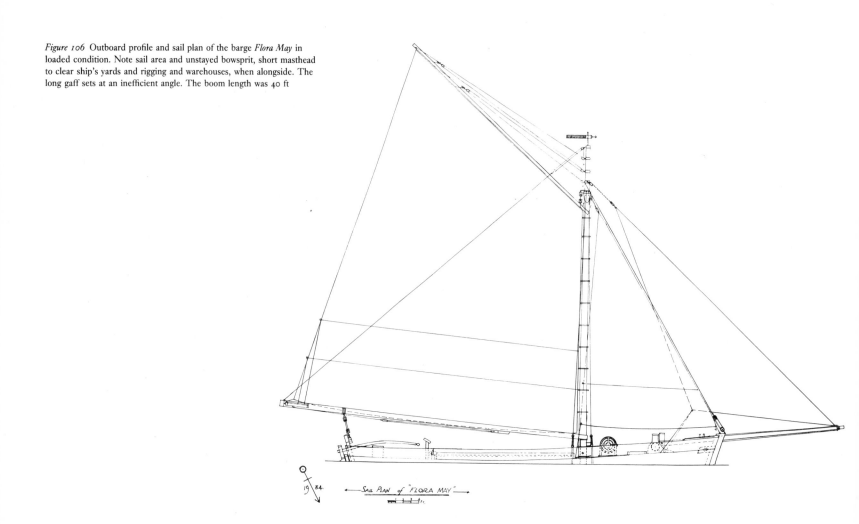

the heel and 9 in at the head. The reeving bowsprit housed against the pawl post and followed the line of the sheer. It averaged 7 in in diameter. The jib halyard was of short link chain but all other running gear was of manilla rope. The halyards were set up with purchases and the topping lift led to a purchase at the masthead. When built the *Flora May* carried a topmast and set a topsail having a short head yard. In later years she was pole masted.

Her hull materials cost about £400 and the sails and rigging a further £100. Like all the barges she had a rowboat from 12 to 14 ft long which was often towed but sometimes was carried on deck in confined waters. The *Flora May* was a good sea boat within the limitations of her form, freeboard, draught and rig, and was fast amongst her type.

During the 1880s numbers of these barges were regularly carrying oak bark from the woods by the Plym to a tannery at Millbrook. Occasionally they traded beyond Plymouth Sound, to the rivers Yealm and Erme and occasionally further. Their capacity was restricted for these passages to preserve a minimum freeboard of 6 in, resulting in a cargo of about 45 tons in the case of the *Flora May*. She once loaded a cargo of old guns at Mothercombe, on the river Erme, to be used as scrap.

In 1914 all the sailing barges became part of the government transport service, and after the war, in 1919, the *Flora May* was sold to a shipbreaking firm to carry scrap steel. This rough trade gradually weakened her hull and she was discarded, being run ashore at Saltash on the Tamar, where her bleaching frames remained for many years.

The cutter rigged sailing barge *Gwendoline* of Plymouth, launched in 1894 was typical of the work of David Banks of Queen Anne's Battery, at the Cattewater, that eastern pool which was home of the Plymouth fleet of sailing trawlers. She was constructed almost entirely of oak, reputedly from trees blown down in the great gale of 1891. Overall length of hull was 55 ft 9 in, beam 18 ft 1½ in and depth of hold 6 ft 5 in. Draughts light were 4 ft 9 in aft and 3 ft 6 in forward. Loaded these were 7 ft 9 in and 6 ft 4 in respectively. Craft of this size were seaworthy and often sailed well, having an easy entrance and some flare forward which helped to keep them dry, and the length made them easier in a seaway than the little flat river sloops. They regularly took the ground and the *Gwendoline*'s framing and floors were strong, spaced at 18 in centres. The double, sawn frames were sided 6 in and were spaced at 18 in centres. The keel was 9 in sided × 12 in moulded, with a similar sized keelson placed on top of the 6 in sided × 8 in moulded depth double floors. The hold ceiling was also, unusually of oak, 3 in thick on the floor and 2½ in at the sides. The ceiling was strapped to the side structure with iron every 6 ft, from the underside of deck to the turn of the bilge. Hull planking was 3 in thick in the bottom and bilge and 2½ in sides, all fastened with wooden treenails. Surprisingly, the deck beam spacing was 3 ft, with the beams 8 in square section but the deck planking was 2½ in thick at the covering board in way of the portable bulwarks, to take the chafe of loading and discharging cargo. The bulwarks were 24 in high above deck. The *Gwendoline*'s mast was stepped through the deck on the keelson and a long topmast was carried. The bowsprit was set in bitts, with a gammon iron at the side of the stem head. Below deck the hull was divided from forward into a fo'c'sle, where stores were kept and the boy slept, then the hold with one long hatch amidships, followed by the after cabin, where the crew of two men lived. As in the *Flora May*,

Figure 107 Lines of the Tamar barge *Kate*, built by Frederick Hawke of Stonehouse, Plymouth. Dimensions 54 ft length of keel × 17 ft 1 in beam × 6 ft depth of hold. Unusual in having a clipper stem profile

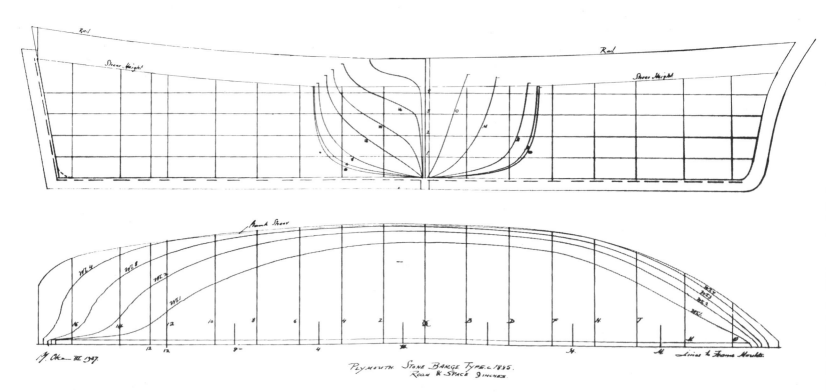

this was entered by a hatch over which the tiller swept when in use. A hand cranked cargo winch stood forward of the mast, with a barrel for whipping cargo.

The cutter rig was lofty, the mainsail was large and the boom well outboard beyond the transom. Generally the rig showed influence of the local trawlers in its arrangements but the small staysail was probably dictated by the difficulty of getting that sail to set well to windward in a cutter having the mast well forward. The bowsprit steeved upwards and did not have a bobstay, which

seems to have been common in west country craft. The jib set on a traveller. Either a jib headed or a yard topsail could be set above the mainsail and these were useful in the rivers and creeks to catch an air above the tree crowded banks. A handspike windlass handled the anchor cable but its working was encumbered by the fore hatch immediately abaft it. Several sailing barges were built by James Goss at Bere Alston, Devon, opposite Calstock on the east bank of the river Tamar where earlier Edward Brooming built. Goss was a mariner from north Devon who left the sea and moved to the Tamar to work in a yard owned by a relative. Having learned something of the shipwright's trade he and his sons set up in business repairing small wooden vessels and occasionally building a sailing barge, besides constructing two ketches and numerous small boats. Their craft had a reputation for sound design and construction. One of their sailing barges, the *Lillie*, was launched in 1899 and like many of her contemporaries was rigged as a cutter with a topsail. Goss continued to build at his yard 17 miles from the sea until the First World War.

The generally full lines of the Plymouth barges made them poor performers to windward in a seaway compared to some of the Cornish craft from the Fal. The *Silex* was bound for Porthoustock quarry, near the mouth of the Helford river, to load stone and crossed the bow of the 47 ft Fal barge *May*, which as the wind freshened was able to carry her sail and romped ahead to berth at the quarry for loading. The *May* was loaded and outward bound before the *Silex* arrived, reefed down and sailing slowly. During the early 1920s, with the radical changes in trade and advance of road transport, many of the Plymouth sailing barges were sold, some to the Fal and others elsewhere. The barges *Industry*, *Gwendoline* and *Yealm* traded under sail late in the 1930s, but were afterwards laid up and sold.

One of Hawke's barges, the *Shamrock*, has survived and between 1975–1978 was restored to her ketch rig of 1926. The *Shamrock* was built in 1899 for Thomas and Frederick Williams, lightermen of Torpoint, on the Tamar, to carry animal manure from Cattedown, Plymouth to the Torpoint chemical works, upriver, where it was converted into briquettes of fuel. The cargo was loaded and unloaded manually. The *Shamrock*,

doubtless named for the Americas Cup challenger of that year, was 57 ft overall length × 18 ft beam and 5 ft 6 in depth. She had full bows, a well rounded forefoot and a transom stern. Reputedly she had two steel centreplates when built and, if so, was exceptional amongst British barges.

The ketch rig simply set a staysail to the stemhead, a gaff mainsail and mizzen. The masts were stepped in tabernacles to negotiate bridges. In 1920 with freights for sailing craft beginning to fall after record wartime levels, Williams brothers sold *Shamrock* and their other barge *J.N.R.* to the West of England Road Metal Co., for whom she continued to carry cargo until the 1950s, principally roadstone. At that time the centreplates are said to have been removed and a false keel fitted. The hatch coamings were raised to Board of Trade load line requirements and a jib was rigged, set to a bowsprit. That year a 22 hp Blake paraffin engine was installed as auxiliary. This gave her 6 knots under power and enabled the barge to make passages under sail and power with some regularity. The hull was strengthened for carrying stone from the quarries on the river Lynher to wharves on the creeks, rivers and harbours of the coast between Falmouth and Dartmouth. During the 1930s until the 1950s the *Shamrock* carried cargoes of crushed stone for road surfacing from the quarry at Porthoustock, on the east side of the Lizard peninsular in Cornwall, to Tresillian on the river of that name. Eventually the mizzen mast was removed as any windward work was usually under the auxiliary engine.

In 1962 she was sold to a local company and was converted as a diving tender principally for work in Plymouth harbour. By 1973 she was laid up in Hooe Lake, a creek near Plymouth and in the following year was acquired by the National Maritime Museum, to be removed to Cote Hele Quay, up the river for restoration to her trading condition as the last of the west country sailing barges.

Several sailing barges were built at Kingsbridge, a Devonshire town at the head of one of the various watery arms of Salcombe's lovely harbour, to the east of Plymouth. Some were by William Date, who also built schooners and ketches, many of which were fast. The Kingsbridge built barges were slightly larger than the average Plymouth craft, varying between 38 and 41 Registered Tons against the Plymouth barges' average 30 to 38. They were finer forward and had a fine entry and run. The stem was usually slightly raked and was sometimes concave in profile. The keel was straight and most had a boxy shaped counter which gave an appearance similar to some of the local schooners.

Salcombe yards launched the smacks or sailing barges *Marie* registered at the port; the *Sirdar* and the *J.N.R.*, which were both registered at Plymouth, besides others. The *J.N.R.* was built by William Date. She was 64 ft × 18 ft 2 in beam × 6 ft 6 in depth of hold and carried 70 tons on a draught of 8 ft. A cargo gaff was used for loading and discharge. The *J.N.R.* was a smart sailer and a stiff barge in a breeze, gaining stability from the broad, flat quarters of her run to the transom stern, though her bows were unusually full.

W. H. Sweet sailed her for thirty years after he became her skipper in 1914. An idea of the work on board for a crew of two is given by the dimensions of her mainsail of heavy flax canvas; luff 24 ft 6 in, head 28 ft 10 in, foot 37 ft 6 in and leach 43 ft. The lowermast measured 43 ft from deck to cap and the top-mast head was about 65 ft above deck. The running rigging followed the usual practice in these barges. The fall of the peak halyards led to the starboard pin rail and

the purchase on the peak halyards, set up with a double block above and a single block below, led to the port pinrail. Throat halyards were a treble sheeve block at the mast crane and a double hooked to the gaff. The fall led to the port pin rail. The topping lift was of wire and the tackle setting it up was a double and single block hooked to a deck eyebolt. The fall belayed to the port pin rail. The foresail halyards led to the starboard pin rail and the lower single block was hooked to an eye on the rail when not in use.

The *J.N.R.* remained fully rigged but about 1932 a 5 hp auxiliary engine was installed to enable her to motor during calms and assist in berthing and manoeuvring in the creeks. A more powerful engine was fitted in the 1940s when canvas was reduced to the mainsail and foresail, though she had a new mainsail in 1953, and at that time her foresail was spread by a boom; an unusual practice in British working craft.

After 1945 the *J.N.R.* was owned at Truro by Mr. May, of Penrose and Son, sailmakers. He ran her in the roadstone trade under skipper Thomas Allen and Alfred Glover was her mate for many years. The *J.N.R.* worked in company with the Plymouth-built barge *Mayblossom* and the ex-Plymouth ketch *Shamrock*. Their cargoes were mainly destined for Tresillian, at the head of the narrow river of that name, near Truro, where a tarmac plant operated until 1950, when it was moved inland and the waterborne stone trade almost ceased. The *Shamrock* was then owned by West of England Quarries and continued to ship an occasional cargo but the others were laid up.

A simple type of barge was built for use on the river Teign, in south Devon, for carrying the ball clay used in making china from Newton Abbot, downstream to load small ships at Teignmouth quays or in the pool off the lovely village of Shaldon, on the west side of the entrance to the river. They also carried granite from the Haytor quarries for transhipment as building stone. The 'Bovey' clay was dug on the edge of Dartmoor, where workings started early in the seventeenth century. At first the clay was carted to tidewater at Newton Abbot and brought downstream by barge. Late in the eighteenth century in the age of canal building enthusiasm, the clay interests decided to reduce the handling costs and time by digging the Stover Canal from Newton Abbot to Ventiford Basin. This was opened in 1782 and provided direct transport of the clay by barge to the waiting ships. About ten barges were built for the trade at this time. These were about 50 ft long × 14 ft beam × 4 ft 6 in–5 ft depth and were capable of carrying around 25 tons of clay in the form of easily handled cubes. The hulls were shapely and had a transom stern. There was a single cargo hatch with shallow coamings as there was little opportunity for a sea to get up in the Teign. Forward and after decks were joined by narrow side decks, and hatches forward and aft gave access to a fo'c'sle and after cabin. The ample rudder had a long tiller and the low bulwarks were supported by the heads of frames carried up above deck, with others serving as mooring bitts. A mast was stepped against the forward coaming of the cargo hatch and on this a single square sail of about 350 sq ft area was set in favourable or reaching winds. Otherwise the barges were poled or were rowed with sweeps in the tidal river. In the canal they were poled but were more usually hauled by their crew, though sail might be set at times. About 1843 the Hackney Canal was also opened for this trade. It closed in 1928.

Ships could load about 100 tons each day from these lighters and about sixteen were working as late as 1931.

They were still built into the twentieth century and one named *George V* was built in 1911. However, from the early 1920s the barges had been towed by the steam tugs *Heron* and *Kestrel* and sails had been laid ashore.

The Teignmouth barge trade continued until 1939, when the Stover Canal closed. The barges were superseded by road transport, direct from pits to quayside. In a creek near Arch Brook bridge, Teignmouth lies in the hull of the *Two Brothers*, the last of the Teign barges. There is hope that she may be preserved.

In north Devon the rivers Taw and Torridge and their estuary supported a number of small sailing barges of mixed size and type, some of which were used to lighter cargoes from small sailing ships anchored in deep water to discharge for the ports of Appledore, Bideford and Barnstaple. The barges also carried local farm and other goods in the area. Towards the end of the nineteenth century and well into the twentieth numbers of these small sloop and cutter rigged barges carried sand and gravel dug by hand from banks in the swift flowing rivers to be delivered to builders' merchants and contractors at the three towns and other places by the riversides. They also were sailed out into Bideford Bay in fine weather to ground alongshore and be loaded with shingle for building work. When the barge dried out the crew went over the side with shovels and dug the cargo from alongside, throwing it into the hold. This primitive method continued into the 1950s.

Many of these barges were built at Appledore, others at Bideford and at Cleeve Houses. At least one came from Prince Edward Island, Canada, with which place the north Devon seafarers had close links through trade and emigration. A few were constructed at Padstow, in north Cornwall, where the sand and gravel trade is also believed to have been carried on in a similar but lesser

Figure 108 Small sloop rigged barges of the rivers Taw and Torridge in north Devon, grounded on a gravel bank to be loaded with hand shovels by their crews. Note that leeboards were not fitted to these shallow craft

Figure 109 An Appledore sand barge shows her uncompromisingly full hull form. By the 1940s almost all these small sailing barges had been converted to motor propulsion and abandoned sail entirely for the short trips to load and discharge

way. Sometimes gravel was transhipped into ketches and schooners for carriage to Cardiff or Barry in south Wales, or to Bristol and Avonmouth on the east side of the Bristol Channel, for use in concrete making for building and dock construction. Many of these barges were not owned by their skippers or crews but by publicans in local towns and other local businessmen, who were notorious for their parsimony towards their crews and craft. Some aged Fal and south Devon sailing barges were sold to the Taw and Torridge owners for this trade.

A typical sand and gravel barge of this estuary was a short, beamy and shallow hull having wide hatch openings and little sheer, making it necessary for care in handling under sail when loaded. These barges regularly used sail but most of the work was undoubtedly done by the strong tides and occasionally also by the crew using sweeps. Motors were installed in some during the 1920s and were increasingly used, but the digging of the cargo by hand continued into the 1950s, after which mechanical diggers were introduced. However, the small sailing barge *J.J.R.P.* was built in 1923 and launched fully rigged. At 37 ft × 13 ft × 5 ft 4 in moulded depth she could carry only 27 tons but continued in service in the 1950s. The smallest barge was the *Tiny Hilda*, a 20 ft. sloop rigged miniature which was the last of the Taw and Torridge barges to work under sail alone until about 1948. The local sand and gravel trade afterwards declined, though some is still dredged by small ships using suction equipment.

14

The Trows of the west of England

The river Severn in western England, formed an important artery of trade for many centuries, reaching from Arlingham in Gloucestershire about sixty miles south-westward where it merges into the apex of the Bristol Channel at Weston-super-Mare on the east shore and Penarth, in Wales, on the west. The major port of Bristol is on the tributary river Avon entering the estuary of the Severn at Avonmouth. Twenty-five miles upstream the river narrows above Sharpness, where the Gloucester and Sharpness Ship Canal avoids the many turns of the Severn stream and, passing through Saul, through which the Stroudwater Canal passes to the east, reaches the city of Gloucester. Above this the river Severn continues to the ancient town of Tewkesbury where the river Avon (the 'Stratford Avon') reaches it as tributary. The main river continues north past Upton on Severn and Kempsey to the city of Worcester, where the Worcester and Birmingham Canal branches off to the north-east. Above this the Severn reaches Stourport on Severn and continues beyond, to the north. Here too the Staffordshire and Worcester Canal links with the river, one of a number of artificial waterways which are still in use in the area, though others once busy with water-borne traffic are closed.

With such a waterways system developing from the river it was natural that local commerce led to the development of several distinctive types of cargo carrying craft, most of them under the generic name 'Trow'. This word appears to derive from the Anglo-Saxon word for trough, and is pronounced as 'Trow' in this part of England. The pointed stern 'canoes' used at Nottingham, in the midlands and in Scotland for fresh water fishing were also called trows. The early Severn Trows were shallow draught craft with pointed sterns and an open hold, used to carry cargo on the river and its tributaries, as water served in the days before locks and attempted regulation of depths in the upper reaches. Waterborne trade on the Severn is as old as the Roman occupation of Britain. Early cargoes were lead, leather, wines, iron, wool, timber, grain, stone, cheese, butter, cloth and hides.

The first cargo of pit coal was carried downstream in 1570 and this quickly became an important cargo which endured until the end of the sailing Trow trade in the 1930s. During the sixteenth century coal began to be increasingly used for domestic heating and cooking instead of wood, as formerly, which greatly increased carriage on the Severn and later also on the associated waterways, as well as from south Wales, across the Bristol Channel. This early Trow trade was increased by a decree prohibiting the use of wood for other than firing for smelting iron, which was then emerging as an important industry in counties bordering the upper part of the river.

During the following three hundred years the Trows were a familiar part of the Bristol Channel and the Severn scene. They were built in a variety of types and sizes to carry cargoes not only on the Severn but also on the tributary rivers Wye, the 'Stratford Avon' and the 'Bristol Avon' and also on associated waterways such as the Kennet and Avon Canal, the Thames and Severn Canal, the Stroudwater Canal and the Droitwich Canal. The Trow in its larger form spread to north Somerset on the Bristol Channel, where many were owned in later years at the port of Bridgwater on the river Parrett. By then the more seaworthy Trows were venturing as far west as Milford in south Wales and Bude in north Cornwall, with reputed occasional voyages as far as Scotland and the south coast of England. However, this was at the end of the Trow's development and far from the simple barges which worked the Severn tides in the sixteenth century. There were several types of these, sometimes called Trows but more usually barges or frigates, a puzzling use of this term. There were also smaller craft which were rowed and sometimes sailed and were also often hauled by their crews from the shore. These were called variously 'wherries' or 'flats' but should not be confused with the larger and later craft of those type names from Suffolk and Norfolk and from Lancashire and Cheshire, respectively.

The carrying capacity of the upper river craft was only about 20 tons in the sixteenth century but increased to about 80 by the nineteenth, reflecting the improvements to navigation. The tonnage of the lower river Trows similarly increased from 40 to over 100 tons during the same period. The upper river craft remained bluffer and of shallow draught but those built for the lower river, and later the Bristol Channel trade, developed into a craft which was decked fore and aft and later had side decks and coamings to be suitable for the wider waters of the estuary and for limited coastal sailing. The open hold Trows were vulnerable to swamping by the short seas of the lower river and the estuary and canvas side screens were rigged on each side from early times in way of the open hold, supported on stanchions and laced to a portable rail. This early and primitive protection was only effective against spray but continued in use in modified forms until the end of the sailing Trow. Some craft had portable boards which were shipped in lieu of the side cloths and some had both.

The rig of the Trows went through various stages of evolution. Early craft had a single mast and a square sail. Some of the larger also set a square topsail and by about 1750 some also set a mizzen which might be a lateen sail or a spritsail. Gradually the rig was changed to the gaff sloop or ketch with either a fixed or a running bowsprit. These rigs were the same as those of many coasting vessels of the time. Trows venturing into the estuary and beyond also often set a topsail on main and mizzen and sometimes several jibs and a jib topsail. Trows owned at Bridgwater in Somerset seem to have mainly carried this ketch rig to suit the longer passages and Bristol Channel conditions. It is believed that a few Bridgwater Trows were rigged as schooners. By the end of the seventeenth century the trade of the river Severn was second only to that of the Thames, with Bristol a major city and seaport. The Severn was then navigated for many miles from seaward without locks and thousands of tons of coal were sent annually from collieries in Worcestershire to towns and villages on the lower river and estuary. Much coal was shipped to Bristol along with pig iron, grain, pottery and timber. Trows made a comfortable voyage downstream but had difficulties getting up against the current.

The earliest known and recognisable illustration of a Trow dates from 1712. A panoramic view of Shrewsbury drawn about 1575 shows two, pointed stern, open hold barges having raked stems and a short mast stepped amidships. One is being hauled upstream by four men with a rope to the masthead; a common method. Another drawing of 1581 shows the single mast stepped about one third length aft and a single squaresail is stowed on its cockbilled yard. A drawing of 1750 shows the single squaresail rig continuing in use and fitted with lifts and braces for the yard, and sheets and a forestay, shrouds and backstays for the mast. A short bowsprit is shown and a foresail may have been set but there is no evidence of this in these Trows until much later.

A drawing of 1778 shows a craft of similar form but having a transom stern of deep tuck form, rather higher than the stem and having the fashion timbers carried up above deck to form bollards. The rudder was long and shallow. It hooked upwards at the after end to increase the area of greatest effect when loaded. This craft had a dolly winch mounted on the short foredeck, which enclosed a cuddy entered by a deck hatch. The single mast was stepped in a tabernacle and there was a forestay and several shrouds on each side and also a single backstay. The halyards were led to the sheer at the shrouds. Cargo was sometimes carried as a 'stack' stowed about 4 feet above the sheer. This encumbered the man at the tiller but formed a surer foundation for the weathercloths on each side.

By the early eighteenth century the Trows had spread to the north Somerset coast where many were owned at Bridgwater. Trows were then voyaging as far west as Swansea on the Welsh coast for coal and at the same time the coal trade from the mines of the Forest of Dean, upstream, was increasing and many Trows were built. By 1756 there were over 370 Trows and barges carrying cargo on the Severn and the adjoining waterways and the Bristol Channel.

Limestone became an important freight from the end of the eighteenth century when more intensive farming needed lime to dress the soil and improve the crop yield. Good limestone was dug in south Wales and the low grade coal used to fire the limestone kilns and convert the raw stone into fertiliser was also mined there, so both formed frequent cargoes for Trows, particularly to north Somerset and Devon. Often these cargoes were unloaded on exposed beaches. By then, Trows of various sizes and types were carrying cargoes anywhere between Pool Quay, the head of navigation on the Severn and Milford on the Welsh coast. Trows also lightered cargoes from ships, often from King Road, to Bristol or up to towns along the Severn. Cargoes became more varied and when the Berkeley Ship Canal and other waterways in Shropshire and Worcestershire were constructed, the range of cargoes was extended to cope with the growth of industry.

In canals the Trows were often towed by a horse or a donkey and their masts could be lowered for the bridges and to reduce windage. A reason for the continued use of square rig in Trows into the early nineteenth century was probably the ease of clearing away the sail and its yard to lower the mast in its tabernacle for canal work. It is much more difficult to clear away the spars, sails and running and standing rigging of gaff rigged or spritsail rigged craft. The simple squaresail rig proved especially useful upriver and it was seen on the Severn into the

1890s. A Trow of 27 tons, the *Fame,* was built at Bridgnorth, Shropshire in 1868 and was square rigged. Barges carrying salt from Droitwich also set squaresails in the 1890s and stone barges on the Bristol Avon set them into the early twentieth century.

The Warwickshire Avon has a confluence with the Severn near Tewkesbury and the river was improved for navigation almost to Coventry, at the expense of Sir William Sandys, who did the same for the river Teme from Powick, near Worcester, towards Ludlow, to enable the carriage of coal, iron and wood. This was about 1636. The Avon was soon navigable for 50 ton capacity barges as far as Stratford, with locks and sluices. In 1661 Sandys was preparing a Navigation Act for the rivers Wye and Lugg and by the 1670s the Wye was navigable for small barges to just above Hay, and to Hereford by larger craft. By 1758 the Severn navigation spread 160 miles inland, without locks, and over 100,000 tons of coal were annually carried from upriver collieries at Madeley and Broseley to villages, towns and cities downstream. An article in the *Gentleman's Magazine* also made a distinction between craft then in use on the Severn:

'This traffic is carried on with vessels of two sorts; the lesser kind are called barges and frigates, being from 40–60 ft in length, have a single mast, square sail and carry from 20–40 tons; the Trows or larger vessels, are from 40–80 tons burthen; these have a main and top mast about 80 ft high with square sails, and some have mizzen masts; they are generally from 16 to 20 ft wide (sic) and 60 ft in length being when new and completely rigged worth about £300.'

There were then about 400 craft of these types carrying cargo on the Severn. These were owned mostly at Broseley (87), and at Bridgnorth (Shropshire) (75). Each carried a crew of 3 or 4 men, probably to cope with frequent towing from the banks and for loading and discharge. These early Trow crews had a reputation for pillage and violence and those of the eighteenth century were little better with frequent theft of cargo, fighting and drunkenness. The early navigation of the Severn was often restricted by lack of water in summer or prolonged drought and the Trow crews had spells of enforced idleness. When several Trows were caught grounded in company the crews often roamed the countryside poaching and playing coarse practical jokes on local inhabitants.

Trow men were not regarded as seamen and their food was provided by the owners. They were paid an allowance but nevertheless many pilfered cargoes and their unsavoury reputation only improved when railways threatened to wipe out waterborne cargoes early in the nineteenth century. Later Trow crews were generally hard working men, the captains engaging the crew but having a habit of promoting a son to succeed them in command, which led to discontent and some incompetence. Many Trows working the lower Severn had crews from upriver Gloucester and Stourport. Bridgnorth, on the Severn above Stourport, was another home of Trow sailors and was typical of these inland 'ports', having quays, stables for the towing horses, the house of the river 'Steward' and the yard of Oakes, who built Trows there. Coalport, Jackfield and Shrewsbury were other Trow ports well inland. Most villages on the river Wye had quays where Trows loaded or discharged, and Trows were occasionally built at some of them. Many vessels of various types were built at Chepstow, where good oak and other timber was available from the surrounding countryside. There was also a yard at Brockwier Bridge.

Canals were built linking the Severn with the early industries of the manufacturing midland counties and those further north. In 1789 Bristol merchants were described as 'having all the heavy goods by water from the north of England by Trows'. It was then reported that 103 Trows from 50 to 130 tons were carrying goods to and from Bristol on the river Severn, which seems a realistic number compared with earlier figures which included all the other smaller craft.

In 1771 the canal from Hawford to Droitwich connected the salt mines of the area to waterborne carriage and there were other feeder canals from Shropshire which connected with Coalport. Various proposals for linking the river Thames to the Severn were mooted over the years and this was first accomplished by a canal from Sapperton to Lechlade, opened in 1789. Then the Kennet and Avon Navigation Canal was completed in 1810, linking the Avon from Hanham Lock via Bath, Newbury and Reading, to the Thames. By 1787 the Trow trade was increasing with records such as 'Severn Trows every spring. Bewdley 2 vessels, Berkeley 1, Bridgnorth 2, Broseley 3, Frampton 1, Gloucester 4, Newnham 1, Shrewsbury 2, Stourport 3, Worcester 13, Tewkesbury 2, Upton 4,' and under 'Wye Trows every spring' recorded 'Abbey Tintern 4, Hereford 2, Langards 3, Monmouth 2, Ross and Wilton 1.' Under 'Market boats every tuesday' were 'Caerleon 1, Chepstow 1, Newport 2, St Pierre 1.' Other notes stated 'Bath barges every week' and under 'Constant coasters', which listed down-channel traders, was the 'Stroud Galley, to Stroud (Gloucestershire) every spring.' Trows then voyaged from 'Bristol to Oxford in 7 days (certain), from thence to London in 7 days more'. Freight of heavy goods from Bristol to Oxford was 12 shillings per

ton and to London 35 shillings a ton. Trows carried goods to Brimscombe port or to Stroud 'in 3–4 days (certain)' at 7 shillings per ton. What a picture of activity through a rural countryside.

Trows worked up the Severn as far as Pool Quay, above Shrewsbury. In 1781 the Trows drew from 3 to 4 feet for upriver work and could carry 50 to 60 tons but the river was only usable for ten months of the year as in the summer it had only 12 to 18 in in some places. In winter it flooded, interrupting the towing and forced traffic to stop. During December many Trows brought cargo downstream and during the January markets, fleets of them were lying at Bristol, starting back upstream loaded with salt or cured fish, hopeful of arriving at their ports in time to sell the cargo for the religious fasting of Lent. Often they were delayed by lack of water and the cargoes were spoiled. The completion of the ship canal to Gloucester in 1827 with a depth of 10 ft affected the Trow trade.

The Trow Birmingham, built at Broadoak in 1790 was typical of her time with hull dimensions of 65 ft 3 in length × 14 ft beam × 5 ft 2 in depth of hold. She probably carried about 90 tons of coal. The Heart of Oak, built at Worcester in 1794 was rigged as a ketch and had dimensions of 64 ft 5 in × 14 ft 9 in × 4 ft 9 in depth of hold and was 62 tons Register. The sloop rigged Good Intent was built at Bridgnorth in 1794 and was 65 ft 6 in long × 14 ft 8 in beam × 4 ft 6 in registered depth and 61 tons Register. These were typical dimensions of the Trows at the time and craft of this size were then being built at many places on the Severn up to the limit of navigation at Pool Quay. The Trow Bratina was launched at Bentall, just downstream, in 1785 and at 70 ft 4 in × 8 ft 10 in × 4 ft 7 in and 106 Registered Tons was one of the largest.

Bridgnorth in Shropshire was a principal place for building Trows, from the end of the eighteenth until the end of the nineteenth century and 166 Trows were launched there between 1786 and 1868. Stourport was second with 109 and yards at Bentall, Bower, Broseley and Worcester built between 10 and 20 each at that time. These upriver yards ceased building above Gloucester after 1869. At that time rail transport was gradually reducing the carriage of cargo on canals and rivers, and the railways took trade from Trows which soon ceased working above Stourport and cargoes except for coal, grain and stone were becoming scarce everywhere. The Trowmen clung to the square rig into the nineteenth century. A drawing of 1781 shows a clinker planked hull with an open hold amidships and short forward and after decks with open wood rails around the afterdeck. She had good sheer and the stern was an early type of counter called a 'lute' stern, then common in small seagoing craft. It had a window on each side and the rudder stock was housed in a trunk. The mast was stepped in a tabernacle and was lowered with a stay-fall purchase on the forestay. A main course and a square topsail were carried and the topmast was fidded. The main and topmast shrouds had ratlines on both sides for the crew to go aloft. The topmast stay led to a short bowsprit which had a bobstay, but a foresail was not carried. The braces for the main and topsail were led to the sheer before the helmsman, who steered with a tiller. Similar contemporary illustrations show the mainsail and topsail to have had two rows of reef points. Some similar Trows had two masts, sometimes with a lateen mizzen. This style of Trow appears to have been influenced by contemporary ship practice.

A painting of 1826 showed two masted Trows with a topmast and having a mizzen with a loose footed, stand-ing gaff brailed to the mast. The hull had a transom stern and side cloths are rigged in way of the hold. Heavy anchors were carried at bow catheads and the cables were handled by a handspike windlass. Trows with a gaff sloop rig were built in the early nineteenth century and possibly earlier and probably reflected the developing trade to and from ports in the lower Severn, the Wye and in the Bristol Channel. These craft were perhaps slightly deeper than the earlier river Trows but retained similar length and breadth to work into the same ports. The rig was the usual gaff mainsail, staysail and one or two jibs set to a standing bowsprit. A topsail and a jib topsail could also be set. Ketch rig also soon came into use and eventually these outnumbered the sloops because of the easier handling of the more divided rig, with its smaller mainsail and shorter boom which made work easier for a smaller crew. The ketches set the usual gaff and boom mainsail and mizzen, a staysail, which sometimes had a boomed foot, a jib on a fixed or a running bowsprit, a jib topsail and a gaff top-sail on the main and sometimes also on the mizzen. A few were rigged as a dandy, with a small lug mizzen. When sailing in the Gloucester Canal and similar con-fined waters the boom of the sloops was often unshipped and the mainsail was somehow sheeted home to avoid damaging locks and other canalside structures.

The ownership of the Trows differed in various parts of the area. Many were owned by syndicates of Trow-men and local small businessmen who were usually shopkeepers, farmers or more often merchants. If poss-ible, a local miller was included as a shareholder so that cargoes of grain and flour would be assured for the vessel. Occasionally Trows were built or bought for trade to a certain mill. Many Trows were owned by merchants, manufacturers and millowners. Benjamin

Danks of Stourport, Worcestershire, owned many built of wood and ten of iron, which were constructed between 1843 and 1876. Four were built with open holds and were later fitted with side decks and coamings.

During the nineteenth century the mercantile expansion of Bristol and the south Wales ports coupled with the rise of manufacturing industry and need for greater coal output in the area served by the Severn and its waterways, led to a need for greater carrying capacity afloat. Steam tugs were introduced and one tug could tow three or four laden Trows with reasonable certainty of passage time and for about twice the cost of one sailing Trow passage. Trows began to be forced from some long established upriver trades and many were unrigged by some owners, to become towed barges.

Many sailing Trows found trade in the lower river and the Bristol Channel. For fifty years after the 1860s many Trows carried salt from Droitwich to Gloucester and many new Trows were built for this purpose, to be known amongst the Trowmen as 'Wich barges'. This trade contributed to the building of Sharpness Docks in 1874 so that seagoing vessels could load there. Many old Trows were sold for the stone trade on the river Avon and supplemented those built on the Wye for the trade, and at Honey Street, a Wiltshire village on the Kennet and Avon Canal, a waterway linking the two rivers and then providing a link between the Thames and Bristol. The barge building yard of Robbins, Lane and Pinnegar was established there in 1811, a year after the canal opened. The yard probably drew workmen from the upper Thames as the Trows built there for the stone trade were similar to Thames spritsail barges, probably with modifications to suit local bargemen. The influences of the two types of craft overlapped as Thames- and Medway-owned spritsail barges were built at Bristol and in Wiltshire and Trows were constructed as far east as Aldermaston, in Wiltshire, about as far from salt water as is possible in England. The 25 ton Trow *Black Rock* and the 29 ton *Avon* were launched there in 1855 and 1856.

Navigation of the Wye above Monmouth ceased after a local railway opened in 1855. Wye Trows carried cinders from Lydbrook blast furnaces to the glass bottle works at Bristol and many returned with esparto grass for paper-making at mills near Landogo. As with all shipping, the bulk of a Trow's cargo affected the freight. A typical Wye Trow of that time carried 80–90 tons of timber or 180 tons of coal. After the opening of the Wye Valley Railway in 1873, Brookwier was the highest place to which Trows traded. At this place, far from the sea yet within reach of good timber, a yard built ships up to 500 tons and many barges and small vessels. The larger hulls were floated down the Wye to be fitted out at Chepstow but the trade died out in the 1870s.

During the mid nineteenth century Trows were still being built in numbers and were rigged as sloops or ketches. Several were built with large centreboards to improve windward performance and perhaps increase speed of passage. Although unusual in British commercial craft, centreboards had then long been used in north America in vessels of all sizes. Another improvement of that time was the use of iron dump fastenings for planking Trows and other types of vessels, replacing the wooden treenails used earlier. The centreboards do not seem to have lasted long in the Trow trade. Perhaps the frequent grounding on sand and shingle led to much time being spent unblocking the cases to free jammed boards. More probably the strong conservatism of the Trow owners and crews led to their early abandonment.

Figure 110 The Trow *Ark* of Gloucester built at Framilode in 1871. She was owned at Bridgwater, Somerset when this photo was taken in 1905

By the mid nineteenth century, if not earlier, Trow owners were ordering decked Trows of substantial size, from 60 to 70 ft long. The ketch rigged *Duke of Wellington*, built at Stourport in 1840 had the usual flat bottomed, bluff bowed and transom sterned hull yet voyaged to many ports as far off as Glasgow, in Scotland. She once ran from St Ives in Cornwall, to Oxwich Bay, 120 miles in $14\frac{1}{2}$ hours. The last great trade of the sailing Trows was the carriage of coal and early in the nineteenth century a considerable traffic arose between the Forest of Dean coalfield and north Somerset and north Devon. Trows loaded coal at the village of Bullo, at the head of the estuary and sailed it principally to Bridgwater in Somerset. Many Trows were owned at Bridgwater on the river Parrett and some were built there, for the coal and other trades. In 1847 the Trow *Thory* was launched at Langport but the little 22 ton sloop rigged Trow *Polly* was the first Trow built at Bridgwater, in 1862. The 16 Trows which followed from the town's yards were larger, two being of 75 Registered Tons. The Bridgwater Trows were usually ketch rigged but some experienced the various changes of rig of other contemporary Bristol Channel coasters. Bridgwater Trows often set a mizzen topsail for their work in longer passagemaking. The masts were stepped standing in most and had fixed external keels to improve weatherliness. One had a counter stern and a few were reputedly rigged as schooners.

The ketch rigged Trow *Norah* was typical of many Trows built and owned at Bridgwater during and after the 1850s and was of a relatively seaworthy type. She was built at Bridgwater in 1868 and was of 59 Registered Tons. Her principal dimensions were 74 ft length × 19 ft 10 in beam × 9 ft moulded depth. The transom stern was well shaped, of generous depth and

Figure 111 Lines of the Trow *Norah*. Built at Bridgwater for Bristol
Channel trading

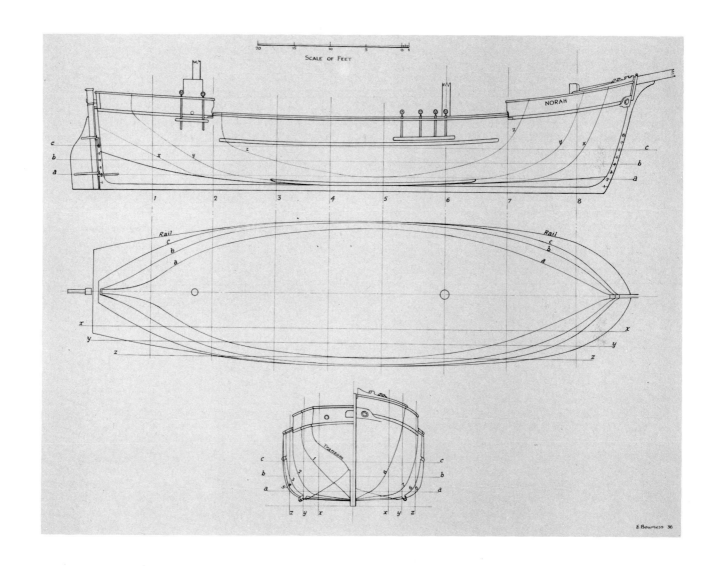

Figure 112 General arrangements of the Trow *Norah*

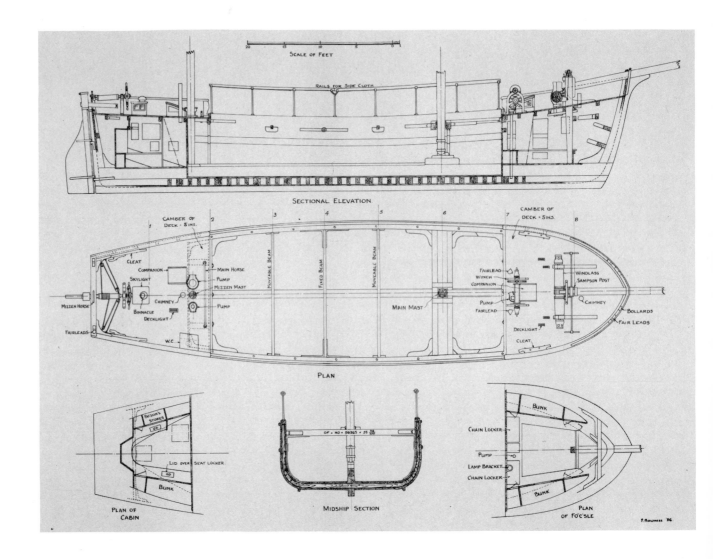

SCALE OF FEET

RAILS FOR SIDE CLOTH

SECTIONAL ELEVATION

CAMBER OF DECK · 5 INS.

CAMBER OF DECK · 5 INS.

CLEAT

COMPANION

SKYLIGHT

MIZZEN HORSE

CHIMNEY

BINNACLE

DECKLIGHT

FAIRLEADS

W.C.

MAIN HORSE

PUMP

MIZZEN MAST

PUMP

PORTABLE BEAM

FIXED BEAM

MOVEABLE BEAM

MAIN MAST

FAIRLEAD

WINCH

COMPANION

PUMP

FAIRLEAD

DECKLIGHT

CLEAT

WINDLASS

SAMPSON POST

CHIMNEY

BOLLARDS

FAIR LEADS

PLAN

PLAN OF CABIN

BO'SUN'S STORES

LID OVER SEAT LOCKER

BUNK

MIDSHIP SECTION

OF · NO · 5035 · 5 · 55

PLAN OF FO'C'SLE

BUNK

CHAIN LOCKER

PUMP

LAMP BRACKET

CHAIN LOCKER

BUNK

had a tuck. The stem had slight rake and the hull had marked sheer forward. The bottom amidships was almost flat and the small bilge radius faired into almost vertical sides. Despite a full deckline forward, the buttocks were sweeping and fair and the waterlines were little distorted. Altogether the *Norah*'s hull was one which would sail reasonably well but would make considerable leeway when going to windward.

The hull arrangements were typical of an open hold Trow. The foredeck ended at the forward transverse bulkhead of the hold and enclosed a fo'c'sle with two berths, chain lockers for the cable and stowages for paints, ropes and spare sails. A wooden barrel windlass and stout pawl post occupied much of the foredeck and a geared hand winch for halyards, warping and cargo handling was placed just forward of the hold opening. The after deck had a hatch and skylight to the after cabin, where the skipper had a berth to starboard, lockers and a table. The coal stove served the dual purpose of heating and cooking for all hands. On deck, the long tiller was in later years replaced by a simple wheel steering gear which had a wooden barrel and rope purchases to a short tiller. Both forward and after decks were enclosed by stout bulwarks but the hold opening, about 40 ft long, stretched from sheer to sheer, protected only by side cloths laced, port and starboard to a wooden rail supported by iron stanchions shipped in the capping at the sheer and laced down to the capping, the bulwarks and the rail. This could easily be cleared away for loading and discharge of cargo but was a crude and vulnerable way of protecting the hold as the cloths would only keep out spray.

Trows were built with sound materials and heavy scantlings, which contributed to their long life, helped by their use in comparatively sheltered waters. Transverse frames and floors were spaced at about 16 in centres and every fifth floor in the *Norah* was doubled. Her keel protruded about 8 in below the carvel bottom planking and was 8 in sided. A keelson about 18 in deep × 10 in siding provided longitudinal strength when loaded aground and helped to resist hogging when afloat. Adequate transverse strength was maintained in way of the hold opening by a pair of heavy beams which supported the mainmast. This was stepped between them, in partners, and the mast heel rested in a chock on the keelson. Heavy lodging knees transferred strains to the gunwales. Two removable and one fixed transverse beams were equally spaced along the hold opening for additional strength.

The ketch rig had the mainmast stepped well aft, allowing a large staysail, which in later years had a boomed foot, which was unusual in British working craft practice. The mainsail and mizzen were gaff sails of the usual pattern, loose footed and with point reefing. A short topmast enabled a yard topsail to be set above the mainsail with a cut typical of the date of build and which does not seem ever to have altered to a taller and more efficient shape as sailing knowledge advanced elsewhere. The jib was set to a traveller on a bowsprit which followed the line of the sheer of the rail and kept the jib from scooping up a Bristol Channel sea.

Like the flats of Lancashire and Cheshire, the Trows do not seem ever to have been fitted with leeboards and relied on a limited ability for windward sailing conferred by the hull's entrance and run and by the strong tides of the area. However, in earlier times some Trows had been fitted with centreboards, as discussed earlier, and many seem to have been equipped with what now seems the impractical device of a removable false keel of wood, which was fitted with lugs on each side and was passed

Figure 113 Sail plan of the Trow *Norah*

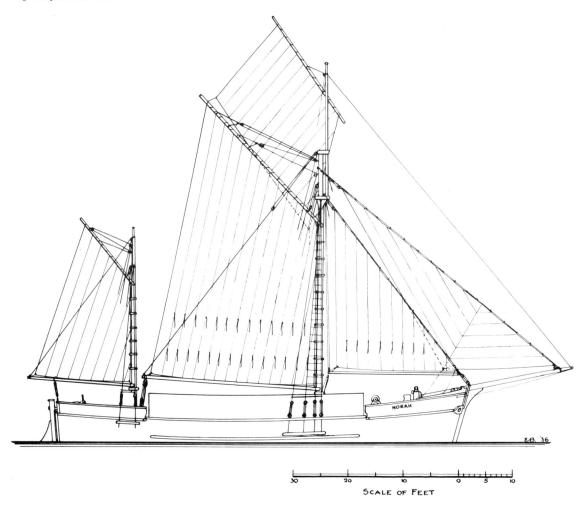

SCALE OF FEET

Figure 114 Stern view of the hull of the Trow *Jonadab*, laid ashore with others in the 1960s to form a breakwater. This shows the typical hull form of the Trow. The *Jonadab* was built at Newport in 1848, was rebuilt in 1895 and was refitted for use as a motor barge in 1948. Photo courtesy A. W. Pyner

under the Trow, afloat, with chains and was somehow guided under the keel until the lugs engaged with the sides of the true keel. Then the upper face of the false keel was drawn to the underside of the keel with the chains, which were set tight. The resulting rounded profile of the false keel, which might be about 35 ft long × 2 ft deep × about 6 in wide would have improved windward performance somewhat on a passage, but how this arrangement worked in practice is difficult to imagine. Presumably the false keel was ballasted to sink, but its positioning must have taken some time and was probably accomplished only with some hard swearing. Similar false keels were fitted to some Norfolk wherries.

Trows which navigated the lower reaches of the Severn and the tide-racked and often rough Bristol Channel, became decked in various ways. Those known as 'box Trows' had side decks of 'waterways' joining the forward and afterdecks in way of the hold, many with coamings around the hatch opening. The resulting hatch opening often did not have wooden covers and then only a tarpaulin was stretched over it, supported on a ridge pole. The 'half box Trow' had the bulwarks built up in way of the hold and the hatch coaming built across the forward and after ends of the hold to the bulwark height, but usually omitting the side decks and any coamings. Side cloths were often retained in these craft and were rigged for protection as in the open hold Trow *Norah*.

Cargoes for the Trows changed with trade and, in the late nineteenth and early twentieth century, many Trows carried coal from Barry in south Wales and other south Wales ports across the Bristol Channel to ports on the opposite shore and elsewhere. Some carried roadstone from quarries at Chepstow on the Wye to Frampton on Severn and bricks from Littleton Wharf. There were cargoes of flour from Tewkesbury to Cardiff and often a cargo from there, and grain to mills at Avonmouth Docks. Trows were then still trading upstream as far as Stourport and occasionally even to Shrewsbury. Large Trows were occasionally sailing beyond the Bristol Channel, to west coast of England ports, to the east coast of Ireland and sometimes to the English Channel coast. The ketch rigged Trow *Topsham*, launched as the *Oliver* at Hempstead, Gloucester in 1871 as an open hold Trow of 63 Registered Tons, was decked and sold to owners at Topsham, south Devon. She occasionally

Figure 115 Bow view of the hull of the Trow *Jonadab*

carried cargoes from Cornwall to Antwerp during the 1920s, having been decked and fitted with coamings and hatch closing arrangements.

However, the usual sea limits for Trows were from Bude in north Cornwall or Milford in south Wales. During the 1890s it appears that the Board of Trade Marine Department prohibited their sailing west of a line from Watchet in Somerset to Barry in south Wales. This probably did not apply to decked Trows with proper hatch arrangements, but several of the more traditional type had then recently been lost by swamping,

which is not surprising with their hold and deck arrangements.

Many of the later Trows were built and repaired at small yards, including those at Epney, Lydney, Framilode, Chepstow and at the Bower Yard at Shrewsbury. The Trow *William,* built at Bower in 1809 was still trading until her loss in 1939 and retained much of her original framing. The last yard which built and repaired Trows was at Saul in Gloucestershire and the last Trow launched there was the *Monarch* in 1900. She was probably the largest Trow ever built, with dimensions of 80 ft 10 in length × 20 ft 6 in beam × 6 ft 9 in depth. She was decked in way of the hold and had hatch coamings.

By 1900 opportunity for the Trows was declining fast and the wider use of towed barges in the river Severn was hastening their extinction. The Bristol Channel coal trade, roadstone and grain and flour cargoes became staples, sometimes with limited coastal passages involved. Some were lengthened to increase capacity and most were competing with the many ketches and small schooners from west country ports, all seeking cargo in a shrinking market for sailing vessels. However, other craft joined the fleet at times and included the Dutch built *Twee Gezusters* and *Arendina,* the Belgian built *Mouzin* and the Danish *Interressenskabet.* The Lancashire flats *June, Miner, Ocean Child, Ark* and at least one other, of from 43 to 66 Registered Tons, were brought to the area by contractors to carry stone for railway maintenance and were soon regarded as Trows. The *June* was built at Runcorn, Cheshire in 1800 and worked on the Severn and the Avon until broken up in 1939.

The last Trow built was the *Gem,* launched by H. Gardiner at Brimscombe, in Gloucestershire, well inland, in 1904. Her dimensions were 68 ft × 15 ft 6 in

Figure 116 A variety of small cargo vessels at Bridgwater, Somerset, early in the twentieth century. Two ketch rigged Trows lie at the right hand corner of the dock and contrast in size with the east coast ketch barge *Parkend*, built at Ipswich in 1873, moored in the foreground with hatch uncovered

× 4 ft 10 in, to suit the Stroudwater Canal. By the 1920s the trade in grain and agricultural produce was seriously affected by the convenient and ever advancing motor lorry, besides the increasing use of towed barges in the estuary trades. All this caused more Trows to be unrigged to become barges. By 1939 there were only three Trows which were rigged; the *Palace* of Chepstow, built at Brimscombe in 1827; the *Alma* of Gloucester, built there in 1851 and the *William* of Bristol, built at Bower Yard in 1809. These were gone a few years later.

Figure 117 General arrangement, lines, structural section and sail plan of
the iron hulled ketch Trow *Wye*, built at Bristol 1860. The rig is typical
but the stern shape unusual. The larger scale profile shows her mast and
derrick as a lighter in later years

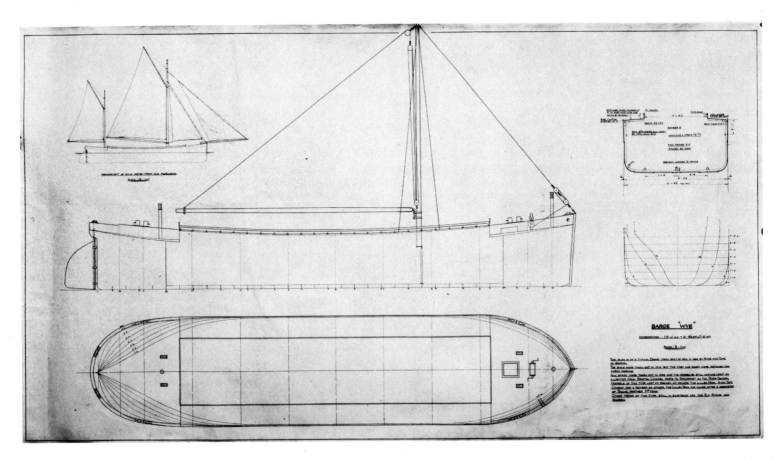

The *Olive Ann* sailed until 1939, when she was condemned. There were then about 100 Trow hulls in use
at the docks of Bristol, Avonmouth, Sharpness and
Gloucester as towed barges. About 42 hulls survived the
war but these were quickly discarded during the 1940s.

The *Hannah* was apparently the last Trow to carry sail,
as a motor ketch in the early 1950s. Several surviving
Trows such as the *Safety* and the *Jonadab* were converted into motor barges towards the end of their useful
lives but were being discarded by the 1960s, usually

being abandoned as breakwaters on the shore at Purton and Lydney. By the late 1960s only the *Hannah* and *Spry* were afloat as hulks and the Severn trade was left to new generations of powerful steel motor barges carrying tanked and dry cargoes.

Since then the hull of the Trow *Spry* of Gloucester has been restored for preservation. She was built in 1894 by William Hand of Chepstow for William Davis, a stone merchant, was launched as a sloop and Registered as of 36 tons. The *Spry* continued in the stone trade until Davis died in 1910 when, with his other Trows *Nelly* and *Eliza*, she was sold to Bristol owners and was re-rigged as a ketch in 1913. In 1923 she was sold to Gloucester owners and was later converted to a towing barge. In 1950 the *Spry* was used as a floating workshop in Diglis Basin at Worcester and eventually sank there.

She is a typical example of a Trow's fortunes; launched as a sloop, converted to a ketch, then a towed barge and finally serving a useful purpose in old age. The *Severn Trow Preservation Society* was formed and in 1977 decided to raise the *Spry* and restore her. Work commenced at Diglis to preserve the last sailing Trow.

15

The sailing flats of Lancashire and Cheshire

The river Mersey and its tributary the Weaver form the boundary between the counties of Lancashire and Cheshire and were probably arteries of trade from medieval times. Their importance for navigation was increased by improvements during the early eighteenth century, mainly directed at trade for the salt producing towns of Cheshire, the coalfields of St Helens and elsewhere, and the textile manufacturers of the city of Manchester. By the mid eighteenth century rivers, several 'improved rivers' and canals connected the port of Liverpool with industrial areas in Lancashire, Cheshire, Yorkshire and with the midland counties where there were growing industries producing coal, salt, cotton manufactures, stone, bricks, grain, timber and other goods, all of which could then only be carried commercially by water. Sailing, rowed or towed barges called 'flats' evolved as local cargo carriers on the Mersey, the Weaver and the associated waterways, and in larger sizes existed, and were developed, for coastal trading on the north-west coast.

The sailing flats were owned in Lancashire and Cheshire and were familiar on the Mersey and Weaver and the Dee and on local waterways. Larger examples sailed to large and small ports, from the north part of Morecambe Bay in the north to the Menai Straits in the south, besides sometimes venturing across the St Georges Channel to the east coast of Ireland. These sailing barges developed during the late eighteenth century and flourished into the 1890s, when steam flats and towed flats began to seriously take their trade. Although much of the flats trade was connected with the port of Liverpool, and the large manufacturing towns on waterways, they were mainly built, owned and manned from waterside towns and villages on the rivers and navigation canals and particularly from the river Weaver.

Development of the river flats was closely linked with that of the various local canals which served manufacturing industry. In 1720 an Act of Parliament was passed for the deepening and improvement of the river Weaver, winding inland into the county of Cheshire, from Frodsham Bridge to Winsford, a salt mining area. In the early days the river Weaver was shallow and the first improvement deepened it to about 4 ft, which allowed cargoes of salt to leave from Northwich and Winsford, bound for Liverpool.

A few years later the Act for the St Helens Canal was passed. This was to run from the river Mersey at the mouth of the Sankey Brook, to the manufacturing town of St Helens, in Lancashire, with later extensions to Fiddlers Ferry. In 1830 another Act gave power to

Figure 118 A typical flat under sail in the river Mersey, 1892. Note the heavily roached foot of the staysail and lack of leeboards

extend a link to the town of Widnes. The Sankey Brook Navigation was one of the earliest canals built in England. It enabled large quantities of coal from the mines near St Helens to be carried to saltworks on the river Weaver and to other places. It was later renamed the St Helens Canal and was taken over by the London and North Western Railway in 1864. Inevitably the coal traffic was gradually transferred to the railway but as chemical factories were established in the area, the canal trade continued and in 1900 it was still carrying 300,000 tons annually. It closed in 1963.

The city of Manchester was a growing industrial centre early in the eighteenth century and efforts were made to improve water carriage of raw materials and goods by the river Mersey and the river Irwell. An Act was passed in 1721 to make these rivers fully navigable but it seems the route was not open until 1736. At Worsley, extensive coal mines owned by the Duke of Bridgewater were linked to Manchester by the Bridgewater Canal which was carried on an aqueduct at Barton over the Mersey and Irwell Canal.

All this activity led to considerable building of flats. For a century after these schemes the Mersey and the Weaver flats were small; about 40 to 50 ft long and about 12 to 14 ft beam. Most appear to have continued to set a simple squaresail on a mast just forward of amidships, were flat bottomed and do not seem to have had leeboards. Some possibly set a topsail above the squaresail in the manner of the keels of Lincolnshire and Yorkshire. Drawings of such craft appear in a 1778 view of Liverpool. These craft carried perhaps up to 50 tons of cargo and it is doubtful that they ever ventured below the lower part of the river Mersey, which is notorious for its swift tides and rough conditions in strong winds. These flats were built in large numbers

and if possible sailed in the narrow canals, otherwise they were hauled by horses.

After the Napoleonic wars the trade of the port of Liverpool increased rapidly and many more flats were built. The closer winded fore and aft rig had replaced the squaresail and although most were rigged as a gaff sloop, some set a spritsail and foresail rig. However, the spritsail did not become popular in the flats. The size of these flats was governed by the locks of the river Weaver which accepted craft up to 68 ft × 16 ft 9 in beam and 4 ft 6 in draught. As much as possible had to be carried on these dimensions. The Mersey and Irwell locks would accept a beam up to 17 ft 6 in. With these restrictions and economic pressures the old pointed stern was replaced by a transom, which increased capacity aft and became a typical feature of new sailing flats for some time after the end of the eighteenth century.

After about 1830 many improvements were made in the canals; wider locks and deeper channels allowed larger craft to use them and the river Weaver was much improved. By then the flat had emerged as a carvel planked, flat bottomed, rectangular sectioned and bluff bowed sailing barge, without leeboards and having a small radius of bilge. A chine was not used despite its apparent advantages of cheaper construction, probably because of the likely damage these would receive from the frequent groundings in strong tideways on hard sand bottom and also in the canals. The rig had developed to a sloop having a high peaked gaff mainsail with a long gaff, a loose-footed mainsail with a boom reaching to the transom or the pointed stern, which had again become used in flats which were built for use in the river Mersey and coastwise.

The flats increased in size for river and coastal work as far as was possible for using the locks on various

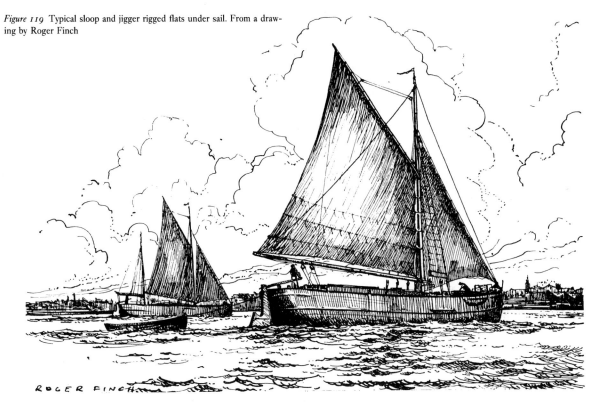

Figure 119 Typical sloop and jigger rigged flats under sail. From a drawing by Roger Finch

canals. At the same time the unrigged, towed lighter type of flat increased in size and numbers. These were towed by horses, later by steam flats and tugs and in the canals often by their crew and other men.

By the early 1820s, and probably long before, flats were coasting to ports on the coasts of Lancashire, Cumberland and Wales, occasionally to eastern Irish ports, and to the Bristol Channel in a few instances, where some are believed to have been sold to local owners. Many early coasting flats were built and owned on the Welsh shore of the river Dee; a shallow, sandy river on which several small ports supported coastal ships, including ketches and schooners and cutter- and ketch-rigged flats, which were much used to carry stone from quarries and coal from Welsh mines to Liverpool and elsewhere on the Mersey.

During the late eighteenth century and up to about 1820, numbers of two masted vessels having flat characteristics were built on the Mersey and the river Weaver for coastal trade and were known as 'Galliots'. These may have developed into the ketch rigged 'jigger' flat, so named for the small mizzen, which was a term borrowed and wrongly so, corrupted from the square rigger terminology for a mast abaft a mizzen.

Over 300 flats were working by the mid nineteenth century, a number which remained fairly constant for many years. Of these the sailing flats were almost all engaged in carrying cargoes to or from the docks at Liverpool, Birkenhead and wharves in the river Mersey and its tributaries. They also worked as tenders to ships carrying bunker coal and ballast of sand or gravel for sailing ships. Some of this work was also done with dumb flats towed by tugs or steam flats, which appeared about 1850. Many dumb flats were owned by coal carrying companies and the *Mossdale*, built for the Shropshire Union Canal Co. in about 1870, was used principally between Liverpool and Ellesmere Port in Cheshire, a typical employment. She is preserved at the canal boat museum at Ellesmere Port.

The river and canal flats generally had a transom stern rather than the pointed one of the coastal flats. Many were built and used on the St Helens, Bridgewater, Bury and Bolton, Manchester, Leeds and Liverpool, Rochdale and the Lancaster canals, also on the Shropshire Union Canal, though of course most of these craft did not use sails.

In the late nineteenth century the sailing flats were finally developed as a type. Generally the flat had a flat bottom, a shaped bow, a transom or a pointed stern and a small bilge radius amidships. The entry and run were of limited length because of the long parallel middle body which enabled them to carry the maximum amount of cargo on the dimensions. However, within the limiting dimensions the ends were as shapely as possible, and often a little hollow was worked into the forefoot to assist when sailing to windward. Some flats of the eighteenth and early nineteenth centuries were built with transom sterns and by 1800 typical dimensions were 66 ft length × 15 ft × 4 ft 6 in draught, in the larger sizes. The pointed sterned flats were usually from 80 to 90 ft long × 19 to 21 ft beam and from 8 ft 6 in to 9 ft 6 in depth of hull. The building of these larger flats increased in the 1860s when the manufacturing potential of the area demanded considerable carrying capacity afloat.

For some reason flats do not seem ever to have been fitted with leeboards, which would have helped windward performance by reducing leeway and by aiding steering on other points of sailing or when being towed. However, probably the owners considered that as a flat could hardly sail over a foul tide in the Mersey, leeboards were not worth the expense and trouble, particularly with the danger of damage when frequently lying alongside ships and dock walls in strong tides and rough water. A loaded flat had a fair chance of beating to windward with a fair tide but would only reach or run over a foul one. The hull construction was strong and mainly of oak, planked on sawn frames, floors and keel, above which was a keelson which might be 24 in high. The deck was softwood on oak beams and was arranged with narrow side and short forward and after decks and a deck between the coamings of the fore and main hatches. Some flats had only one large hatch.

Carvel planking appears to have been used from at least the mid eighteenth century, and probably earlier. The keel protruded only a few inches below the bottom

Figure 120 A flat with reefed mainsail preparing to anchor or enter a dock on the Mersey

planking to avoid grounding damage when setting across hard sands in a tideway, and the keelson provided much longitudinal strength. In small flats this was often of 12 in square section and in larger was often built from two pieces as a keelson and a rider. Some flat builders fitted a hog to take the garboard fastenings, which seems good practice with the frequent grounding. Others relied on a rebated keel. The transverse frames were spaced about 16 in centre to centre and were double with a shift of butts for strength. The forward and after frames were usually canted to reduce bevel on the faces. Many flats had the four or five bilge strakes shaped from 4 in thick Canadian Rock Elm to achieve the bending and to resist wear. The decks were usually of Columbian Pine but some were of pitch pine.

The mast was stepped abaft the small forehatch and abaft the mast the main hatchway opening and its coamings took up most of the deck space. A strong-beam was fitted at mid-length of the main hatch and it had the usual wooden hatch covers and tarpaulin cloths which were secured to the coamings with battens and wedges for rough weather sailing. The heavily cambered hatch covers spanned the hold opening from coaming to coaming and were stacked at each end of the hatch when unshipped for loading or discharge. A low footrail ran around the deck and wooden stanchions supporting a rail were often fitted around the after end as some protection for the helmsman and crew in rough water. River and estuary flats had various arrangements of open rails and only those regularly making coastal or short sea passages had bulwarks. Many river flats had a stern rail and a short portable rail on each side in way of the mast. Others had a rail from the quarters to the mast.

Until the mid nineteenth century a simple barrel windlass was worked by handspikes. Later the windlass varied in arrangement and was often a double handled, geared type with a wooden barrel between substantial posts with a centre pawl and ratchet. Above this up to four hand cranked barrels might be mounted for warping ship and for heaving up the mast if lowered. Sometimes the main barrel was worked by a system of gearing from one of the upper barrels. The windlass had no brake and no gypsy, just a barrel around which three turns of the anchor cable were taken, as in many contemporary small coasting and fishing craft. Thirty fathoms of chain cable were usually carried and an anchor of about 900 lb weight. The cable was carried flaked on deck abaft the windlass and the anchor was hove up at the bow, the weight of its crown being taken by a devil's claw in the cable at the hawse. Some flats had a cast iron windlass with a chain gipsy and a warping drum for the considerable warping which had to be done in locks and docks. Then the cable was held clear of the windlass by hooks. Several timber heads were let through the deck forward and aft as bollards and were often fitted with a horizontal bar driven through them to prevent ropes lifting and for catching a turn when entering a lock or going alongside. Heavy rope fenders were hung from these when in port or against a ship. The rudder was of strong construction to withstand use in confined places and the pintle was a rod passing through gudgeons on sternpost and rudder. The tiller was long and had relieving tackles to aid the helmsman under sail or when being towed in a tideway.

The sloop rigged flat had a loose footed gaff mainsail with a short luff and a long gaff; a shape used in the mainsails of the Lancashire and north Wales fishing craft. The staysail was relatively small and was often cut with a pronounced roach in the foot, rather as that of an Essex or Kent sailing barge. The crew of two managed the cumbersome gaff rig which, even when arranged as a ketch, which might carry three hands, had a fair sized mainsail for the men to hoist and reef in some conditions.

The single headsail gaff sloop, the gaff cutter and the gaff ketch, with or without a bowsprit, were the rigs of the flats. Until about 1870 many of the larger flats had a cutter rig, but the large mainsail and the small crew encouraged a change to ketch rig, which was probably first fitted to the flats working up to Morecambe Bay, the Welsh coast or across to Ireland. In sloops and cutters the mast was stepped about one third of the length from the stem and was about 15 in diameter at the heel. Many sloop rigged flats had the mast stepped through the deck on to the keelson.

Flats built for much canal work usually had one long hatch. The mast was arranged for lowering and stepped in a wooden tabernacle formed by two stout cheek pieces set on the keelson and against the forward coaming of the hatch. With this arrangement the mast could only be lowered when the cargo was clear of it and when the hatch covers were removed. It seems to have been a primitive method and its use was not widespread. Towards the end of the nineteenth century fixed masts became almost universal as the flats were seldom taken into canals, which were mainly worked by dumb flats and tugs, in the form of steam flats. Many masts were made of pitch pine (Georgia Pine or yellow pine) and the masthead was painted in various colours. Masts were lowered with an eight-fold purchase tackle. Sloop rigged flats had three shrouds on each side set up with deadeyes and lanyards. The jigger rigged flats often had four (sometimes three) on the mainmast and two on the jigger.

Most estuary and coastwise flats did little work in canals or under dock bridges and did not usually have a stay fall tackle to lower the mast, if in a tabernacle. If necessary a tackle was rigged. In some cases the rope forestay was replaced with an iron bar but the foretopmast stay remained of wire rope. Sails were of flax canvas, sometimes white but often tanned with cutch. The mainsail halyards were handled by small winches mounted on the sides of the tabernacle. That to port was usually for the throat halyard and the starboard one for the peak and the foresail halyard. These were needed to hoist the large mainsail and its heavy gaff, which was hard work for a crew of two men, sometimes with a boy on board to help. Some flats had chain peak halyards leading from a span on the gaff, through a block at the masthead and down to a purchase led to the winch on the tabernacle. Others had the usual arrangement of blocks on the gaff and at the masthead, with a purchase at the lower end of the fall. Some flats also had a chain throat halyard.

The staysail of the sloop- or cutter-rigged flat was fairly large and was sheeted to an iron horse across the foredeck or to a wire rope shackled to eyebolts in the covering boards. A bowline was used when tacking to get the head round and this needed tending when coming about. For some reason the flatmen called a sheet horse a 'transom', which defies logical explanation.

Flats came about relatively quickly when unladen but were sluggish when loaded. The mainsheet was rove through a block on the boom, through another on an eyebolt on the after coaming of the main hatch, then up to a block on the boom and the fall to a cleat mounted on the heavy wooden barrel of a pump on the centreline aft. A metal horse protected the rudder head from being fouled.

Jigger flats often set a jib topsail when reaching or

running. This was hanked to a topmast forestay and almost filled the area between it and the luff of the staysail. Cutter rigged flats carried a bowsprit on which the jib set on a traveller. It is believed that some coasting, jigger-rigged flats also carried a bowsprit and jib.

The blocks in flats were of large sheave diameter and shell size for ease of working. In calms or in docks sweeps were used to move a flat for short distances. The accommodation aft was for two and was entered by a sliding hatch. If a third man or a boy was carried he berthed in the fo'c'sle. The after cabin had a bunk for the skipper and a locker top on which the mate slept, also lockers, cupboards and a stove on which meals could be cooked. Forward, the third hand spread his mattress on a locker top and shared the small, dark space with vegetables, stores, ropes, spare gear and sails. Fresh water was carried in a barrel on deck chocks. A small cock boat was towed as tender. This was much used for running off lines and also to lay out a kedge, often in turbulent water. The cock boats were about 16 ft long and were carvel planked on sawn frames, making them heavy but strong, to resist damage in locks or canals or when alongside the flat. The boat was usually towed on the starboard quarter and probably affected the helm of the flat under sail.

The crews of the flats were frequently from small villages and towns up the river Weaver, the St Helens Canal and the upper Mersey. Many came from Northwich, Runcorn, Warrington, Widnes and Winsford. They were from families which had owned and sailed flats for many years. Others were men of varied origins and some had served in deep-water sailing ships. The flatmen had a hard life, working in an area subject to strong tides and the more open waters some of which could be

rough. Passagemaking required keeping watches at night, particularly when sailing up the Lancashire and Cumberland coasts, across the St Georges Channel and to the river Dee and north Wales. Though river flats were usually sailed by two men the coasting flats carried three in accordance with Board of Trade requirements and the master had to have a certificate of competence. Flatmen were competent seamen in their own waters. It was said that a sailor could be made of a flatman but not a flatman from a sailor. One who had sailed in them and went on to become master of large ships wrote:

'It was marvellous to see them make the locks, especially the Canada dock lock (in Liverpool) in a stiff north-west breeze and bring up all standing without an anchor – just the turn of a line here and there on different timberheads. Going up the Mersey the soundings were by pole, with three signals: "Coming up", "More on it" and "Lost it". If you grounded, silt formed on the lee side to within a foot of the deck and then you had to wait to float over it. The flatmen scorned the use of steam, and hand-winched their flats through the dock; the master could be and was generally an old man but the mate had to be young and active.'

The river flatmen had little knowledge of navigation, though excellent men in their own waters. In about 1900 the Northwich Carrying Co. bought some small coasters to extend their previous river Mersey and river Weaver trade to bring tarmac from Penmaenmawr in north Wales to the river Mersey. Their skippers had never been outside the Rock Light so they engaged pilots for a few trips to provide experience and particularly to enable them to find the entrance of the Queens or the Horse

Channel from the Great Ormes Head. One of the skippers, who had made his first trip without aid of a pilot was in the pub at Widnes being asked how he had managed. 'Nowt to it lad', he said, throwing out his chest, 'Tha needn't be particular to a handful of points. Let her go as much one way as t'other and tha'll mak as good a fetch as most of em!'

Gradually two types of sailing flat emerged; those for coasting and estuary use and others for working the river and adjoining canals. The first type were the largest in size and many were rigged as ketches, but this group also included many 'single masters', as the sloop rigged flats were known locally. The river flats were almost all sloops and were of a fuller hull form than the coasters to gain maximum capacity on the dimensions. The larger flats could carry 200 tons on about 9 ft draught in the smooth water of the river. They were limited to 175 tons when coasting. The size, rig and general arrangements of the rigged flats were similar to those of the Humber sloops described in Chapter 10.

Flats were owned by chemical works, collieries, salt producers, soap manufacturers, bunkering firms, builders' merchants, explosives manufacturers, small shipping companies and some by their skippers. A variety of cargoes were carried. Coal and salt were always staples but others included glass, timber, grain, limestone, sand, ores, slates, building stone, bricks, roadstone, and various manufactured products. Salt-making in Cheshire was the foundation of much of the river and estuary flats heyday. The many saltworks needed much coal for fuel and there was a large coal-field around St Helens in Lancashire, across the river Mersey. Attempts were made to link the two by improving the navigation of the river Weaver to Winsford and Northwich and by constructing a canal from the river

Mersey to St Helens. When these works were completed there was a considerable increase in trade for flats with coal up the Weaver and salt outward for Liverpool, which remained the distribution centre for the salt trade into the twentieth century, a time when it was being shipped all over the world.

As well as the expanding manufacture of salt, other industries grew along the Weaver; ironworking, small shipbuilding and engineering. Several European salt-makers arrived in the area and one, a German named Hermann Falk, had interests in many local businesses and was largely instrumental in having steam propelled flats built. He also owned a number of sailing and towed flats. Brunner and Mond were Swiss and German respectively and set up a firm manufacturing soda ash at Northwich. This was even more successful than saltmaking and provided many cargoes for flats. Another two Germans, Castner and Kneller started the manufacture of caustic soda at Weston Point and needed coal for their generators and boilers, so a further fleet of flats was needed. Across the narrow river Mersey from Runcorn is the town of Widnes, where many chemical firms were sited. Some combined with Castner–Kneller to form the United Alkali Company which also had a works at Fleetwood, up the Lancashire coast and owned many flats which were mainly of the large coastal type. These lingered in trade until the early 1930s, some being fitted with auxiliary motors. These firms were some of the principal constituents of the large combine forming Imperial Chemical Industries.

Soapmaking came to the area soon after the expansion of saltmaking and soda ash. Many flats were used to carry coal and other materials for this industry. The last few sailing flats were mainly employed carrying coal from Point of Ayr in north Wales to Bromborough

Dock, for Lever Brothers' soap-making plant. Another large industry began to grow at the end of the eighteenth century when cotton manufacturing, particularly in the Manchester area, was boosted by power-driven machinery which needed coal for its boilers. So more work for flats resulted, as well as for canal craft. Raw cotton was brought upstream from ships unloading at Liverpool and products were taken down to the port for shipment abroad.

So the flats found most of their cargoes in coal for factories, for ships' bunkers, for domestic use and for many industries in the area. However, there was competition from rail carriage and the building of the Manchester Ship Canal from the river Mersey to Manchester itself brought a radical change in the fortunes of many flats. Traffic on the Bridgewater Canal was immediately affected and declined and the inland water flats suddenly had little need of sails and had a much shorter passage to make.

Carrying sand from dredgers in the Mersey was a long established trade for some river flats. Much of this was taken to Liverpool and sailing flats were still working this trade in the 1930s. One, the *Keskadale*, was the last sailing flat to work, being withdrawn in 1946.

A fleet of flats owned by the United Alkali Co. carried limestone from quarries in north Wales to Fleetwood on the north Lancashire coast, where the firm had a soda manufacturing plant. Return trips were usually made with freights of soda products for Liverpool, where they were exported. Many craft in this fleet were jigger rigged, including the *Santa Rosa, Winifred* and later the *E.K. Muspratt*.

The Liverpool Magazine Co. owned four flats which carried explosives from Garston (Liverpool) to the powder hulks moored off Bromborough and to ships anchored in the 'powder grounds' of the Crosby Channel. The usual precautions against explosion, of no naked lights and non ferrous fittings and fastenings in the flats, were observed.

Flats were built in small yards in the counties of Lancashire and Cheshire. They were constructed at Tranmere, Birkenhead, Warrington, Ellesmere Port, Runcorn, Garston, Fiddlers Ferry, Sankey Bridges, St Helens and beyond the river Mersey and its associated waterways at Chester on the river Dee and at Lytham St Annes on the river Ribble. Several were built at Rhyl on the Welsh shore of the river Dee, including the *Elanor* in 1865 and the *Humber* and *Pilgrim* in 1878. Flats often survived many years' service, such as the *Eccleston*, built in 1815 and still trading in 1918, though she had been rebuilt in 1887. The oldest flats seemed to have been owned by the Mersey Docks and Harbour Board who, before 1914 were working the *Chester*, built there in 1818 and the *Betsey*, built at Liverpool in 1825.

Others were built in Lancashire at Widnes, Woodend, Anstey and Slattocks and in Cheshire at Runcorn, Over and several other places. Many of the sailing flats were built on the Cheshire river Weaver at Winsford and Northwich. Weaver flats were limited in dimensions by lock sizes to 68 ft length × 14 ft beam × 6 ft depth. The family Cross built many at Winsford in the 1860s. W. Cross was proprietor. Later came R. G. Cross and then G. and R. G. Cross. The *Rising Star* launched in 1891 was one of the last flats launched by them. Others included the *Avon* and the *Riversdale* of 1874. They also built many of the steam barges which soon usurped the sailing flat in the salt trade. Also at Winsford, the yard owned by Ann Deakin was busy with flat building during the 1870s. It was later owned by George Deakin. They built some sailing flats and many steam propelled flats, locally known as 'steam packets'. Many of these were for their own carrying business. In 1872 the Deakin yard launched the sailing flat *Lady Delamere* which worked for the Salt Union fleet until the late 1940s as a towing barge but in 1884 was fitted for a time with steam propulsion. In 1880 Hermann Falk, the local industrialist, had built at his yard at Winsford the steel flat *Corona*, probably the earliest constructed in that material and at 89 ft 10 in length and 21 ft beam a large flat. She was still working as a towed barge in the Salt Union fleet in the late 1940s. At Wharton, also on the river Weaver by Winsford, the yard of Dobson also built flats for the salt trade. Verdins and Stubbs, salt merchants at Winsford, had their own building and repair yard there.

Northwich was a centre for building flats and other vessels for many years. The 48 ton *Phoenix* built there in 1792 was still at work almost 100 years later. Several small yards have flourished at Northwich, usually briefly, then closed. The longest lived were W. J. Yarwood and Isaac Pimblott, who ended business in the 1960s and 1970s respectively, leaving a reputation for good work. These yards built many flats, including some large steel ones, but later turned to building small steel ships, tugs and barges. Yarwoods built several towing flats for the Rochdale Canal Co. between 1906 and 1914. These were unusual in being of composite construction with steel frames and wooden hull and deck planking, bolt fastened.

Isaac Pimblott built many flats including the large *Pilot* for T. and J. May and Co. of Liverpool who owned a fleet of coasting craft which were all registered as separate companies. A fine model of their jigger flat *Pilot* is in the collection of the Merseyside Museums. This 103 tonner was still under sail in 1940, aided by an auxiliary engine. She frequently worked to Welsh ports before

1914 and also to Fleetwood. An auxiliary motor was installed in 1925 and she continued in the costal trade into the 1930s, carrying cargoes of fertiliser to Holyhead and to other north Wales ports.

Other Northwich builders were J. Woodcock and J. Thompson and Sons, who built many craft in iron and some of composite construction with steel frames and wooden planking. The *Bertie* and the *Lord Stanley* were iron hulled flats from that yard. Also at Northwich were the yards of William Okell and at Whitton Dock others were built by Gibson. Clare and Ridgeway built flats at Sankey Bridges on the St Helens Canal and as late as 1905 launched the jigger flat *Eustace Carey*.

Several flats were built at Burscough, on the Leeds and Liverpool Canal and others were built at Runcorn, where J. Davis also built schooners and steam propelled craft. At Runcorn, Brundrits yard was bought in 1891 by the Manchester Ship Canal Co. and was afterwards used to repair and maintain their craft. Some flats were built at Rhyl and at Connah's Quay, on the river Dee and at least one at Amlwch on the Isle of Anglesey, where schooners were also built. The flat *Confidence* was built at Danzig in 1860, the only one recorded as being built abroad. For many years she was owned by H. Bramall of Liverpool and later by the Wadsworth Lighterage Co.

During the nineteenth century sailing flats developed as larger coasting barges, while numbers of unrigged flats increased as towed lighters for canal and river use. The sailing flats of large size carried cargoes to the coasts of Wales, Lancashire and what is now Cumbria. Also to the Isle of Man and to the east coast of Ireland, across the often stormy St George's Channel. As flats became increasingly used for local coasting work they were usually built with a round or pointed stern for improved seakeeping. Transoms were rare on the coast.

Figure 121 A ketch rigged or jigger flat lowering her mainsail in a squall.
The mizzen is of almost equal height to the mainmast

About 1882 several larger flats were built of about 80 ft length × 20 ft beam, mainly rigged as ketches, the mizzen mast being known as the 'jigger'. Sometimes many of these set a jib topsail and a yard topsail above the mainsail, which had the low peak of the north-west coast fashion. Most of these larger flats traded out of the Mersey to the rivers Ribble and Wyre to the north and to the river Dee south of the Wirral peninsular, where flats traded to Connah's Quay, where some were owned. Usually flats did not sail further south along the Welsh coast than the Menai Straits ports but at least one, the *Sarah*, traded to Aberdovey. North of the Mersey, flats often worked as far as Lancaster.

The *E.K. Muspratt* was one of the largest flats. She was built for Captain W. Heaps, who also owned the *Herbert* and another flat, mostly working for the United Alkali Co. between Burn Vage, Fleetwood and Liverpool, carrying soda ash. The *E.K. Muspratt* was jigger rigged and had a fairly fine after body, as did several of the larger jigger flats as the length allowed some refinement of form. William Heaps was an enterprising man and like contemporary flat owners Joseph Monks and W. S. Savage, he also built up a fleet of steam coasters. The jigger flats were frequent visitors to the river Dee in their heyday. The *Sarah Latham* was one built and owned there. She was a gaff ketch with the mainmast stepped well aft, a good sheer and ample freeboard and draught. Her masts were stepped on the keelson and the mainsail had roller reefing gear. She had wheel steering and continuous bulwarks of modest height. Connah's Quay saw regular trade by several flats with names ending in *Star* which traded to Liverpool, Mostyn and Flint. The jigger rigged flat *Transit*, sailed by Captain Amos Matshall made many trips to Ireland with coal. She had no bulwarks and was tiller steered and was a wet craft at sea.

In the 1880s quarry owners at Llandulas, north Wales, had four large flats built to carry stone; the *Federation, Protection, Reciprocity* and *Free Trade*. It is believed that all were built with cutter rig, having a bowsprit and jib and, if so, must have been a handful for their crews in coastal sailing. They carried limestone from the quarry to Widnes and usually remained in this trade, though some voyages were made to other places in the area. The master of one of the quartet was asked by his wife if she could make a trip on board in the summer. He told her she could go in the winter to see how the money was earned, then she would be more careful in spending it! These flats were difficult in stays and if beating up the Horse or the Rock Channels, the skippers let them go in towards the ground until they felt the interaction forward, then put the helm down, when, curiously, they came round well. The *Protection* was built at Connah's Quay, that tiny port on the south shore of the river Dee, in 1887, and was Registered at Liverpool. Her dimensions were 73 ft 2 in long × 18 ft 2 in beam × 7 ft 7 in depth of hold. Her full bodied hull could load up to 150 tons and she spent many years carrying stone from the Welsh quarries to Liverpool and Widnes and other places in the area. The cutter rig with a large mainsail and stout bowsprit was heavy work and when deep loaded she was a wet ship. Sometimes in bad weather her crew had to smash away the bulwark planking aft to let the seas run overboard to relieve her. Later she had a Board of Trade loadline. Usually she and her sisters loaded at Penmaenmawr, at a jetty where they dried out and the crews hoped the wind would not blow strongly onshore. Overloading was a common hazard when loading aground and frequently some of the cargo had to be thrown overboard alongside in a hurry to get the hull to lift on the flood.

Some years later the *Protection* was re-rigged as a ketch and so became a jigger flat. By then she was trading from the quarries to Fleetwood in north Lancashire and to Widnes and Runcorn, up the Mersey, with cargoes of limestone and sometimes carrying soda ash from Fleetwood to Liverpool. The *Protection* retained her rig after the First World War and in 1925 was fitted with a 44 hp Kromhout oil engine which in smooth water propelled her at about 7 knots. She also carried slates to Sankey Bridges, an involved trip for her deep draught hull. She was then owned by builders' merchants Clare and Ridgeway of Warrington who used her to carry slates from the Welsh quarries. In 1936 the *Protection* was due for a Board of Trade survey for continuance of her loadline assignment, but probably because of the cost of repairs to meet it, she was laid up at Sankey Bridges until sold in 1937 to Captain S. Kirby of Hale Shoal. He ran her in the river Mersey trades, for which a BOT certificate was not required, until 1948. Until the war started in 1939 the *Protection* was loading grain at Liverpool or Birkenhead for a mill at Frodsham, up the river Mersey to Weston Point, through the ever shifting channel of the upper Mersey, which proved fatal to many flats which grounded and were washed over in the strong tidal scour. After locking in, the *Protection* proceeded up the river to Frodsham, carefully negotiating its narrow and winding channel.

In 1939 and during the war years the *Protection* carried chemicals for the I.C.I. works at Northwich and discharged these to ships at Liverpool, Birkenhead and Manchester. She also carried general cargoes including copper, lead and various ores; a trade to which she was suited, having been strongly built for grounding. Lying in the Canada Dock at Liverpool during the waves of German air raids on the city at Christmas 1940, several incendiary bombs landed on the *Protection*, setting her alight. The crew beat out the flames and kicked the bombs overboard but some went through hatches into the hold. However, these burst the bags of bicarbonate of soda with which she was loaded and the flames were extinguished, saving the ship. In a heavy snowfall that winter her crew arrived at the dock to find the deck full to the bulwarks with snow. They had to dig their way to the cabin hatch and shovel it all overboard before trying to get the halyards cast loose and the sails unstowed from the frozen tyers.

Soon after, the owner decided to unrig the flat and she became a motor barge. The rig was often in the way when loading or discharging and as an auxiliary she was under motor power most of the time and the engine was reliable. So the *Protection* was taken to the Old Quay yard at Runcorn and the masts, spars and sails were lifted out of the last flat to sail on the Mersey and the last one worked by an owner-skipper. She was sold in 1948 to William Adams and Co. of Newport, Monmouthshire for work in the river Severn, carrying stone from quarries at Chepstow, on the tributary river Wye, to river wall work along the banks of the Severn. Her port of Registry was changed to Newport.

Competition by railways and steam flats took much of the carrying trade from sailing flats by the late 1880s and afterwards only the larger sailing flats kept up a steady trade. Some of the smaller flats were sold to suppliers of bunker coal to the large numbers of ships then using the river Mersey. Many ended as hulks. One of these was the pretty little flat *Avon*, built at Winsford in 1868 and the subject of a fine model by a Liverpool lock gate man, which was destroyed when the Liverpool museum collection was bombed during the Second World

Figure 122 Model of the flat *Avon*, built at Winsford on the river Weaver, Cheshire in 1868. She was still afloat in 1930

flats, in some trades. This trend was particularly marked on the river Weaver, which had a sinuous course, was narrow and on which head winds impeded sailing progress considerably. Some sailing flats were converted to steamers and the sails and gear were left ashore. Others were built as 'steam packets' as these craft were whimsically known. Gradually more and more sailing flats were towed in rivers and canals and the process of discarding sail began early in this area. However, early in the twentieth century the sailing flats were still working into the Canning dock at Liverpool, masts, sails and rigging a tracery against the domed bulk of the Harbour Board offices and the twin towers of the Liver Building, symbols of the port's heyday.

The building of flats declined at the end of the 1890s but as late as 1906 the jigger flat *Santa Rosa* was built by Clare and Ridgeway at their yard at Sankey Bridges for the United Alkali Co. Because of restricted launching width Clare and Ridgeway, like most other canal based shipbuilders, had to launch broadside, usually on only three ways, which were sufficient for the small vessels they constructed. The last sailing flat built was launched by Clare and Ridgeway in 1910 for the United Alkali Co. The fender pieces had to be removed from the bridge nearby to get her through.

By 1914 the day of the sailing flats was almost done. When war commenced in 1914 all the sailing flats on the coast were ordered back to Liverpool and by 1916 most had been laid up or were unrigged as being unsuitable for trade in war conditions. There were more than 300 flats at work in 1916 and most were unrigged, including the largest fleet, that of the Liverpool Lighterage Co. By 1920 only a few remained trading under sail. The jigger flats *Pilot* and *Sarah Latham* had auxiliary engines fitted in 1919, followed by some others.

War. The *Avon* was broken up at Tranmere in 1931.

In such an industrial area and in an age when deliveries were increasingly needed on time and often to meet the loading schedule for a ship, sailing flats were gradually replaced by towed flats or by steam propelled

By the early 1930s there were between 20 and 30 flats still working under sail, principally between Widnes and Liverpool but over 150 remained in use as towed lighters. As a small boy in Liverpool during the early 1930s I remember seeing many unrigged wooden flats being towed about the dock entrances and the tideway, but I never saw a flat under sail. In 1939 three flats remained with sails, of which two had auxiliary engines. Shortly before the Second World War the large flat *Herbert*, which had long laid up at Warrington was recommissioned for Richard Abel and Sons, sand and ballast merchants, and was renamed *Keskadale*. She was the last flat to work under sail alone.

PART THREE

American barge types

16

The gundalows and scows of eastern America

The original North American gundalow appears to have been evolved late in the eighteenth century as a pointed stern, shallow draught hull with a flat bottom, a chine and curved side sections. These were used to carry goods and men on lakes and rivers. Some larger gundalows set a single square sail and a few were rigged as sloops or even schooners. These, with shallow draught sloops, scows and flats were used in many parts of New England and Canada before 1800.

Scows were built on the lower Kennebec River, at Woolwich, where early settlers are believed to have used flats and gundalows for transporting goods. Simple river scows were rigged with a single spritsail set on a mast stepped well forward and had short decks or platforms at bow and stern. These were used to carry light goods and for general transport and were common throughout North America during the eighteenth century. At the battle of Brooklyn, in 1776, similar craft were used to save Washington's army.

Wherever possible, river transport was used for carriage of goods in New England before the railroads were laid early in the nineteenth century. Henry Thoreau, philosopher, naturalist and dreamer, mentioned trade by scows and sailing barges in his *Week on the Concord and Merrimac Rivers* published in 1849. The Concord river flows through Sudbury, Concord and Billerica to join the larger river Merrimac at Middlesex, from where the Merrimac runs 35 miles to the sea at Newburyport. Before the railroads spread during the 1840s, scows and canal barges moved quantities of goods on these rivers, to and from the manufacturing towns of the district. These included Lowell, the 'Manchester of America'. The Merrimac was navigable by sizeable vessels for 20 miles upstream and scows, barges and gundalows sailed their cargoes well inland. Concord, about 75 miles from the sea, was reached via sets of locks, making the lower part of the river Concord the earliest canal in north America. Raw materials and imports were carried upstream and products of the many factories from the towns of Haverhill, Lawrence, Lowell, Nashua, Manchester and Concord were brought down to Newburyport for transhipment in seagoing vessels. Perhaps some loaded the fine sand, favoured for building mortar, dug from the beach of Plum Island.

Gundalows have a name of uncertain origin. They were built at Newbury, Salisbury, Amesbury and probably at Haverhill, Bradford, Rowley, Ipswich and Newburyport, where shipbuilding survived long after other yards on the river had given up.

In 1839 Thoreau wrote:

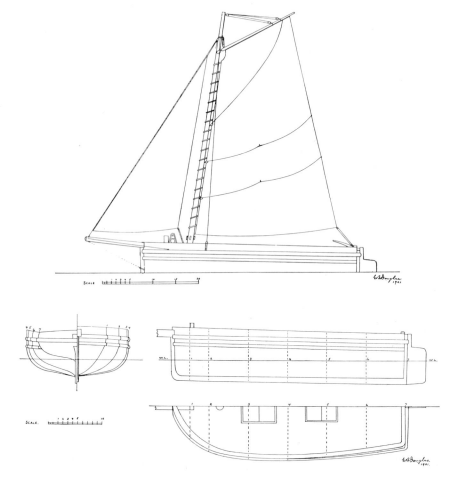

Figure 123 Lines and sail plan of a sailing lighter of New York harbour. Period 1870–1910. Typical dimensions 95 ft × 40 ft × 9 ft draught unladen

'The canal boat is of very simple construction, requiring but little ship-timber, and, as we were told, costs about two hundred dollars. They are managed by two men. In ascending the stream they use poles fourteen or fifteen foot long, pointed with iron, walking about one third the length of the boat from the forward end. Going down, they commonly keep in the middle of the stream, using an oar at each end; or if the wind is favourable they raise their broad sail, and have only to steer. They commonly carry down wood or bricks, fifteen or sixteen cords of wood, and as many thousand bricks, at a time – and bring back stores for the country, consuming two or three days each way between Concord and Charlestown.'

Thoreau gives several pleasant glimpses of the boatmen's life:

' . . . ere long another scow hove in sight, creeping down the river; and hailing it we attached ourselves to its side, and floated back in company, chatting with the boatmen, and obtaining a draught of cooler water from their jug. They appeared to be green hands from far among the hills, who had taken this means to get to the seaboard and see the world . .'.

There was an atmosphere of rustic voyaging on the fresh water of the Concord where the boats sometimes ventured above the town:

'I have seen them in the summer when the stream ran low, mowing the weeds in mid-channel, and with hayer's jests cutting broad swaths in three feet of water, that they might make a passage for their scow . .'.

Below Litchfield he noticed:

'Some carpenters at work here mending a scow on the green and sloping bank. The strokes of their mallets echoed from shore to shore and up and down the river, and their tools gleamed in the sun a quarter of a mile from us, and we realised that boatbuilding was as ancient and honourable an art as agriculture, and that there might be a naval as well as a pastoral life. The whole history of commerce was made manifest in that scow turned bottom upward on the shore. Thus did men begin to go down to the sea in ships.'

At Cromwell's Falls, Thoreau spoke with a canal boat man:

' . . . a brawny New Hampshire man, leaning on his pole, bareheaded and in shirt and trousers only, a rude Apollo of a man, coming down from that "vast uplandish country" to the main; of nameless age, with flaxen hair and vigourous, weather-bleached countenance, in whose wrinkles the sun still lodged, as little touched by the heats and frosts and withering cares of life as a maple of the mountain; an undressed, unkempt, uncivil man, with whom we parleyed awhile . . .'.

In 1849 Thoreau observed:

'Since our voyage the railroad on the bank has been extended, and there is now but little boating on the Merrimac. All kinds of produce and stores were formerly conveyed by water, but now nothing is carried up the stream, and almost wood and bricks alone are carried down, and these are also carried on the railroad. The locks are fast wearing out and soon will be impassable, since the tolls will not pay the expense of repairing them, and so in a few years there will be an end of boating on this river. The boating at present is principally between Merrimac and Lowell, or Hooksett and Manchester. They make two or three trips in a week, according to wind and weather, from Merrimac to Lowell and back, about twenty five miles each way.'

Nevertheless, some scows and gundalows survived on the Merrimac and developed to shapely-hulled 50 to 70 ft sailing barges, having a single leeboard and a unique, single sail rig. The type sailed the river until the end of the nineteenth century and identical gundalows were used on the nearby Piscataqua River, which enters the sea between Portsmouth, New Hampshire and Kittery, Maine. The Piscataqua is a salt water river, flowing inland and dividing New Hampshire from Maine, on its eastern bank. It is wide and tidal to the head of navigation, about 30 miles inland.

The gundalows sailed to and from Portsmouth and Kittery with coal and other cargoes, to Dover and Great Bay, returning with manufactured goods, timber and farm produce. Occasionally one made a voyage along the coast with cargo, in settled weather, perhaps to York, Maine. These shallow hulled sailing barges had shaped ends and an only slightly rounded chine amidships. One leeboard was fitted. The rig was distinctive and was probably adopted from the rig of the shallops brought to the area in colonial times (fig. 125). It had a superficial resemblance to a lateen. A single triangular boomless sail laced to a long yard, the heel of which was slung from a short, stout mast by a chain halyard. The peak of the yard was adjusted by a tackle to its heel, leading to the mast, which made it stand almost vertical when set. The yard could be lowered to pass under low bridges, which was the reason for the rig. A light line led from the after deck to the peak of the yard to enable it to be hauled down. Some gundalows had the heel of the yard weighted to balance it for lowering.

Piscataqua gundalows varied from 60 to 80 ft length. The hulls were heavily constructed from prime timber and usually lasted well. Many were designed and built by their owners. A complete record exists of the shapely gundalow *Fanny M*, built in 1886 by Edward H. Adams at Adams Point, New Hampshire, for his own use. The resourceful Adams, who had designed and built other river craft, made a scale model of his new gundalow and sailed it until he was satisfied with the form and balance, then took off the lines to build the new craft. She was 68 ft 10 in overall × 19 ft 2 in beam × 5 ft depth. The sides had considerable flare and the bottom was slightly cambered athwartships. The bilge amidships had a very slight radius, almost a chine, but the ends of the hull were spoon shaped in section and profile and were well formed. The mast was stepped 13 ft abaft the stem and a stout mooring bitt was set between it and the stem-head, which protruded above the deck in the manner of the old Chebacco boats.

The single leeboard was hung on the port side and had an iron retaining rod to keep it to the side when it was being raised on the windward side. It was hoisted by a single part lift with a simple purchase. She drew 4 ft 6 in with the board raised and the hull draught was 3 ft 2 in. The cargo, often coal, was loaded on deck amidships and was confined by stout and removable box bulkheads, stayed to the deck. The deck in way of the cargo was covered with asphalt to protect the wood planking against the chafe of loading and discharge. The hull

below the box hold was sometimes used to carry cargo, but was entered only by a small hatch abaft the mast, so stowage was difficult and confined to small items, with most cargo carried on deck. The trunk cabin aft housed the crew, which in the larger gundalows was a skipper and one or two men and the inevitable dog. The *Fanny M* was usually sailed by the owner and his wife. Mast height was dictated by clearance below the lowest bridge on the river; for many years that at Great Bay. The mast of the *Fanny M* was 19 ft 2 in above deck and 15 in diameter. The yard was 68 ft 10 in long, 21 in diameter at heel and 6 in at head. The chain halyard led through an 8 in diameter sheave at the masthead but was really a standing lift, made fast to a pin driven through the mast. The lower part of the yard, where slung against the mast, was protected from chafe by battens. The sail was laced to the yard and had an outhaul at the peak, made fast to a cleat on the yard. The sail sheeted to a horse across the top of the trunk cabin, similarly to the main-sheet of a Norfolk wherry. The sail could be furled to the yard by five brails, working through wooden sheaves on the sides of the yard and led to a cleat at its heel. There were also two rows of reef points parallel to the yard, which was lowered to the deck for reefing. The mast to yard heel tackle was led through double blocks at the heel of the yard and the mast, with the fall belayed to a mast cleat. This peaked the yard almost vertical when set. Sometimes the heel of the yard was weighted with a counterbalance and very little of the yard protruded before the mast when the sail was set.

The gundalow rig was arranged to allow quick lowering of the yard to pass bridges on the way up and down river. Gundalows sailed well in river conditions as the tall sail plan caught the breeze above the rivers' hilly banks. They were fast and handy in narrow waters. In calms the crew rowed them with two sweeps worked in thole pins forward of the mast. Railroads and powered craft took away the gundalows, trade by the early twentieth century and most were laid up. The *Fanny M* ended her days abandoned at Dover Point, New Hampshire.

One of the last of the Piscataqua gundalows was built by Chet Hatch in the 1880s but by 1900 she could not pay her way and was laid up. Her owner went ashore to work his father's farm, by the river. Eventually it became his and as the years went by he looked longingly at the glittering tideway from his fields and like many another sailor stranded ashore, wished he could again feel the drive of a hull under sail. About 1928 he decided to design and build for himself another gundalow; a small one for pleasure sailing. He carved a scale model for a 45 footer, 40 ft on the waterline × 15 ft beam and 5 ft 9 in depth, which would draw about 2 ft. He sought suitable timber in nearby forests and two years later had assembled sufficient in a waterside meadow, where the keel blocks were laid. Construction was typical for these craft. The keel was in one length of white oak, 12 in × 14 in section and had a rock maple shoe against chafe. Frames were white oak, 6 in × 6 in section, spaced 10 in centres and the bottom planking was white oak, 4 in thick. The chines were from 12 in square white pine and the side planking was also white pine, 4 in thick. All the planking and the many knees were fastened by 1½ in diameter treenails of white oak. Beams and carlings were 6 in square, with heavy deck clamps and the deck planking was 3 in thick, white pine.

Working mainly alone with simple hand tools: adze, handsaws, augers, chisels, planes, maul and hammers, Chet built the gundalow, which became an object of wonder to river users. After five years' work she was ready to caulk but was never completed by her ageing owner, who had intended to fit two auxiliary engines.

Sloop rigged scows and others rigged as schooners and a few with square sails were in use at the time of the American revolution. Most of these are thought to have used leeboards, as the centreboard or pivoted 'drop keep' was not devised until 1774 by Lieutenant Shuldham, Royal Navy. Although this attracted little attention in Britain, centreboards were to be widely used in America, where the first patent for a pivoted centreboard was granted to Joshua, Henry and Jacocks Swain in 1811. By the 1820s centreboards were in widespread use there in craft of many types. Sailing scows were built in numbers from Nova Scotia to Mexico on the eastern seaboard, on Lake Champlain, the Great Lakes, some inland waterways and rivers and at San Francisco and in Canadian north-west waters.

The term 'scow' appears to derive from the Dutch 'Schouw'; a swim ended craft with bow and stern transoms; really a large form of pram. North American scows differed considerably in size and proportions to suit the intended trade and local conditions. In general all were of light draught and were inexpensively and quickly constructed, sometimes by carpenters with little skill. Most had the basic characteristics of a midship section having a flat bottom, little depth, great beam and flared sides. The ends are swims ending in a small transom and the half breadth of deck line has moderate curvature throughout. Cargo was carried either in a hold or on deck inside portable bulwarks. Some scows had a rounded forward swim, convex in profile. Rig was sloop or two masted schooner and leeboards or a centreboard were fitted.

Economy of construction stemmed from the rectangular hull sections allowing floors, frames and beams to be got out of straight timber. They were also usually easy to plank. The bottom planking was often fitted transversely but in scows built by shipwrights and those built on the coast of the Gulf of Florida it was often longitudinal. Transverse planking allowed shorter lengths to be used but longitudinal planking better withstood shocks of grounding on a hard bottom and was sometimes nailed over a transverse planked bottom. Some were built with transverse bottom camber to withstand drooping at the chines. In these shallow hulls of about 5 ft depth, the sides were an important strength member and the side and bottom planking were of comparable thickness as a result. In Canada some scows were built with clinker planked sides and flat, carvel planked bottoms. Sometimes the side planking was edge fastened with drift bolts for added strength. The side frames were usually butted to the chines in cheaper construction, provided the chines were rockered fore and aft. Other scows had the heel of the frames notched over the chines to resist movement. The chines usually had to be cut to profile from large pieces of timber and were the most expensive items in the structure and one of the most important to resist hogging. The keel was backed by a substantial keelson and was slotted in way of the centreboard case, if a centreboard was fitted. Many were fitted with leeboards, sometimes a single board on one side in preference to widespread use of a centreboard in contemporary craft of round bilge form or in the more soundly built chine hulls.

Leeboards were usually fitted to scows in Maine and the Bay of Fundy area of Canada. Sloops usually had one on each side, schooners frequently only one, possibly because these did not attempt beating to windward so often. The arrangement used in many scows was to hang the leeboard from a chain, passed through the head of the board and set up on a timber head or through a reinforced part of the bulwark, allowing the board to flow out from the windward side before it could be hauled up. Some leeboards were pivoted on heavy bolts through the sheerstrake or the low bulwarks; a bad practice as unless the weather board was hoisted promptly in strong winds, it might be pulled from the side and cause damage to the hull. Most scows with this arrangement had an iron rod strap fitted to resist lateral movement of the board. The leeboard also bore against a horizontal wooden ledge which maintained the board vertical when the scow was upright. Both strap and ledge were close to the light waterline and, as scows were not sailed at large angles of heel, the offset position of the leeboard did not seriously affect windward performance. Most of the leeboards had flat faces but some were shaped with a convex surface on the inboard side, the outboard one being flat. In many, the forward edge of the boards was arranged to be slightly more inboard than the after edge to improve windward efficiency. This angle was maintained by the shape of the ledge. In smaller scows the leeboards were sometimes handled by a single part lift, belayed to a cleat on the deck or bulwark. Larger scows had a purchase and many had an 'arm' at the head of the board, protruding above the deck edge when lowered, to assist in lowering and raising the board to the desired depth.

Most scows had a rudder without a stock, hung on the after end of a budget and turned by a purchase from each quarter, leading to an upright horn at the after upper corner of the rudder blade. The falls of the steering purchases were led inboard through sheaves to the barrel of a steering wheel mounted on 'A' frames on deck. This gear gave sufficient power to steer a scow in strong winds, when part of the rudder might be out of the water. Small scows frequently had stocked rudders with the tiller passing through the stock in the usual way.

The sloop rig, with gaff and boom mainsail, was hoisted with the usual throat and peak halyards. The single headsail, usually termed the jib, was often set on a short bowsprit and its clew came abaft the mast. The headsail sheets were led aft to belay within reach of the helmsman, who could tack the scow single handed in ordinary weather. The mainsail had several rows of reef points as scows needed to be sailed as upright as possible. When the deck edge neared the water the crew reefed quickly, for the range of stability was limited. Some scows were fast in smooth water and strong winds and pointed well to windward, but most were dull sailers in light weather and in calms the crew rowed them with the tide, using long sweeps which were stowed up and down the shrouds when not in use. Some scows were fast and occasionally were surprisingly seaworthy, within their limitations. These craft carried a large sail area for their displacement and some had sweeping lines at chine and deck, resulting in good speed when light. If the bottom profile at the swims was correctly designed, many would almost plane when reaching or running in strong winds and smooth water. The small scows were not suitable for deepwater sailing but larger ones made coastal passages in reasonable weather, when necessary.

Many of the scow sloops used on the rivers and coast of Maine and Nova Scotia were between 35 and 45 ft long, rigged with a single headsail. Larger scows were generally schooner rigged and carried topmasts and topsails. Some also set a jib topsail. These were used for a variety of cargoes and dimensions varied. The smallest often carried firewood, ice, farm crops and supplies and some tended fish weirs along the coast. Larger ones car-ried bricks, stone, timber, hay and ice. Some made coastal passages with these cargoes, many worked mainly in the bays, estuaries and rivers of that magnificent coast.

The boom in the timber trade from Maine between 1820 and 1880 led to the building of many craft to carry the then apparently inexhaustible cutting from the forests along the coast to cities and towns and down the large rivers to load deep water ships awaiting cargoes for abroad. The Penobscot river was the centre of a vast timber trade, much of which was carried in schooners and small square riggers, but many schooner rigged scows were built for trade on the river and for limited coastal voyages. These were intended to have a short life but could carry astonishing quantities of timber. Wood in many forms was shipped from the Penobscot; long lumber, laths, shingles, deals, fence posts, clapboard, ship timber, bark for tanning, box parts and railroad sleepers amongst them. Schooners and scows staggered out of the river deep loaded and jostled at river ports such as Bangor, at the head of Penobscot navigation canal, 24 miles from the sea. At times perhaps 250 vessels crowded the river to load timber.

Scows carried firing wood to limekilns on the river and its bay, particularly to Rockland, a centre of the lime making trade. One of the oldest jokes 'down east' concerns these cheaply built craft. The skipper of a smart coasting schooner hailed the helmsman of a passing scow with 'Where's the other one?'. 'What other one'? Came back. 'Why, the one they turned to and sawed that one off'n'.

Many scows joined in the carriage of baled hay from Penobscot watersides to coastal towns and to Boston. The deck stack needed a man on top to direct the helmsman. However, most of these coastal hay voyages

Figure 124 A two masted schooner rigged cargo scow on Lake Champlain

were made by the more seaworthy but equally laden round bottom schooners. Granite was extensively quarried in Maine after the 1870s and the inhabitants of Chebeaque Island, in Casco Bay, specialised in carrying it with sloops. At first they carried stone ballast for ships building at yards along the coast but as granite ship-ments for public buildings and civil engineering projects in coastal cities increased, so did the size of the Chebeaque Islanders sloops, culminating in one which was the pride of the island with a mainsail of 4,000 sq ft.

Centreboard scows 35–45 ft long were used to tend fish traps in Casco Bay in the 1880s and 90s. Many were built at South Portland, Maine, by shipwrights and were well constructed, with soundly fitting members. Similar but usually smaller sloops and cat rigged scows were used to tend pound nets elsewhere on the Maine coast, around Cape Cod and on the Great Lakes, carrying loads of poles to the fish weirs and driving these into position; however, these do not qualify as barges. Scow sloops about 60 ft long sailed from Quincy, Massachusetts in the stone trade, loaded with granite from local quarries and nicknamed 'square toed frigates'. Many scows were built there and like the sloops were strongly constructed for this arduous trade. Small scows and sloops carried bricks, timber and hay on the rivers of Massachusetts and sometimes made short coastal passages. The Connecticut river scows were about 40 ft long and were sloop rigged with a topsail and sometimes a jib topsail, set to catch a breeze above the wooded shores. A few scows were converted for pleasure sailing in the late nineteenth and early twentieth centuries and one or two were built as yachts, with large cabin tops, which almost made them sailing houseboats. Several craft of this type were used by wildfowlers.

Two-masted schooner scows of considerable size sailed on Lake Champlain, a fine stretch of fresh water between the states of New York and Vermont, on which a good sea can arise in strong winds. Some of these were perhaps 120 ft long and had centreboards. The swim-ended hull had slight sheer, shaped half breadth,

Figure 125 A gundalow with a deck load on the river Merrimac. Note the stump mast and lateen sail with brails

low bulwarks, a trunk cabin top aft over crew accommodation and a gaff and boom foresail and mainsail. The masts had two shrouds on each side and the tall, tapering mastheads allowed topsails to be set above fore and main. A single headsail was set to a stout bowsprit and its foot was spread by a short boom sliding on a horse on top of the bowsprit (fig. 124). These scows carried varied cargoes between ports on this 90 mile long lake. Shorter, relatively deeper hulled sloops also sailed the lake under a tall rig with fidded topmast, but much of their trade was taken by steam tugs towing lighters by the end of the nineteenth century.

Scow sloops and schooners sailed Chesapeake Bay. The sloop *Elsie* was built at Philadelphia, Pennsylvania, in 1874, probably for trade on the river Delaware. She was rebuilt at Harve de Grace on the Chesapeake in 1890 and this was her home port in later years. She remained under sail into the 1940s. Her cargo hold was abaft the mast and had a long, narrow hatch. Accommodation was forward under a trunk top and she steered with a tiller. The *Elsie* carried a topmast and could set a jib headed topsail. She was nimble enough to turn out on workboat race days in the 1930s. Cargoes throughout her long life were probably very varied and might have ranged from watermelons to slag for roadmaking. Scow schooners for commercial shooting of wild duck on the Chesapeake were built at Harve de Grace in the 1880s and the place seems to have been a centre of scow construction and use on the bay.

Scows were used in North and South Carolina and in Louisiana from colonial times. Small, sloop rigged scows carried crops and supplies for the river plantations of the Carolinas. Larger scows, up to 80 ft in length, carried tobacco and cotton crops to southern coastal ports and returned with goods, particularly in the New Orleans area.

After the early nineteenth century, many of these craft were built with a centreboard but the introduction of steamers for freight and passengers, which spread quickly from the western rivers to the southern coast, led to a rapid decline of the large scows after the 1830s. It is difficult to determine the extent of use of these large craft but fig. 126 is drawn from a detailed and accurate illustration of one under sail. The 80 ft long hull had little sheer or freeboard when loaded with cargo, which was carried on deck between 5–6 ft high bulwarks of a box hold which extended from forward of the mast to a stern deckhouse of similar height and width at the stern. A steering shelter was built above this to keep sun and rain off the helmsman. A fixed awning was carried at bulwark height above a shallow forward cockpit which may have been used to seat 6 or 8 slaves who assisted in working the scow and rowed her with sweeps in calms. They probably also slept under the awning. The narrow side decks barely provided working space on each side and the crew also walked on top of the cargo to work the scow. The mainmast of the sloop rig was stepped 20 ft from the stem and a loose footed gaff and boom mainsail was set, with a staysail tacked to the head of the stem, which protruded above deck. A fidded topmast and square topsail were unlikely features of this rig. The mainsail is shown with two rows of reef points and the topsail has one reef, so these scows were sailed in strong winds, though great care would be needed with the low, loaded freeboard. It is possible that some of these craft were built with a shaped bow and swim stern, and the type worked to and from plantations and landings along the coast adjoining New Orleans where there were many shallow semi-protected waters, bayous and inlets.

This coastline stretched along the coasts of northern Florida, Alabama, Mississippi, Louisiana and Texas and

Figure 126 A sloop rigged box scow carrying cargo above deck on the
Mississippi river, early and mid nineteenth century

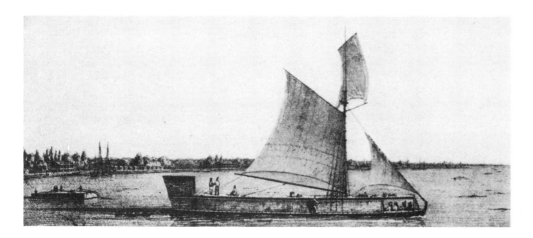

these shallow waters led to the building of many smaller
scows with varying bottom shapes, many having a rise of
floor at the ends, making them shapely examples. These
were built up to about 60 ft but most were 40–50 ft
long. Many sailed the Louisiana coast and westward to
the Mexican border. The hulls had well flared sides and
curving deck and chine lines, sweeping up to shapely
ends. Some were rigged as schooners and a typical craft
was about 50 ft long and known locally as a 'butt
header'. These sailed well in smooth water and were fast
when only partly loaded, like most sailing barges. Quality
of construction varied but a well-built scow of this form
lasted for many years. Similar scows were also built on
the coast of Texas, some having round bilges. Many
chine scows were owned at Houston and sailed cotton
cargoes down the shallow rivers to Galveston for shipment. A typical 40 footer would draw only 9 in with the
centreboard raised. Scows of this type frequented Bayou
St John in New Orleans and some of these affected a
knee or beak head to the stem, which was fitted on the
forward side of the bow transom. They were gone by the
1930s.

17

The scows of San Francisco Bay

The concept of the cargo scow used on the east coast and the inland lakes of North America spread to San Francisco in the mid nineteenth century. San Francisco Bay is the largest harbour on the Pacific coast of the United States. Even at low water it covers 450 square miles of water and has a shore line of about 100 miles. The Bay stretches about 40 miles south-east from the Golden Gate, which channels through the coastal range from the Pacific Ocean and spreads a further 10 miles northwards before merging into San Pablo Bay. Its general width is about 13 miles, with depths up to 36 fathoms. The north end of the bay merges into San Pablo Bay, which connects with Sisun Bay by Carquinez Strait. This shallow water has the rivers Sacramento and San Joaquin leading into its eastern side in a common channel. Sacramento, the head of commercial navigation on that river, is about 100 miles from the Golden Gate and Stockton, on the San Joaquin river, is about 70 miles inland.

The area was little populated until about 1846 and San Francisco Bay appears to have remained undiscovered by Europeans until 1775, when it was charted by a Spanish ship. Until the 1830s the principal settlements on San Francisco Bay were Presidio, overlooking the Golden Gate and at the mission San Francisco de

Asis. Then Englishman William Richardson built a house at Yerba Buena Cove in 1837 and by 1846 this had grown to the hamlet of Yerba Buena. The American flag was raised there by a party from the sloop of war *U.S.S. Portsmouth* in 1846. Shortly after the hamlet was renamed San Francisco and wharves were soon built out into the bay to attract trade. Ships called to load hides and tallow and small craft carrying these commodities from inland watersides used the anchorage.

The discovery of Californian gold in 1848 caused a rush of settlers to the goldfields to prospect and the village was almost deserted for a time. Then came the goldseekers of '49, the clipper ships, the needs of thousands of incomers who swamped the village, which became a town, then a city very quickly, with all the undesirable elements of a place of mushroom growth coupled with the lust for wealth; rocketing prices, labour troubles, overcrowding, extortionate prices, vice and crime.

During the gold rush days of the early 1850s, scores of merchant ships lay off San Francisco, abandoned by their gold-happy crews. In 1857 over 800 vessels lay at Yerba Buena Cove for a time. The surrounding steep hills and tidal marshes were against the development of a major city, but the gold fever and consequent business

Figure 127 Hay scow on San Francisco Bay. A painting by Gideon
Jacques Denny. Courtesy San Francisco Bay Maritime Museum

and population expansion caused an ever increasing flow
of goods to the wharves of the city. Other settlements
were established in many parts of the bays and rivers,
located in those pre-railroad days by navigable water,
however shallow, to allow transport of their produce and
goods to and from San Francisco.

Sailing scows were a practical and inexpensive solu-
tion of local water transport problems posed by the
waterways off San Francisco Bay. Shallow, tidal rivers,

creeks and sloughs which prohibit the use of deep
draught vessels, divided the land and made wheeled
transport impractical. The scow form offered relatively
quick and inexpensive construction with a minimum of
skilled labour with its flat bottom combined with shallow
draught and upright discharge. A centreboard enabled a
blunt ended scow to beat to windward and the short
ends assisted harbour manoeuvring and berthing. Scows
were a major link between the harbour of San Francisco

and the outlying bay area communities. They carried cargoes of grain, hay, potatoes, stone, coal, fruit, farm crops, logs, sawn timber, bark, bricks, salt, fertiliser and other goods. Many scows carried hay in the days of horse transport in the city and this caused them to be termed 'hay scows'. A few ventured along the coast to Alaska or southern California, but these were infrequent and hazardous passages.

Most scows were rigged as two masted schooners with a gaff foresail and mainsail, a single jib and a jib headed topsail set on the main topmast, sometimes on both masts. A main topmast staysail was also often set in light reaching winds. A few were sloop rigged. Size ranged from the *Little Star*, 37 ft × 15 ft to the big *Mono* at 89 ft × 31 ft. Depth of hold varied little, despite length variation and was generally 5 ft or a little more. The 69 ft 10 in *Robbie Hunter* was a typical schooner scow, built at San Francisco in 1870. Her beam of 23 ft 3 in and depth of hold of 5 ft 3 in were typical of the type. The rectangular sections of the parallel middle body swept up in swim ends having a rounded bottom profile, the stem swim being slightly the finer. Her bow transom was plumb but the stern transom raked above the rudder, which was hung on a stout budget. Subtlety of form was in the shape of the swims and the half breadth. The greatest beam was slightly aft of amidships and the hull had a slight sheer. Eighteen inch high bulwarks around the deck merged into coamings for the cabin top which was carried across the full breadth of the hull abaft the mainmast. It was entered by a sliding hatch at the aft end. The bowsprit came inboard between stout bitts on which a geared hand windlass was mounted. A small deck hatch led to the fore peak. The wood centreboard was 26 ft × 5 ft and worked in a wooden case between the masts, extending from keel to deck, dividing the

hatch into two openings, with portable hatch boards over. The centreboard was raised and lowered by a tackle from the main hounds in a schooner and by a purchase on deck in the sloops. Hull construction was heavy with 3 in thick bottom and side planking on 6 in × 6 in floors and side frames, spaced at 18 in centres. There was a 2 in thick hold ceiling. These shallow hulls had considerable tendency to hog and the chine longitudinals were 10 in moulded × 20 in sided to resist deformation, backed by a keelson of 16 in × 18 in section. Deck beams were 8 in × 12 in, lodged on clamps 4 in × 6 in and the deck planking was 3 in thick. The 6 in thick hatch coamings were supported at each corner by a 10 in square stanchion. The centreboard case sides were 5 in thick and the longitudinal strength of the hull was continued aft with an 8 in sided budget, which gave the hull directional stability under sail and supported the rudder.

Most scows had the rudder hung on the aft end of the budget. It was strongly constructed and was moved by two purchases shackled to an iron horn at its after, upper edge. The falls led inboard through sheaves on the transom to the barrel of a steering wheel, giving powerful control to steer these boxy hulls in strong winds, when the rudder became partially ineffective.

Two substantial fenders were fitted around the sides as a scow had to take considerable chafe in her work alongside wharves and shipping. Many scows, such as the 73 ft 8 in *Regeina S* had a smaller trunk cabin top which allowed a second, smaller cargo hatch to be arranged between it and the mainmast. The chain cable led from the chain locker, over the gipsies on each side of the windlass, through fairleads and over wooden catheads on each side of the bow transom. The steamhead was continued as a knee supporting the bowsprit, which had two chain bobstays.

The rig of the *Robbie Hunter* was that of a gaff schooner with a single jib set on a stay to the bowsprit end. It was spread by a boom which pivoted on an iron horse on the upper side of the bowsprit. The jib had one row of reef points and lazyjacks gathered it when lowered. Each mast was supported by two shrouds on each side, set up with deadeyes and lanyards. The gaff foresail and mainsail were cut with little peak in the head of the sails. The mainsail had three rows of reef points and a system of lazyjacks gathered it when lowering. The foresail also had three reefs and a topping lift with a purchase led to the main hounds. Some schooner scows carried a topmast and jib headed topsail on each mast but others had a topmast on the mainmast only. The topsails were not intended to be carried well to windward but were useful on a reach or run, or on inland waters where banks or trees might obstruct the wind. Many scow sails were made by C. J. Hendy and Co. who also supplied chandlery. Scows sailed reasonably well to windward when light. They bubbled along like huge pram dinghies and on a reach or run were fairly lively, providing they had a clean bottom.

Scows were built in many yards around San Francisco Bay. Hunters Point, earlier known as South San Francisco, was a principal centre of scow construction, where Emil Munder and Hans Anderson built, repaired and refitted scows and other small craft. As elsewhere, an owner placed an order on carrying capacity, with a limit of dimensions. Few if any plans were drawn and the type evolved and continued by the experience and skill of the yard owners, or more probably their foremen. Some scows were built by their owners, others by house carpenters. By 1867 many scows were being built and were repaired at 'south beach', where they were drawn up on greasy ways under the shanties on the low cliff, overlooked by the forbidding blocks of St Mary's hospital. J. S. Nichols built at Hunters Point and the 50 ton *Albertine* was one of his best known scows, launched in 1884. Later that year J. Dirks built the *Paul and Willie* at the Point. Emil Munder built the scow schooner *Annie L* there in 1900 and many scows were repaired by Hans Anderson, a Dane who established his yard in 1893. The firm later became Anderson and Christofari.

Scows of considerable size were built at San Francisco in the early 1900s. A few had a shaped bow, including the *Margaret C.* The *Lizzie R* was one of the few scows built with a full poop having crew's quarters below, with stern windows, instead of the usual coach roof, or cabin trunk as Americans call it. The sloop rigged scows, such as the *D.N. Darlington* built in 1900, had the same hull form as the schooners and carried a similar bowsprit on which a single headsail was set without a boomed foot. The mainsail boom and gaff were long and these craft pointed higher than the schooner scows.

Normally scows were handled by a crew of two or three men, sometimes two men and a boy. The owner was often the skipper. They sailed and maintained the scow and helped with loading and discharge. All lived in the cabin aft. Scows sailed during spring, summer and autumn; seasons when the prevailing westerlies gave a fair or reaching wind for sailing most of the local waters. In calms or narrows, with a head wind, where possible, the crew towed the scow from the bank, which they termed 'Jay hawking'. Alternatively, she was warped along with a long line run out from the windlass and made fast to a tree. Sometimes they kedged with an anchor, poled in shallow water with a hard bottom or towed her with the rowing yawl boat carried in stern davits.

In spring the scows were hauled out to have the bottom cleaned and painted and to fit out for the season's work. When re-launched, the owner often had a party on board for the crew, relatives and friends, and made a day of it, perhaps sailing to Paulse Cove in Richardson Bay, a favourite place for picnics and a swim. Occasionally groups of local people chartered a scow for a day's outing.

Scows gathered their cargoes at city wharves and at river landings, at creeks and sloughs where deeper craft such as the conventional round bottomed schooners could not float. The Sacramento and San Joaquin rivers are principal tributaries of upper San Francisco Bay waters and were arteries of waterborne trade. Rail and road transport met at Sacramento and in the 1860s scow schooners were carrying logs there; a cargo 'staged out' over the sides by about one third of the beam to increase carrying capacity in smooth water. Cargoes were discharged alongside a wooden wharf by wooden cranes and the Central Pacific Railroad ran to the town. Many cargoes were brought to and from Sacramento by sloop rigged scows, locally termed 'river sloops', but in early times, at least in 1849, ships and schooners, river steamers and sloops crowded its wharves. The Sacramento river was still then unsilted by the later hydraulic mining upstream and deep water vessels regularly traded there as the upper depot for the prospectors and mines. Broderick, on the opposite bank, was another port for the scows and some were built there in the early 1890s.

After about 1850, scows carried logs and sawn timber from the wharves of Redwood City, on Redwood Creek, at the south-west end of San Francisco Bay. The timber was cut from forests of the coast range and became an important trade of the lower bay in those days of wooden buildings and wood shipbuilding. Scows with deck stacks of timber threaded the narrow creek to the open bay, bound for the lumber yards of San Francisco.

At the turn of the century at Tiburon Cove, inside Angel Island, scows loaded timber alongside a long pier, the big logs rumbling out on flat railroad cars, hauled from the redwood cuttings by pantingly picturesque engines of the San Francisco and North Pacific Railroad. The clapboard cottage houses of Belvedere peeped out amongst trees on the far shore of the cove and the hills beyond Sausalito rose as a backdrop. Others worked into the open marshlands and tidal creeks off San Leandro Bay, where piled wharves and wooden sheds were tucked away on shallow, meandering rills with scows and schooners alongside, reminiscent of the English river Medway area. More creeks led off the bay's southern end, where Alviso landing was the port used by scows, schooners and steamboats. After the railroad arrived, the small vessels continued to load fruit, farm produce and other odd cargoes, but waterborne trade had seriously declined by 1900.

There were many of these little ports, such as Napa, at the head of navigation in the river of that name. It is a sluggish stream, entering San Pablo Bay at Vallejo, at the entrance to Carniquez Strait. Many scows traded to Petaluma, on the upper reaches of the creek of that name which leads off the north side of San Pablo Bay. Stage and freight lines ran from there to Santa Rosa, Healdsbury, Tomales and Souoma. The Straits of Carquinez led to Suisun Bay, with ports at Crockett, Port Costa, Martinez, Pittsburg and Antioch in the upper reaches, from which the Sacramento and San Joaquin rivers branch. Scows wriggled up to Stockton, on Stockton Slough, off the San Joaquin River. This originated as a gold rush landing and scows brought goods for the mines, steamboats towed barges and it was alive with the bustle and turbulence of these communities. Steamboat Slough and Cache Creek were creeks leading off into the delta lands from the mouth of the Sacramento River and there were other little waterways used by Bay shipping.

Growth of the city of San Francisco and its horse traffic created demand for fodder and bedding and the hay trade flourished until the early 1900s, much of it carried by scows. Stacks of hay were frequently 7–8 bales above deck, extending forward of the foremast. The fore shrouds were let into the stack and some scows regularly in the trade had a taller rig than others to set sufficient sail when loaded. Scow schooners beat to windward with a deck load of hay under full jib and a small mainsail specially set for stack work. The foresail remained bent to its spars but was not set. The helmsman of some stack scows stood in a 'pulpit' at the stern to see ahead over the load. Many scows unloaded at the San Francisco hay wharf, on Third Street Channel in the city.

The San Francisco waterfront extended steadily into the bay after the initial filling in of Yerba Buena Cove. Scows and many other types of ships and craft loaded and discharged from wooden piers, and wharves thrust out into the bay below Telegraph Hill, many were square riggers, including big wooden 'down easters' and the later large steel sailing ships of many nations, besides steamers. When the Central Pacific Railroad arrived at Oakland, to the east of San Francisco, in 1869, the long wharf served as transhipment for goods from trains to ships bound for ocean voyaging, besides handling cargoes for shipment to the bay ports.

Sometimes the coming of the railways created work for local shipping. The Central Pacific Railroad completed a connection to Martinez in 1879 and the deep waters of Carquinez Strait offered ample berthing for big ships to load grain. By 1889 ocean going vessels, mostly square riggers of many nations, loaded grain at wharves which almost continuously lined over four miles of shore, and half the ships clearing from the port of San Francisco with grain loaded there. For a time wheat became a new gold for California and the scows, sloops and schooners were busy. Much grain was brought down from upriver ports in scow schooners, loaded in the hold and on deck in sacks. The *Wavelet* was one in this trade, built in 1878 by John J. Dirks with dimensions of 57 ft × 20 ft × 4 ft 1 in depth. Port Costa and Vallejo were also important grain shipping ports, and scows, sloops and schooners brought wheat to these places for transhipment. The volume of the trade is suggested by the operations of the Port Costa Warehouse and Dock Co., owned by G. W. McNear and Co., whose warehouses could store 70,000 tons of grain at a time when a ship loading 2,000 tons was usual.

Manning of the San Francisco Bay scows and other small commercial craft suffered from fluctuations in the local labour requirements and lack of an established coastal seafaring tradition. Seafaring and waterside labour was scarce after the gold rush days and there was no definite part of the population looking to the sea for its living, as in the New England states, Britain, Europe or Scandinavia. Opportunities ashore were so attractive that a maritime tradition did not emerge and the large numbers of deep water ships arriving at San Francisco with crews often ill-used and accustomed to harsh conditions, led to most coastal vessels and waterside facilities being manned or influenced by them. This background, alien to the traditions of manning small craft, led to labour strikes as early as 1850. In 1885 the Coast

Seamans Union was formed and a year later a serious strike disrupted the waterfront and affected shipping, including the scows and sloops, and the small ports they served. Others followed at intervals. The Boatmens Protective Association held a regatta for working craft on 4 July 1867 and this became an annual event. After 1868 it was organised by the Master Mariners Benevolent Association. Scows, schooners and sloops, coasting schooners and the few yachts then owned locally, started off Mission Rock to compete in boisterous racing. These regattas were held from 1868 until 1877 and then infrequently, in 1879, 1884, 1885 and 1891, when they ceased for commercial craft. In 1884 the deep water barquentine *Makah* raced against the scows and other entries. The scows had the advantage in the beat to windward. Races were also held at Mertinez, where scows competed.

There were approximately 400 scows sailing in the 1880s and there were mentioned by Jack London as background in his description of bay activity in one of his books. Over 200 were sailing in 1900 and many were still building. Fully rigged schooner scows were still working from San Francisco in the early 1920s, but advancement of petrol and diesel engines early in the twentieth century led to construction of small cargo craft with hull forms suited to screw propulsion and hastened the decline of sailing scows. Many were being unrigged in the early 1920s and others followed, to be converted to powered barges or towed lighters.

Interest in the scows has revived in recent years and the schooner rigged *Regeina S* has been preserved at San Francisco as a good example of these useful sailing barges. Principal dimensions are 73 ft 8 in × 25 ft 8 in × 5 ft 7 in draught with centreboard raised. Her hull has a springing sheer and is shapely for a scow. The

Alma is another surviving sailing scow which was built by Fred Siener, a German emigrant from Bremerhaven, who had worked in shipyards there. He emigrated to San Francisco and for a time worked at shipyards before buying a small yard at Hunters Point. In 1891 he built the *Alma* for his son-in-law, James Peterson, for whose three-year-old daughter the scow was renamed. As Mrs Alma Sooman she was until recently living near Hunters Point. Siener's yard continued on repair work and he built only one other vessel, the scow *Adelia*, also for Peterson and named for his wife. The *Alma*'s principal dimensions are 59 ft × 22 ft 7 in × 3 ft 11 in draught. Registered Tonnage is 41. She is constructed almost totally in Oregon pine. The bottom is planked transversely as this economised in construction time and was considered to be stronger than longitudinal planking used by some builders.

James Peterson was a typical scow owner. A native of Sweden, he deserted from a ship in San Francisco when aged 14, with a capital of fifty cents. Eventually he served in the scows and later owned six at one time; an unusual number for one man. The *Alma* had a typical career in local trade under Captain Erik W. Carlson, another Scandinavian. In April 1909 she was run into by the steel steamer *Kvichak*, owned by Alaska Packers, which ran off her helm in clear weather with no sea and a light breeze, ramming the *Alma* which was loaded with sulphate of ammonia fertiliser worth $5,500. The *Alma* capsized. She was towed in by a tug and cost $20,000 to repair. There was no loss of life. She continued to sail until July 1918 when with five other Peterson scows she was unrigged to be used as a barge. She carried salt and fertiliser until 1926 when she was sold to Frank Resech of Petaluma who installed an engine in her and, like many other dismasted scows, she began a long battle to carry freight in competition with road transport. Petaluma was a centre of poultry farming and large quantities of chicken feed were carried. Many scows entered this trade, loading oyster shell from the east and south shores of San Francisco Bay. At first the scows were allowed to dry out on the banks and beaches and the shell was loaded in wheelbarrows run up a plank. Later, suction pumps enabled scows to dredge shell at high water and washing belts were a final refinement. The *Alma* sprouted 8 ft high bulwarks to contain the deck load of shell and the owner had a deckhouse built aft so he and his wife could live on board, adding a wheelhouse above.

Resech was content to jog along with a 40 hp petrol engine. He sold the *Alma* in 1944 to Peter J. Gambetta who in 1951 re-engined her with two diesels totalling 220 hp and installed more elaborate dredging gear. The scow could dredge 150 tons of shell in 6 to 8 hours with a crew of two, usually working the shell banks off Oakland, landing at Petaluma and elsewhere. She continued in the trade until 1957.

During the 1950s a group of San Francisco maritime researchers and other preservation conscious people wished to obtain a scow for preservation at the San Francisco Maritime State Historic Park, associated with the San Francisco Maritime Museum. They considered the scows *Matthilda* and the *Hermione Blum*, but chose the *Alma*, which in some ways is an unrepresentative scow, although cherished for her age and service. Restoration by shipwrights began in 1964 and continued at odd times. In 1969 the *Alma* sailed again, in the revived Master Mariners Regatta after fifty unrigged years and continues to sail and give pleasure to many, reminding them of the hard working little craft which played a part in the growth of a city.